GW01368459

NEW STEPPING STONES 2

TEACHER'S GUIDE

Julie Ashworth John Clark

LONGMAN

Syllabus

	Unit	Main Structures	Vocabulary	Main Communicative Functions	Tasks and Activities
	The Alphabet	How many …? What colour's …? What's your name? How old are you? Have you got a pet? How do you spell …? You are 'it'.	*Revision of Level 1 vocabulary* *The alphabet* bottle	Ask/Answer questions about a picture. Use the alphabet in English. Recognise words when spelt out. Spell words out.	Revision Quiz. Word search. Song. Group Survey. Make and play word stones. Game: *You are 'It'.*
Clothes	**1a**	What's this? What are these? [Gary] is wearing a [T-shirt]. Is [Suzy] wearing [shorts]?	hat jacket jumper shoes shorts skirt socks T-shirt trousers *colours*	Identify clothes. Ask/Say what someone is wearing. Ask/Say what colour someone's clothes are. Identify people from a spoken description.	Action Game. Role play. Crossword. Listening Task.
	1b	Whose is this? Whose are these? *Possessive*'s	off on dress tie shirt sweatshirt	Ask/Say what someone is wearing. Ask/Say what colour someone's clothes are. Ask someone what colour their clothes are. Ask/Say who clothes belong to.	Colour a picture. Rhyme. Role play. 'Clothes' Bingo. Make and play word stones. Group survey. Word search.
	1c	What colour is/are …? Where's …? Where are …?	cold snowman boots cardigan coat scarf bed wardrobe	Ask/Say what colour someone's clothes are. Understand descriptions of people and their clothes. Ask/Say where objects are in a room.	Quiz. Decipher coded words. Colour a picture. Anagrams. Draw a member of your family. Make pictures with clothes cut-outs.
	1d	Is he tall? Is he wearing …? Yes, he is. No, he isn't. Whose [T-shirt] is this? Whose [trousers] are these? My [socks] are [white]. My [hat] is [red]. The boy/girl is wearing …	spy my	Ask/Say what clothes people are wearing. Say who clothes belong to. Describe oneself.	Action Game. Find the spy. Match pictures and descriptions. Mark statements 'right' or 'wrong'. Crossword. Make pictures with clothes cut-outs. Personal file: My clothes.
	1e	He/She is wearing an [orange jumper]. *Plural* s	dungarees jeans sandals trainers glasses earrings necklace belt button zip	Say what clothes people are wearing.	Make and play word stones. Stepping Stones game. Jigsaw reading. Read and colour. Spelling game. Vocabulary games. Anagrams.
	1f		school badge	Understand descriptions of school badges.	Listen and number the badges. Make a school badge. Project: *Clothes.* Evaluation. Supersnake.

Food

Unit	Main Structures	Vocabulary	Main Communicative Functions	Tasks and Activities
2a	What's [Butch] eating? Where's the …? Is the [chicken] on the …? Do you like …? He likes/doesn't like … bottle of [lemonade]	food picnic garden kitchen apple banana fish biscuit cake cheese chicken hamburger sausage on in under bottle lemonade milk ice-cream chocolate	Identify food items. Ask/Say what food you like/don't like. Talk about differences between two pictures. Ask/Say where objects are in a picture.	**Listen and draw. Group survey. Spot the difference. Quiz. Listening task. Personal file: *My picnic.***
2b	I like/don't like … Does [Butch] like …? What does [Slow] like?	eggs meat bread apple grape orange cauliflower carrot potato bean onion tomato fruit vegetable	Identify food items. Ask/Say what food someone likes/doesn't like.	**Rhyme. Anagrams. 'Food' Bingo. Listening task. Mystery photos. Crossword. Personal file: *I like/don't like …***
2c	How many letters are there in …? There are ten letters in … Do you like …? What's your favourite [fruit]? My favourite [fruit] is …	hot-dog cheeseburger chip cabbage strawberry orange juice milk shake water	Say which is your favourite fruit etc. Say which is the odd one out in a group and why.	**Board game. Word stones. Personal file: *My favourites.* Group survey.**
2d	good/bad for you What would you like? I'd like … We'd like … Do you want …? Anything else?	vanilla chocolate ice-cream hair teeth	Say what someone's favourite food is. Say what food is good/bad for you.	**Ask questions about a picture. Listening task. Personal file: *My monster.* Role play: *In a restaurant.***
2e	I like/don't like … He likes/doesn't like … What's your favourite [food]?	a/an computer game roller skates bike ball sweets	Express personal likes/ dislikes.	**Make and play word stones. Stepping Stones Game. Jigsaw reading. Crossword. Spelling game. Class survey. Personal file: *My favourite food.***
2f	What's your favourite colour/toy?	kite yo-yo xylophone crisps pizza salad	Ask/Say what your favourite colour/toy is.	**Listening task. Group survey. Project: *Scrapbook.* Evaluation. Supersnake.**

Syllabus

Animals

Unit	Main Structures	Vocabulary	Main Communicative Functions	Tasks and Activities
3a	What colour are …? Are they big or small? They're very big. Do they eat meat? [Elephants] can swim. Can [tigers] swim? [Penguins] can't fly.	animal bird crocodile elephant kangaroo monkey panda penguin tiger can can't climb trees fly jump swim eat drink big biggest small long trunk tusk Africa Asia	Ask/Talk about animals. Ask/Talk about ability using *can*.	Listen to information about animals. Complete an information table. Identify pictures of animals. Personal file: *Animals.* Groupwork. Card games.
3b	[Camels] eat … They don't eat … What do [lions] eat? Do [hippos] eat [meat]?	camel crocodile giraffe hippo lion rhino seal zebra fish fruit meat big dangerous	Ask/Say what animals eat. Understand descriptions of animals.	Role play. Identify animal noises. Find animals hidden in a picture. 'Animal' Bingo. Crossword. Make word stones. Personal file: *My animal and what it eats.*
3c	Is it big? Can it swim? Has it got four legs? Does it eat [grass]? Have you got a [tiger] in your zoo? Which cage is it in? What's next to the [tiger]? Where does the [crocodile] live? What's wrong with …?	next to body head legs tail	Ask/Answer questions about animals. Describe animal characteristics. Describe the position of objects in a picture. Describe imaginary animals.	Animal knowledge quiz. Describe a zoo. Identify animals from a description. Create your own zoo. Song. Draw an imaginary animal.
3d	Where do [giraffes] live? What colour are …? He likes … She doesn't like …	spots stripes body ears head legs mouth tail teeth toes big short small enormous favourite	Understand descriptions of animals. Discuss animal characteristics. Ask someone what their favourite animal is. Describe your favourite animal.	Discuss giraffes, tigers and hippos. Write a description. Mystery photos. Describe photos of animals. Animal card games. Class survey. Personal file: *My favourite animal.*
3e	[Penguins] can swim. [Monkeys] can't swim. [Tigers] eat meat. [Monkeys] don't eat meat.	can can't fly jump swim beak claw feather fin fur shell whiskers wing	Talk about ability using *can* and *can't*. Talk about differences between two pictures.	Make and play word stones. Stepping Stones Game. Jigsaw reading. Spot the difference. Spelling game. Vocabulary games. Draw your favourite animal and label it.
3f	It's got [four legs]. It can't [fly].		Ask questions about animals.	Listening task. Animal guessing game. Project. Evaluation. Supersnake.

	Unit	Main Structures	Vocabulary	Main Communicative Functions	Tasks and Activities
Homes	4a	Does [Julie] live in a flat/house? Do [Kev and Kate] live in a flat/house? What's the biggest room in [Julie's] house? Have you got a …? How many rooms are there? How long/wide is your …? What's your telephone number?	house flat room live (*v.*) bathroom bedroom kitchen garden living room balcony biggest between next to plan upstairs downstairs	Identify rooms in a house. Describe your house. Ask someone about their house. Ask/Say where rooms are in a house. Ask for/Give your telephone number.	Listening task. Personal file: *My home.* Make a telephone. Class survey. Measure a room. Personal file: *A plan of my home.*
	4b	Where's …?	between next to under on door floor wall *Furniture*	Say where objects are in a house. Say where furniture is in a room.	Read and draw. Listening task. 'Furniture' Bingo. Make word stones. Make pictures with furniture cut-outs.
	4c	What's on the [table]?	next to in on bookcase clock lamp plant tap telephone toilet washing machine	Identify rooms and furniture. Ask/Say where objects are in a room. Ask/Say what furniture is in your bedroom.	Draw and describe a room. Count the furniture in your house. Sentence memorisation game. Mystery photos. Board Game. Group survey. Personal file: *My bedroom.*
	4d	There's a … There are …	in next to on under aerial balcony chimney door roof window	Describe a room.	Play word stones. Stepping Stones Game. Jigsaw reading. Say what's wrong with the picture. Spelling game. Vocabulary games. Listening task. Word search.
	4e	The [pencil] is on the [table]. The [apples] are in the [fridge].	*Classroom furniture*	Say where objects are in a room.	List the furniture in your classroom. Draw a plan of your classroom. Dice game: Draw a house. Project: *Houses.* Evaluation. Supersnake.
Festivals			Halloween ghost witch Bob Apple apple water hat		Play Bob Apple. Make a witch's hat. Halloween project.

New Stepping Stones

is a four-year English course for young learners beginning English at Primary level. The course is carefully constructed around a conceptual framework in which the tasks, activities and language points reflect the interests and development of young learners.

The key features of **New Stepping Stones** are as follows:

A syllabus geared to the child's development
The *New Stepping Stones* syllabus has been designed to meet the specific needs of young learners, providing four achievable years of English. The syllabus takes into account the cognitive development of children this age. The choice of themes therefore reflects children's developing awareness. For example, in Year 1 of the course, the topic about animals focuses on pets. In Year 2, the same topic relates to wild animals.
The syllabus also grades the tasks and activities in which children participate. This is related to a thorough coverage of appropriate structures, functions, words and pronunciation. All the language points are regularly revised and reviewed to ensure maximum progress for all learners.

Topic-based learning
Level 2 of *New Stepping Stones* is divided into four topics. Within each topic, the language items are carefully selected and graded. Pupils are presented with language which allows them to communicate in a genuinely meaningful way about each topic. The topic-based syllabus also offers maximum opportunity for project work.

Personalisation
Children get great motivation and satisfaction from talking and writing about themselves. *New Stepping Stones* offers many opportunities for pupils to do this in English.

Variety of learning styles
It is generally acknowledged that all children learn in slightly different ways. To accommodate this, *New Stepping Stones* exploits a wide range of tried and tested techniques and activities to allow all pupils to fulfil their maximum potential.

Teaches positive learning habits
One of the purposes of learning English at Primary level is to provide positive motivation for future studies. This includes not only laying foundations in terms of language and enjoyment but also developing positive learning habits in young learners.
New Stepping Stones teaches pupils organisational skills; the importance of co-operation; referencing skills; and the need to use language for real purposes. The Activity Book contains innovative learner-training sections with self-assessment activities.

Comprehensive coverage of skills
The syllabus in *New Stepping Stones* is carefully graded in order to ensure comprehensive coverage of all four skills. Within each lesson pupils are engaged in listening, speaking, reading and writing in English, with listening and speaking having prime importance in the early years.

Interdisciplinary
The topics and activities in *New Stepping Stones* provide an interdisciplinary approach to language learning, enabling teachers to link the study of English with work in other areas of the curriculum. The projects, which are built into the Coursebook, actively encourage such links.

Simple to use
The teaching notes to *New Stepping Stones* include a step-by-step guide to every activity in every lesson. Reproduction of both the Coursebook and Activity Book alongside the teaching notes provides an immediate reference for teachers.

Pupils learn by doing
The activities in *New Stepping Stones* require the active participation of the pupils. There are games which practise the language through physical involvement, tasks which involve making things and emphasis upon learning through concrete activities. The unique new 'word stones' sections involve pupils in active vocabulary development.

Learning is fun
New Stepping Stones is based on the belief that learning is most effective when it is fun and moreover that enjoyment provides motivation and encourages pupils to continue in their studies.

Introduction

ORGANISATION

Contents of the course

Level 2 of *New Stepping Stones* consists of:

Coursebook

64 lively, full-colour pages, featuring stories, cartoon strips, vocabulary and project work, games, songs and rhymes and numerous activities for presenting and practising the language.

Activity Book

76 pages, providing practice in all the skills, with questionnaires, puzzles, games, tests and self-assessment activities to fully involve pupils in the learning process.

Cut-outs

Each Activity Book comes complete with its own centre pull-out section of cut-outs. These include playing cards and story strips for use in a wide variety of games and activities.

Teacher's Guide

A simple to use, lesson-by-lesson guide giving instructions on all activities. Reproductions of both Coursebook and Activity Book pages greatly simplify preparation and classroom use, while the **Resource File** at the back of the book provides a wealth of additional ideas. Photocopy masters are provided to support pupils' self-assessment work in the Activity Book.

Cassettes

The cassettes feature both adults and children and provide a wide range of natural listening material including stories, dialogues, songs, rhymes and listening tasks.

Objectives of the course

The main objectives of *New Stepping Stones* are as follows:

- To instil the idea that learning languages is enjoyable.
- To encourage pupils to want to go on learning English in secondary school.
- To enable pupils to talk and write about themselves.
- To lay the foundations for future study in terms of basic structures, lexis, language functions and basic study skills.
- To enable pupils to use English for a purpose and to regard English as a means of communicating real information.

Organisation of the course

New Stepping Stones Level 2 is made up of four topics:

CLOTHES
FOOD
ANIMALS
HOMES

Pupils explore each topic in sufficient depth to enable them to talk and write about themselves, their family, their classmates and their possessions. Each topic contains an introductory story, four or five units and project and evaluation work.

There is also an introductory unit on the alphabet and a 'Festivals' lesson at the end of the Coursebook, for use as appropriate. Each unit is divided into three lessons (of approximately one hour) which, together with story, project and evaluation lessons, provides a total of 70 lessons. Further suggestions for projects and a wealth of ideas in the Resource File supplement the core material. There is constant revision throughout the course, four progress tests and four self-assessment sections.

Adaptability of the course

New Stepping Stones is designed to be as flexible as possible: the Coursebook and Activity Book are divided into units rather than lessons because the time available will vary from situation to situation, according to factors such as class size and age of pupils.

Simply work through the material in the order shown in the Lesson Notes. The topic-based structure and in-built revision make it possible to begin a lesson at any point.

The extra ideas in the **Resource File** also give the teacher greater flexibility in managing time.

Organisation of the Coursebook and Activity Book

Each unit consists of two pages in the Coursebook and three pages in the Activity Book. The text of the introductory story is reproduced in the cut-out story strips in the Activity Book.
Key vocabulary and classroom language is given in wordlists at the back of the Coursebook.
Colour games material is provided in the centre pull-out section of the Activity Book.

Organisation of the Teacher's Guide

Each two-page spread is devoted to one lesson, i.e. approximately one hour's worth of material. There is a step-by-step guide giving detailed teaching instructions for each activity. Reproduced pages from both the Coursebook and the Activity Book allow teachers to see instantly which exercises are being referred to. Tapescripts and answers are also included. The symbol // is used in some tapescripts. This is an indication that the teacher should either stop the tape temporarily or use the 'pause' button.

Resource File

The Resource File is at the back of the Teacher's Guide. It contains suggestions and ideas for extra games, activities and projects. Many of these activities can be used at any stage; others are more applicable to particular lessons. Suggestions as to when extra activities are appropriate are given in the syllabus box at the top of each page of Lesson Notes. The numbers of appropriate activities from the Resource File are given here.

Main Language Items		Resource File	Materials Needed
What colour ...? How many ...? Who's this? What's this?	bottle wall	3 51a	cassette/cassette player

These extra ideas will also be helpful in dealing with mixed-ability groups, since they include suggestions for remedial work and expansion activities.

TEACHING PROCEDURES

The following notes deal with how to use *New Stepping Stones* in the classroom. Pupils are required to learn only a limited number of techniques, which can be applied to a wide range of activities in the Coursebook (called CB in the Lesson Notes) and the Activity Book (AB). All variations upon these techniques are given in the Lesson Notes.
The activities in *New Stepping Stones* can be loosely divided into those which concentrate on one of the four skills (SPEAKING, LISTENING, READING and WRITING) and those which practise two or more skills simultaneously.

Speaking activities

Pair Work (Ask and answer)

The **Pair Work** exercises provide much of the initial presentation and practice of new language and range from very controlled exercises (i.e. drills in which both questions and answers are given) to free exercises based on picture prompts.
For controlled exercises the following procedure is recommended, although as a first step it may be useful to demonstrate exercises with one pupil, or get more able pupils to show the rest of the class.

a Divide the class into pairs and give each pair question and answer roles (for suggestions on organising pupils into pairs see **Classroom management**).
b Each pair uses only one book, placed between them, open at the appropriate page. The words should *always* be covered. Pupils must not read while listening.
c Pupils repeat after the tape. All pairs work simultaneously. P1 repeats the questions, pointing and referring to pictures as appropriate to contextualise the questions. (This is necessary since, for example, **'What's this?'** is meaningless unless it is clear what is being referred to.) P2 answers.
As the course progresses, pupils can be encouraged to test themselves by trying to answer before the tape.

What's this?
What's this?
A dog.
What's this?
A ...

d Practise without the help of the tape. P1 now uses the words in his book as prompts to ask the questions. (NOTE Simply reading the question aloud destroys natural rhythm and pronunciation, so encourage pupils to adopt a 'Look and Say' method here, i.e. pupils read the question silently before looking up at their partner and asking the questions.)

P2's book should remain on the table with the words covered. He/she answers the questions using the pictures as prompts and help from P1, if required.

What's this?
A dog.
What's this?
Er... a dog.

e Change roles and repeat step **d**.

f Practise until the whole exercise can be done using only the pictures as prompts. (This stage will be reached gradually as skill and confidence increase.)

g During the practice phase the teacher's task is to circulate and help the pupils where necessary. Praise and encourage natural speed and intonation; the use of 'Look and Say' techniques; co-operation between pupils – helping and checking etc.

The above procedures are goals to be worked towards. Pupils will take time to get used to working in pairs. Therefore during **Pair Work** it is important to keep a few points in mind:

Take your time ...

All pupils vary in ability; some will instantly grasp the technique while others may need a little longer.

Communication before correctness ...

Don't expect instant perfection. Communication is more important initially: correctness will come gradually.

Timing ...

Controlled **Pair Work** will usually take about fifteen minutes. Pupils will vary in terms of what they can achieve in this time. More able pupils will be able to produce both questions and answers without the help of the words, while less able pupils should at least know key vocabulary items and question words.

Noise levels ...

Pupils working simultaneously in pairs will inevitably generate some noise. The sound of a class working is a healthy learning environment but only tolerate noise that relates to the task in hand.

These techniques are invaluable in maximising the involvement of all pupils. Individual capabilities vary, but even less able pupils will be more active and involved in their own learning than if the teacher is asking all the questions. Initially **Pair Work** may be time-consuming, but a little initial patience in using the above techniques will be greatly rewarded.
In freer **Pair Work**, the basic practice procedures are the same from the teacher's point of view although the model questions and answers are not on the tape. Demonstrate by asking appropriate questions to the whole class until pupils understand the nature of the exercise and the language forms needed.

Groupwork: Questionnaire

Questionnaires provide pupils with a real purpose for communication and an opportunity to talk about themselves. Always demonstrate **Questionnaires** to the class first, so that pupils know exactly what they have to do. Quickly draw a grid on the blackboard. Select one or two pupils. Write their names on the grid. Then ask the questions to be practised and write each pupil's answers alongside their name.

Name	dog	cat	other	no pet
Alex				
Anna				

a Divide the class into groups of three or more, depending upon the nature of the questionnaire. Ensure that pupils are not always in the same groups, so that Questionnaires are less predictable. (For suggestions on the organisation of groups see **Classroom management**.)

b Then pupils complete their own questionnaires. Set a 5–10 minute time limit for the task.

c The teacher's task is to circulate, giving assistance if required. Ensure that pupils are using English and that they are asking questions and not simply copying each other's answers. Communication is more important than correctness here.

d When pupils have completed their questionnaires, ask the class questions about the information they have collected.

Role Play

Two types of **Role Play** are used in *New Stepping Stones*; conventional Role Plays and Role Plays using puppets. Both can be used to bring more life to the language. The following points offer guidance on procedure:

a Set the scene by telling pupils to look at the pictures and then asking questions about who and what they can see.

b Play the tape. Pupils listen to the whole dialogue, looking at the pictures at the same time.

c Give roles. Name badges can be used to clarify the concept of playing a role.

d Role Plays usually involve two characters. All pairs work simultaneously. Pupils should be standing or sitting, according to the relative positions of the characters in the picture.

e Pupils then repeat the dialogue two or three times after the tape.

f During the repetition phase insist upon intonation and gesture. Demonstrate to pupils by 'overacting' yourself, if necessary. Alternatively, to focus attention upon gestures, pupils can act out the dialogue using mime.

g Pupils then act out the dialogue without the help of the tape. All pairs practise simultaneously. Allow pupils between five and ten minutes to practise the Role Play.

h Volunteers can then be allowed to act out the Role Play in front of the class. However, it is best to restrict such activity to enthusiastic volunteers.

i If time allows, pupils can change role and repeat the Role Play.

Listening Activities

Story presentation

The **Presentation** phases of lessons usually relate to the story cartoon strips in the Coursebook. These are used to contextualise all the language to be practised and provide listening and reading practice.

Draw pupils' attention to the pictures and ask some simple questions to set the scene before playing the tape.

The focus of the **Supersnake** strips is on reading and listening. Encourage pupils to read silently to themselves before listening to the tape.

Listening (Task)

These exercises provide a contrasting type of listening exercise to the **Presentation** strips. Rather than listening for general meaning, pupils are now required to listen for specific detail and carry out a set task. The activities themselves vary from simple, directed colouring and drawing in the early units, to chart-filling activities as the book progresses. Procedures for individual activities are given in the Lesson Notes. All **Listening (Task)** exercises are on tape.

Reassure pupils that they do not have to understand all the words, but only listen for specific information.

Action Game

The **Action Games** are an adaptation of Asher's Total Physical Reponse method. The aim is to improve listening comprehension through the active involvement of the pupils.

The teacher gives instructions in English. Demonstrate the meaning by acting out the instruction with the pupils, not by translation.

Detailed guidance on the language to be used is given in the Lesson Notes. Obviously the physical layout of the classroom will determine to what extent instructions can be used with the whole class simultaneously or only with individual pupils. Most of the games can be adapted to suit the environment and those instructions which require pupils to **'Walk'** can be practised with individuals. The **Action Games** are very important since they introduce a great deal of functional classroom English which is later recycled in the CB itself. (The written forms of the language introduced in the **Action Games** are given in the AB.)

The following points offer guidance as to procedure:

a Pupils should not repeat the instructions. **Action Games** are silent listening games!

b Always demonstrate all new words by acting them out with two or more pupils at the front of the class. It is not sufficient to show the meaning by demonstrating yourself. Pupils must do each action.

c Continue to act out each new instruction until pupils can do it without your help. To check pupils are comfortable with a new instruction, delay your own response slightly to give them a chance to act on their own.

d Always practise a new instruction with the whole class at some stage. All pupils should be active as much of the time as possible.

e Combine words previously introduced with new words to make your own original instructions. Perhaps note these down before the lesson.

f Do not try to progress too fast. It may take a little time for pupils to understand some instructions.

g Speak at natural speed and do not split sentences to make it easier for pupils. Simply repeat the instruction, if necessary.

h Do not try to trick pupils. Your aim is that they should always succeed.

j **Action Games** should last about ten minutes, depending on the particular game. Games are better repeated in a later lesson than twice in the same lesson.

Reading Activities

Reading (Task)

With the **Reading (Task)** exercises, pupils are directly involved in performing a task, this time based upon a written passage. They may be asked to 'Read and colour' or 'Read, then write.' Once again, the pupils do not have to understand all the words, but only that information which will enable them to complete the task.
Pupils should work individually and the ability of the group will dictate the amount of time each activity takes. The cut-outs also can be used to provide extra practice for faster pupils.
Encourage pupils to compare their work when they have finished. Round off the activity by going over correct solutions on the blackboard.

Stepping Stones Game

This is a simple sentence-making game. The object of the game is to make as many sentences as possible. Pupils work from left to right and select a word, or words, from each column. Each sentence must be true or be a correct description of a picture or pictures in the CB. Pupils may choose not to select a word from a column if they wish, but must still work across from left to right. One pupil from each pair should write their answers on a piece of paper. Demonstrate the game by constructing a similar grid on the blackboard and asking pupils to make sentences. Write these on the board.
Set a time limit of ten minutes. Then ask each pair how many sentences they have made. Check that all sentences are correct and appropriate. Correct any mistakes. Pupils must deduct incorrect sentences from their total. The pair with the most sentences are the winners. Pupils' answer sheets can be collected to assess progress.

Look and Find

The **Look and Find** exercises require pupils to use more than one skill, but are always introduced by reading a series of written instructions. These instructions direct pupils to look at a picture and find specific things. Pupils work in pairs and discuss where the things can be found in each picture. These exercises are basically a form of guided discussion. The teacher's role is to circulate, encourage pupils to speak in English and provide help, if required.

Writing Activities

Word stones

The 'Word Stones' section is another example of pupil-centred work in *New Stepping Stones*. Pupils start their own collection of 'word stones' either by writing words as directed on real stones or on stone-shaped pieces of card. The 'word stones' are a tangible collection of vocabulary items chosen for work on sentence building. They can be stored in a box (such as an old shoe box) or in a large, strong envelope. Pupils use them in matching activities and games in later lessons, and they can also be used for revision and self-testing. Pupils should be encouraged to add their own words and build up their own collection of word stones for future reference.

Puzzles

A variety of **Puzzles** provide valuable revision and reinforcement of vocabulary and structures in an enjoyable way.

Personal File

The **Personal File** gives pupils the opportunity to write about themselves. These exercises are always based upon models in the CB and pupils' attention should be drawn to these models both before, during and after the exercise, to allow them to monitor their own work.
The **Personal File** involves pupils drawing and colouring pictures and then describing them. It is often helpful if the teacher provides a model on the blackboard first, giving personal information about herself as an example.
The **Personal File** makes excellent wall displays, providing motivation and the opportunity for follow-up work involving the whole class. (See **Resource File** for suggestions.) Pupils derive satisfaction from seeing their own work displayed, despite differences of ability.

Other writing exercises

Most of the other **Writing** exercises in *New Stepping Stones* are there to provide reinforcement of the spoken word. These include answering questions in writing and simple sentence-completion exercises. It is important to encourage pupils to monitor and check their own written work. Models are always given in the CB and pupils should be referred to these to compare their own answers, rather than having their work corrected by the teacher. Pupils can also be encouraged to check each other's work. This adds a game-like element to such correction.
Freer writing exercises, in which pupils write questions or messages for their partners to answer, are an effective way of dealing with mixed-ability classes, since they ensure faster pupils always have something to do. (See **Resource File.**)

Integrated skills

Cut-outs

The cut-out material is located in the centre pull-out section of the AB. The cut-outs consist of four colour pages and two black-and-white pages. There is one sheet of 'clothes pieces', eight playing cards linked to ANIMALS, four 'menu cards' and one sheet of 'furniture pieces'. There are also four sets of story strips, containing the text to accompany the introductory stories in each topic.

All pieces have to be cut out before they can be used. (See **Classroom Management** below.) They provide an added element of physical manipulation in practising the language. A wide variety of games and activities using the cut-outs are described in the Lesson Notes. The cut-outs can be used at any time to provide extra practice of words and structures, and are particularly useful as a source of extra activities for faster pupils, in mixed-ability classes.

Games

The games in *New Stepping Stones* provide variety in the presentation and practice of the language. Although they are there to be enjoyed, they all have a linguistic purpose. Some of the games are traditional children's playground games and introduce an element of cultural study.

Songs & rhymes

All the songs and rhymes in *New Stepping Stones* are traditional English songs, providing an important element of authenticity in the course.

They are activities for the whole class. Always use the pictures to clarify meaning and use actions wherever appropriate.

The Lesson Notes indicate when the song is to be first presented, but once pupils know the tune and words they can be repeated in any lesson.

Phonics (Listen and match)

These exercises, which appear in the AB, have a dual function. They present the most common sound-letter correspondences in English, particularly the vowels, and they provide valuable pronunciation practice. The following procedure is recommended:

a Play the tape, one phrase at a time. Pupils listen and draw a line to match the phrase and picture.

b Listen to the presentation phrase on the tape again and pause for pupils to repeat.

c Play the tape again. Pupils repeat the phrases as quickly as they can.

d Pupils practise saying the phrases as quickly as they can. Volunteers then say the phrases as fast as they can in front of the class.

e Pronunciation will develop systematically through the use of these exercises and the teacher should not over-correct pupils.

Projects

Project work calls upon the pupils to work independently or in small groups. It allows them to explore their immediate environment, tailor the task to their learning style and personal preferences, use their prior knowledge and experiences, and integrate the four skills. Pupils should state their objectives before they begin, or at least have a clear idea of what they intend to do. Once they have chosen their own work, they should also be encouraged to continue it outside their English class. Display as much of the work as possible.

Other activites

All other activities in *New Stepping Stones* are fully explained in the Lesson Notes. These include: **Bingo**, **Number Dictations**, **Find more words**, **Quizzes**, **'Making' Activities** and **Surveys**.

Evaluation

Although evaluation in **New Stepping Stones** is continuous, there is a teacher-administered test and a self-assessment activity at the end of each of the four topics.

Teacher-administered tests

The teacher-administered test is useful in that it signals some stages in the learning process and allows both teacher and pupils to look back on what they have achieved up to that moment.

Some pupils are easily discouraged by their mistakes; avoid using red ink to correct tests and try to focus on the improvement in their work rather than on their deficiencies. In this way, they will be able to appreciate the positive aspects of their school experience.

Test yourself

The self-assessment activities help centre pupils' attention on what they have learned and the score which they must circle at the bottom of the page gives them instant feedback on their performance. To test themselves, pupils use a set of cards with words and pictures on them. (Photocopy masters for these are at the end of the Teacher's Guide.)

Self-assessment is essential in that it allows pupils to become more aware of their own strengths and weaknesses. Point out to them that errors are a natural part of the learning process and remind them that you can be sure of avoiding mistakes only if you learn nothing.

Classroom management

The organisation of your classroom is very important.
Always ensure pupils know exactly what they are doing before they start an activity. A demonstration is often more satisfactory than an explanation. Although this can be time consuming with new activities, a little time spent before an activity can save a lot of time and effort later.
Organising pupils into pairs and groups is another important job for the teacher. Pair pupils with the person sitting next to them, if possible. This can be done if pupils are sitting around tables:

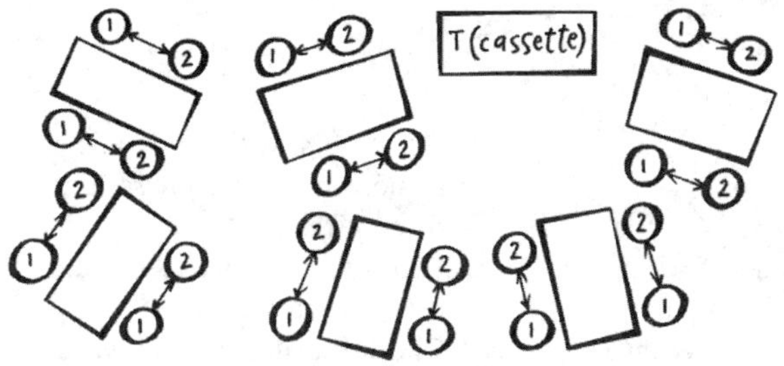

T (cassette)

or in rows:

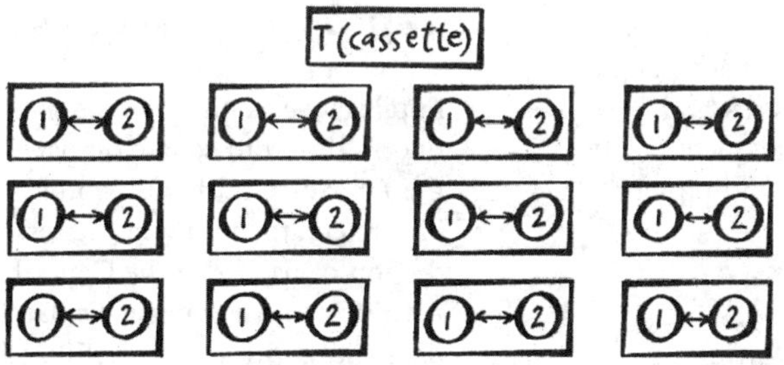

T (cassette)

Pupils can always turn to work with the person behind them:

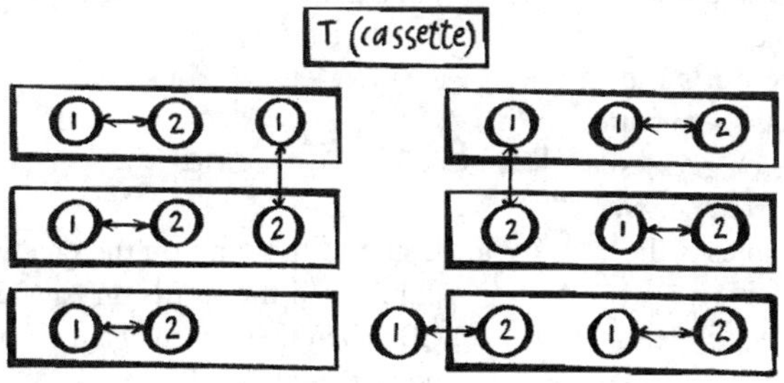

T (cassette)

Give pupils roles. Since the questions and answers in *New Stepping Stones* are colour-coded, this can be used as a prompt when giving roles. Say to each pupil in turn **'You are blue. You are red.'** Next ensure pupils understand the roles they have been given. Say **'Blue stand up!'** etc. Then write the first two questions on the blackboard in coloured chalk. Initially use these as prompts while pupils repeat. (Cards with the word **'QUESTION'** and **'ANSWER'** or the letters **'Q'** and **'A'** can be given to all pupils to clarify roles, if necessary.) Pupils will quickly learn to get themselves into pairs and this procedure can soon be abandoned. Above all, be patient during early exercises and give pupils time to learn the procedures.
For **Groupwork**, ensure that pupils are facing one another and not spread out in a line, making communication impossible.
Organisation of equipment is another important responsibility for the teacher. A list of items required for each lesson is given in the syllabus box in the Lesson Notes. Encourage pupils to be responsible for bringing their own coloured pencils etc., but try to have a class set available to avoid time wasting.
It is probably a good idea for the teacher to look after the cut-outs and word stones, if they are to be used most effectively. Collect the cut-outs and word stones and store them in envelopes or boxes in the classroom. They can be returned to pupils at the end of term. (See **Resource File** for further ideas on the storage of cut-outs.)

Language in the classroom

Using English in the classroom is a very good way of both introducing and constantly recycling language. *New Stepping Stones* encourages this in two particular ways:

a Through the Action Games.
b Through the teacher's script, which is given in the Lesson Notes.

Extensive piloting has shown that *New Stepping Stones* can be used equally effectively with or without the mother tongue. The mother tongue may be useful for classroom management, although a demonstration is often an equally effective substitute. Use English wherever possible and encourage pupils to do the same. Pictures or actions can usually be used instead of translation to explain meaning. As pupils become familiar with English expressions and classroom language, such phrases should always be used.
Pupils need to become familiar with the following phrases as quickly as possible, if they are not already.

Hello.	**Goodbye.**
Give me ...	**Thank you.**
Come here, please.	**Listen.**
Read.	**Write.**
Draw.	**Colour.**
Repeat.	**Cover the words.**
Good.	**Well done.**
Quiet.	**Hands up.**
You ask the questions.	**You give the answers.**
Get into pairs.	**Get into groups.**
Good morning/afternoon/evening.	

Starter lesson 1

Main Language Items		Resource File	Materials Needed
What colour ...?	bottle	3	cassette/cassette player
How many ...?	wall	51a	
Who's this?			
What's this?			

Step 1 Quiz

a Say **'Open your Coursebooks at page 2. Look at the picture.'** Point to various objects and characters and ask **'Who's this?'** and **'What's this?'** to see if pupils can remember the English names.

b Divide the class into two teams. Play the first question on the tape. The first pupil to raise their hand gets a chance to answer, and if correct, wins two points for their team. If the answer is wrong, the other team may answer the question for one point.

c Do all the questions in the same way.

Tapescript (with answers):

1 **How many legs has the monster got? // (1)**
2 **What numbers are in the picture? // (30, 8, 1)**
3 **How many girls are there in the picture? // (6)**
4 **What colour's the kite? // (Orange)**
5 **What colour is Bill's hair? // (Black)**
6 **Is the pencil brown or blue? // (Brown)**
7 **How many pets are there in the picture? // (5)**
8 **What colour's the plane? // (White)**
9 **Is the box red or green? // (Red)**
10 **What colour's the snake? // (Red and yellow)**

Step 2 Pairwork

a Elicit questions from pupils about the picture on page 2. Pupils may use any question forms they know, ranging from simple questions such as **'What's this?'**, to more complex ones such as **'How many boys are there in the picture?'** Write the questions on the blackboard.

b Divide the class into pairs. Each pair uses one book and pupils ask and answer questions about the picture.

c Encourage pupils to help and prompt each other.

Step 3 Memory game (Pairwork)

a Pupils remain in pairs (P1 and P2). P1 in each pair takes the book and asks P2 the colours of three objects in the picture by asking **'What colour's the *pencil*?'** P2 does not look at the picture but answers from memory (or guesses). P2 gets a point for each correct answer.

b Then P2 takes the book and asks the questions.

Step 4 Look and find

The instructions at the top of CB page 2 ask pupils to look carefully at the picture and find specific objects.

a Do the first with the whole class to demonstrate the exercise. Say **'Find three girls.'**

b Pupils then work in pairs and complete the other tasks.

c Check the answers and write them on the blackboard.

Step 5 Find the words

a Pupils circle as many words as they can find in the word square on page 4 of the AB. Some of the 37 words are illustrated around it and the rest are at the top of page 2 in the Coursebook. **Answers:** thirty, Supersnake, Duffy, Sam, Slow, girl, bag, arm, Bill, table, badge, pencil, pencil sharpener, boy, eight, dog, ruler, foot, kite, pen, Gary, head, hat, hair, rat, monster, leg, Wow, Julie, plane, Suzy, cat, box, chair, pet, Butch, Kate

Step 6 Song

a Listen to the song on the tape while pupils read the words on page 2 of the CB. Then they listen again with the book closed.

b Play the first verse again line by line. Pupils repeat.

c Finally pupils sing as many verses as they can.

Step 4

Step 6

The Alphabet

NEW STEPPING STONES 1
Who's this ?
30
8
How many ?
What's this ?

Look and find

1 Find three girls.
2 Find six animals.
3 Find five red things.
4 Find six things beginning with 'b'.

Sing

Ten Green Bottles

Ten green bottles standing on a wall.
Ten green bottles standing on a wall.
And if one green bottle should
accidentally fall,
There'd be nine green bottles standing
on a wall.

Nine green bottles standing on a wall ...

2

Sing

The Alphabet

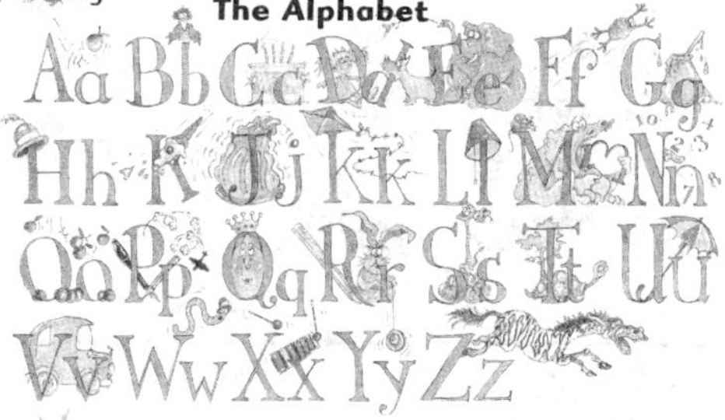

Aa Bb Cc Dd Ee Ff Gg
Hh Ii Jj Kk Ll Mm Nn
Oo Pp Qq Rr Ss Tt Uu
Vv Ww Xx Yy Zz

Make

Word Stones

bird
dog
worm
tree
cake
glue
plane
rabbit
frog
monster
hat
kite

3

Step 5

The Alphabet

1 Find the words. Look → ↓ ↘

Look at the pictures here and on page 2 in your Coursebook.

NEW STEPPING STONES 1

Y	E	L	E	B	T	H	I	R	T	Y	K	E	S	P
E	B	U	R	S	U	P	E	R	S	N	A	K	E	V
D	U	F	F	Y	H	T	S	A	M	S	L	O	W	J
K	G	I	R	L	E	O	C	B	O	N	E	R	O	U
I	A	B	A	G	A	H	E	H	N	Z	G	A	W	L
T	R	Y	A	N	D	A	R	M	S	B	I	L	L	I
E	Y	N	O	K	A	T	E	D	T	A	B	L	E	E
F	B	A	D	G	E	J	C	P	E	N	C	I	L	S
P	E	N	C	I	L	S	H	A	R	P	E	N	E	R
E	L	A	O	S	G	K	A	Q	T	E	B	O	Y	O
N	E	A	R	V	U	E	I	G	H	T	D	O	G	B
G	R	E	N	E	W	Z	R	U	L	E	R	G	X	O
F	O	O	T	E	D	O	Y	S	T	S	H	I	R	N

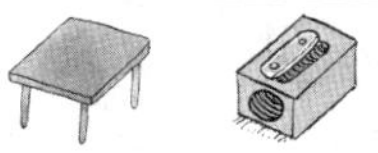

2 Ask your friends. Then write.

name	age	number of brothers	number of sisters	pet

4

The Alphabet

3 Write the letters and make sentences.
Then number the pictures.

1 I/A M/S I X/Y E A R S/O L D.
2 _ _ _ _ _ _ _ _ _ _ _ _.
3 _ _ _ _ _ _ _ _ _ _ _ _.
4 _ _ _ _ _ _ _ _ _ _ _ _ _ _ _ _ _.
5 _ _ _ _ _ _ _ _ _ _ _ _ _ _ _.
6 _ _ _ _ _ _ _ _ _ _ _ _.

Kate
Julie
Gary
Kev
Bill
Suzy

4 Join the dots.

i
d
o
a
t
j
l
w
y
r
m
g
e
x
p
c
f
v
k
q
n
b
s
h

5

Starter lesson 2

Main Language Items			Resource File	Materials Needed
What's your name?	bird	kite	23	cassette/cassette player
How old are you?	cake	monster	25	materials to make and store word stones
How many brothers/sisters have you got?	dog	plane	25a	
	frog	rabbit		
Have you got a pet?	glue	tree		
The alphabet	hat	worm		

Step 1 Action Game

a Briefly revise a variety of the following commands:

Point to …	**a boy**
Touch …	**a girl**
Stand on …	**the floor**
Sit on ...	**a chair**
Stand up!	**a/the table**
Turn around!	**the door**
Walk to …	**pencil**
Pick up …	**pen**
Put down …	**Activity Book**
Open your …	**Coursebook**
Close your ...	**blackboard**
Write …	**chalk**
Put your … on …	**window**
Put your … under …	

b Then play a variation of the traditional English game 'Simon Says'. When you give a command the whole class should act it out. When you say **'Don't'** before the command, it should be ignored. Any pupil who carries out the command when you say **'Don't'** must leave the game. The last player remaining is the winner. Keep the action very brisk and if commands are not obeyed immediately, then pupils must also leave the game.

Step 2 Groupwork

a Ask various pupils in the class the following questions:

What's your name?
How old are you?
How many brothers have you got?
How many sisters have you got?
Have you got a pet? If yes, **What is it?**

b When pupils are familiar with the question forms, ask them to look at the grid on page 4 of their AB. Copy the grid onto the blackboard. Ask one pupil the questions again. Write his or her answers in the grid.

c Then all pupils work simultaneously, asking each other the questions and filling in their charts.

d Finish the exercise by asking pupils questions about other class members, e.g. **'How many** ***brothers*** **has** ***Maria*** **got?'**

Step 3 Song

a Listen to the whole song on the tape and look at the letters of the alphabet at the top of page 3 of the CB.

b Listen to the song again line by line, and repeat the words.

c Finally play the whole song and sing along with the tape.

Step 4 Word stones

a Pupils continue their own collection of 'word stones' from Level 1, either writing on real stones stored in a box (such as an old shoe box) or stone-shaped pieces of card stored in a large, strong envelope. The 'word stones' are a tangible collection of vocabulary items chosen for work on phonics and rhyme. Pupils use them in matching activities and games in later lessons and they can also be used for revision and self-testing.

NOTE As well as making the word stones shown in each topic, pupils can add their own words to their collection individually, for example when doing project work.

b Each pupil requires twelve 'stones'. Pupils write one word on each stone in felt-tip pen as shown in the pictures on CB page 3, to start an alphabet collection. Pupils may use just one colour felt-tip pen or a variety of colours.

c When all pupils have made their twelve stones, they look at the pictures at the top of page 3 of their CB. Pupils then match their word stones to the appropriate letter and picture.

d Divide the class into pairs. Pupils place their stones face down on their desks. P1 then turns over one stone from each set to try to make a matching pair. If he/she is successful, he/she keeps both stones and has another turn. If not, he/she turns the stones face down again in the same position and P2 has a turn.

e Pupils then store their stones for future use.

Step 3

Step 4

The Alphabet

Look and find

1 Find three girls.
2 Find six animals.
3 Find five red things.
4 Find six things beginning with 'b'.

NEW STEPPING STONES 1
Who's this ?
30
8
How many ?
What's this ?

Sing

Ten Green Bottles

Ten green bottles standing on a wall,
Ten green bottles standing on a wall,
And if one green bottle should
accidentally fall,
There'd be nine green bottles standing
on a wall.

Nine green bottles standing on a wall ...

2

Sing

The Alphabet

Aa Bb Cc Dd Ee Ff Gg
Hh Ii Jj Kk Ll Mm Nn
Oo Pp Qq Rr Ss Tt Uu
Vv Ww Xx Yy Zz

Make

Word Stones

bird
dog
worm
tree
cake
glue
plane
rabbit
frog
monster
hat
kite

3

The Alphabet

1 Find the words. Look → ↓ ↘

Look at the pictures here and on page 2 in your Coursebook.

NEW STEPPING STONES 1

Y	E	L	E	B	T	H	I	R	T	Y	K	E	S	P
E	B	U	R	S	U	P	E	R	S	N	A	K	E	V
D	U	F	F	Y	H	T	S	A	M	S	L	O	W	J
K	G	I	R	L	E	O	C	B	O	N	E	R	O	U
I	A	B	A	G	A	H	E	H	N	Z	G	A	W	L
T	R	Y	A	N	D	A	R	M	S	B	I	L	L	I
E	Y	N	O	K	A	T	E	D	T	A	B	L	E	E
F	B	A	D	G	E	J	C	P	E	N	C	I	L	S
P	E	N	C	I	L	S	H	A	R	P	E	N	E	R
E	L	A	O	S	G	K	A	Q	T	E	B	O	Y	O
N	E	A	R	V	U	E	I	G	H	T	D	O	G	B
G	R	E	N	E	W	Z	R	U	L	E	R	G	X	O
F	O	O	T	E	D	O	Y	S	T	S	H	I	R	N

2 Ask your friends. Then write.

name	age	number of brothers	number of sisters	pet

Step 2

4

The Alphabet

3 Write the letters and make sentences.
Then number the pictures.

1 I/AM/SIX/YEARS/OLD.
2 _ _ _ _ _ _ _ _ _ _ _ _ _.
3 _ _ _ _ _ _ _ _ _ _ _ _ _.
4 _.
5 _.
6 _ _ _ _ _ _ _ _ _ _ _ _ _.

Kate
Julie
1 Gary
Kev
Bill
Suzy

4 Join the dots.

5

Starter lesson 3

Main Language Items			Resource File	Materials Needed
How do you spell ...?	apple	queen	16	cassette/cassette player
How many letters ...?	elephant	snake	22	materials to make word stone collections
The alphabet	ice-cream	umbrella		
	jelly	van		
	lamp	xylophone		
	nose	yo-yo		
	orange	zebra		

Step 1 Write the letters

a Listen to each of the sequences and write down the letters in the spaces provided in the AB, page 5.
b Separate the letters into words to make a sentence.
c Do each sequence in the same way. The first one is given as an example.
d Then number the picture which corresponds to the sentence.

Tapescript (with answers):
1 I-A-M-S-I-X-Y-E-A-R-S-O-L-D // (Gary)
2 M-Y-N-A-M-E-I-S-B-I-L-L // (Bill)
3 I-V-E-G-O-T-A-M-O-U-S-E // (Kev)
4 I-V-E-G-O-T-T-W-O-B-R-O-T-H-E-R-S // (Suzy)
5 M-Y-H-A-I-R-I-S-B-L-O-N-D-E // (Julie)
6 S-A-M-I-S-M-Y-S-N-A-K-E // (Kate)

Step 2 The Alphabet Quiz

a All the questions in this quiz are about the letters of the alphabet.

Tapescript (with answers):
1 How do you spell 'cat'? // (C-A-T)
2 What do these letters spell? B-O-Y.
3 How do you spell 'car'? // (C-A-R)
4 How many letters are there in 'tortoise'? // (8)
5 How many 'l's are there in the word 'yellow'? // (2)
6 Is there a letter 'z' in the word 'dogs'? // (No)
7 Which of these words has got a letter 'p' in: 'kite', 'doll' or 'elephant'? // (elephant)
8 What do these letters spell? H-E-L-L-O. // (Hello)
9 How do you spell 'pencil'? // (P-E-N-C-I-L)
10 How many letters are there in the word 'alphabet'? // (8)

b Divide the class into two teams. Play the first question on the tape. Pause the tape immediately after the question and before the answer! The first pupil to raise their hand gets a chance to answer, and if correct, wins two points for their team. If the answer is wrong, the opposing team may attempt the question for one point. Play the answer to check.
c Play all the questions in the same way. Be prepared to replay the quiz questions several times.

Step 3 Join the dots

a Pupils listen to the tape, look at page 5 of their AB and join the dots in the sequence given, to form a picture.
b Ensure that pupils start at the letter 'd'.

Tapescript:
d-t-o-i-a-g-x-q-e-v-m-c-r-y-j-w-p-k-n-s-h-f-b-l-d

Step 4 Game

a 'You are it!' is a traditional playground game that is used to choose a person for further games (to be 'it' or the 'chaser', for example). The players stand in a circle and one child says the chant, pointing at a different child in turn round the circle as he or she says each letter of the alphabet. The child who is pointed at after letter 'T' is 'it' ('U/you are it').
b Say **'Open your Activity Books at page 6. Look at the picture at the top of the page.'** Then listen to the chant on the tape, reading at the same time.
c Listen again with books closed and repeat the words. Play the tape again and chant along with the tape.
d When pupils are familiar with the chant, play the game in small groups.

Step 5 Words and pictures

a Pupils look at the puzzle and draw lines to connect the appropriate words to the pictures.

Step 6 Make word stones

a Pupils add fourteen more word stones to their collection to complete the alphabet, using the words in AB activity 6 (Step 5 above).

b Say **'Open your Activity Books at page 6.'** Point to the words. To make the word stones, each pupil requires fourteen 'stones' (either real stones or stone-shaped pieces of card, as before). Pupils write one word (**apple**, **elephant**, etc.) on each stone in felt-tip pen.

c When pupils have made all fourteen stones, ask them to put them together with the twelve stones they made earlier on their desks in alphabetical order.

d Now listen to the tape to check all the stones are correctly in order.

e Pupils then store their stones for future use.

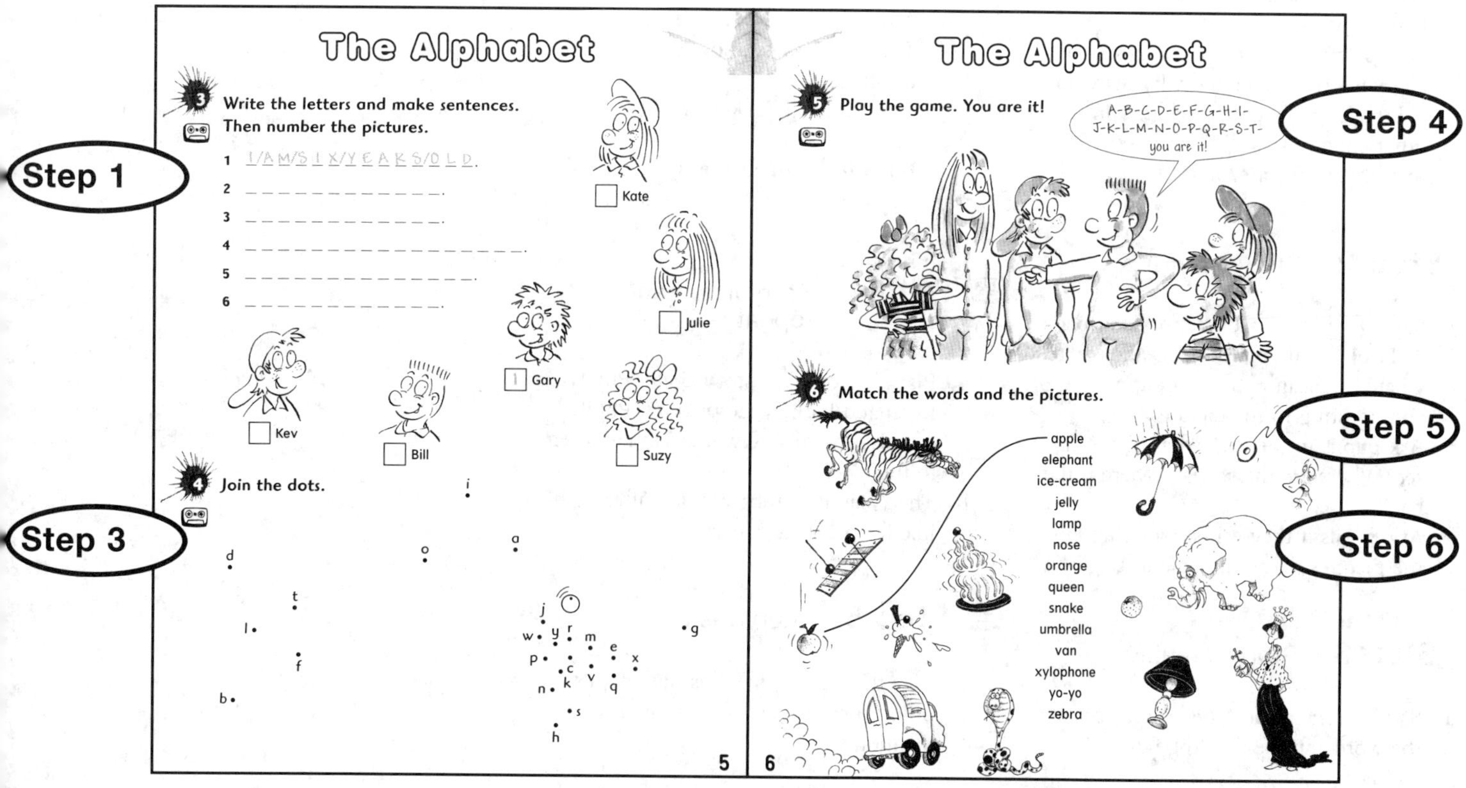

Step 1
Step 3
Step 4
Step 5
Step 6
The Alphabet
3 Write the letters and make sentences. Then number the pictures.
1 I/AM/SIX/YEARS/OLD.
Kate
Julie
Gary
Kev
Bill
Suzy
4 Join the dots.
5
The Alphabet
5 Play the game. You are it!
A-B-C-D-E-F-G-H-I-J-K-L-M-N-O-P-Q-R-S-T- you are it!
6 Match the words and the pictures.
apple
elephant
ice-cream
jelly
lamp
nose
orange
queen
snake
umbrella
van
xylophone
yo-yo
zebra
6

1 Story lesson

Main Language Items			Resource File	Materials Needed
There are ...	bed	shoes	45	cassette/cassette player
There's a ...	cupboard	coat		
clothes	floor	hat		
under	chair	skirt		
on	wardrobe	trousers		
table	socks	jacket		

Step 1 Topic warm-up

a Tell pupils in their L1 that they are going to continue their English lessons by looking at clothes. Introduce the word **'clothes'** at this point.
b Then ask pupils what words they think they might learn.
c Ask pupils what they are wearing. Can they name anything in English? Ask if they always wear the same things or if sometimes they wear different clothes. If so, why?
d Discuss what they can wear to school and what they can't and why/why not.
e Ask pupils if they think clothes in other countries are the same. Why do they think they are/aren't?

Step 2 Story warm-up

a Say **'Open your Coursebooks at page 4. Look at the pictures.'** Demonstrate what you mean by holding up your CB and pointing to the pictures.
b Ask pupils in their L1 what they can see. Where are the shoes? Where is the hat?
c Ask pupils if they can see anything in the pictures they can name in English.

Step 3 Story listening

a Say **'Listen to the tape.'** Pupils cover the words on the wardrobe door, look at the pictures and listen to the tape at the same time.
b Play the tape again.
c Ask questions in the pupils' L1 to check they have understood the story.

Tapescript:

What a Mess!
There are socks under the table, //
There are shoes under the bed, //
There's a coat on the cupboard //
And a hat on Rover's head. //
There are skirts and trousers on the floor, //
And there's a jacket on the chair, //
But when I open the wardrobe, //
I've got no clothes to wear. //

Step 4 Story listen and repeat

a Play the complete story again. Pupils listen and look at the pictures. Pupils can also mouth the words as they listen to the tape.
b Then play the story, pausing after each line for pupils to repeat.

Step 5 Story task

a Play the tape again. This time pupils point to each item of clothing as it is mentioned.
b Pupils can either point to clothes that are being worn in the classroom or you can draw pictures of the clothing on the blackboard.
c Repeat the above procedure once more.
d Pupils then close their CB. Ask pupils if they can remember where each item is. Say each item, e.g. **'socks'**. Pupils say where they are. **(Under the table.)**
e Play the tape again. Pupils listen and try to join in.

Step 2

Step 3

Step 4

Step 5

1 Clothes

STORY

What a Mess!

There are socks under the table.
There are shoes under the bed.
There's a coat on the cupboard.
And a hat on Rover's head.
There are skirts and trousers on the floor.
And there's a jacket on the chair.
But when I open the wardrobe,
I've got no clothes to wear.

GET THIS!
T
4
5

1A Lesson 1

Main Language Items		Resource File	Materials Needed
What are you wearing?	You look like a banana!		cassette/cassette player
Come on!	shoes		
getting dressed	jumper		
Where's my ...?	trousers		
Where are my ...?	jacket		
It's ...	*Parts of the body*		
They're ...			

Step 1 Action Game

a Briefly revise the names of the parts of the body using the commands **'Point to ...'** and **'Touch ...'**.

b Then play a variation of the traditional English game 'Simon Says'. When you give a command the whole class should act it out. When you say **'Don't'** before the command it should be ignored. Any pupil who carries out the command when you say **'Don't'** must leave the game. The last player remaining is the winner. Keep the action very brisk and if commands are not obeyed immediately then pupils must also leave the game.

c Other instructions can be added where they are appropriate to the body, e.g.
Stand on one leg!
Sit on your hands!
Don't close your eyes!
Put your hand under the chair!
Put your hands on your head!

Step 2 Presentation

a Say **'Open your Coursebooks at page 6.'** Hold your book up for the class. Very quickly ask some preliminary questions about the picture. Use **'Who's in the first picture? Is Suzy in the bedroom? Where's Bill?'**

b Play the tape. Pupils follow the dialogue, reading at the same time.

Step 3 Role play

a Divide the class into pairs and assign roles. One pupil in each pair plays Bill's role and one pupil Suzy's. Say **'Close your books and repeat after the tape.'**

b Play the first part of the dialogue. This time pupils repeat after the tape. Do this twice. Change roles and repeat the procedure.

c Pupils act out the dialogue without the help of the tape.

d Repeat steps **a–c** for the remaining part of the dialogue.

e Then pupils practise the whole dialogue. Insist upon actions to make the dialogue realistic, i.e. 'Bill' should be searching for his shoes; 'Suzy' pointing and handing 'Bill' his jacket.

f Volunteers can be invited to act out the dialogue for the class if they wish.

Step 4 Pairwork

a Divide the class into pairs. All pairs work simultaneously, with only one Coursebook between each pair, open at page 6. Say **'Cover the words at the bottom of the page. Look at the pictures.'**

b Pupils repeat after the tape. P1 repeats the questions, P2 repeats the answers. Repeat four times, changing roles.

c Then pupils ask and answer the questions without the help of the tape. P1 asks the questions using the words in the book to help, P2 answers using only the pictures, P1 must check and correct his/her partner's answers.

d Change roles and repeat the procedure.

Step 5 Crossword

a Pupils look at the picture clues and write the answers in the crossword on page 7 of the AB.

Step 2

Step 4

Getting Dressed

Listen

Bill, are you ready?
No!
Where are my yellow shoes?
They're under the bed.
Where's my yellow jacket?
It's in the wardrobe.
What are you wearing?
My yellow jumper, yellow jacket, yellow trousers and yellow shoes.
You look like a banana!

Ask and answer

What's this?	What's this?	What are these?	What are these?
A jacket.	A jumper.	Socks.	Shoes.

6

Clothes 1A

Listen

Suzy, Bill and Gary are ready for school. Bill is wearing his yellow clothes. Suzy is wearing a T-shirt, a skirt, socks and shoes. Gary is wearing a T-shirt, shorts, socks and shoes.

Ask and answer

Is Suzy wearing shorts?	No, she's wearing a skirt.
What colour is Gary's T-shirt?	Blue and white.
Are Suzy's socks red or white?	White.
What colour are Bill's clothes?	Yellow.

Listen

What number is on the sweatshirt?

32
68
51

7

Step 5

The Alphabet

5 Play the game. You are it!

A-B-C-D-E-F-G-H-I-J-K-L-M-N-O-P-Q-R-S-T- you are it!

6 Match the words and the pictures.

apple
elephant
ice-cream
jelly
lamp
nose
orange
queen
snake
umbrella
van
xylophone
yo-yo
zebra

6

Clothes 1A

1 Crossword. Write.

Across → 1 2 3 4

Down ↓ 1 2 3 4 5

2 Write.

jacket	jumper	shoes	shorts
skirt	socks	trousers	T-shirt

7

1A Lesson 2

Main Language Items		Resource File	Materials Needed
Is … wearing …? Are they … or …? He's/She's wearing …	skirt T-shirt shorts socks clothes	14 35	coloured pencils cassette/cassette player

Step 1 Presentation

a Say **'Open your Coursebooks at page 7. Look at the picture of Suzy, Bill and Gary.'**
b Play the tape. Pupils listen to the passage, reading at the same time.

Step 2 Pairwork

a Divide the class into pairs. All pairs work simultaneously. Say **'Cover all the words. Look at the picture of the children again.'**
b Pupils repeat after the tape. P1 repeats the questions, P2 repeats the answers. Repeat four times, changing roles.
c Then pupils ask and answer the questions without the help of the tape. P1 asks the questions using the words in the book to help, P2 answers looking only at the picture. P1 should prompt and check his/her partner's answers.
d Change roles and repeat the procedure.
e Then pupils ask and answer other similar questions about the children's clothes.

Step 3 Listen

a Say **'Look at the pictures at the bottom of page 7 of your Coursebook. Listen to the tape.'** Play the tape.
b Pupils listen to the first description and decide which picture is being described. Play the description twice then ask pupils **'What number is on her sweatshirt?'**
c Repeat the procedure for the other descriptions.

Tapescript (with answers):

1 **She's small and she's got brown hair. // She's wearing a yellow sweatshirt and blue trousers. // What number is on her sweatshirt? // (68)**
2 **She's wearing a blue sweatshirt, a green skirt and pink shoes. // The number on her sweatshirt is red. // What number is it? // (32)**
3 **She's the tallest of the four girls. // She's wearing a skirt and red shoes. // Her hair is brown. // What number's on her sweatshirt? // (87)**

Step 4 Write

a Pupils label the picture on page 7 of the AB, using the words in the boxes.
b Faster pupils can colour the picture.

Step 5 Read and colour

a Working individually, pupils read the description at the top of AB page 8 and colour the children's clothes.

Getting Dressed

Listen

Bill, are you ready?
No!
Where are my yellow shoes?
Where's my yellow jacket?
They're under the bed.
It's in the wardrobe.
What are you wearing?
My yellow jumper, yellow jacket, yellow trousers and yellow shoes.
You look like a banana!

Ask and answer

What's this?	What's this?	What are these?	What are these?
A jacket.	A jumper.	Socks.	Shoes.

6

Clothes **1A**

Listen

Suzy, Bill and Gary are ready for school. Bill is wearing his yellow clothes. Suzy is wearing a T-shirt, a skirt, socks and shoes. Gary is wearing a T-shirt, shorts, socks and shoes.

Ask and answer

Is Suzy wearing shorts?	No, she's wearing a skirt.
What colour is Gary's T-shirt?	Blue and white.
Are Suzy's socks red or white?	White.
What colour are Bill's clothes?	Yellow.

Listen

What number is on the sweatshirt?

32
68
51

7

Step 1

Step 2

Step 3

Clothes

1A

1 Crossword. Write.

Across →

1
2
3
4

Down ↓

1
2
3
4
5

2 Write.

jacket	jumper	shoes	shorts
skirt	socks	trousers	T-shirt

7

8

1A

Clothes

3 Read and colour.

Number five is wearing a blue T-shirt and yellow shorts. His socks are blue and his shoes are white. Number twelve is wearing an orange T-shirt and a black skirt. Her socks and shoes are grey. Number nine is wearing green shorts and a pink T-shirt. His shoes are red and his socks are pink.

9
12
5

4 Colour. Then ask and answer and write.

The Clothes Shop
OPEN
What colour's the ________ in your picture?
What colour are the ________ in your picture?

clothes	me	friend 1	friend 2

Step 4

Step 5

1A Lesson 3

Main Language Items	Resource File	Materials Needed
Who's wearing ...? She's/He's wearing ... What colour is/are the ... in your picture?	29 54	coloured pencils cassette/cassette player

Step 1 Presentation

a Practise the new vocabulary items introduced in this unit by asking pupils what they are wearing. Say '**Who's wearing trousers?**'

b Pupils who respond by raising their hands should be asked '**What colour are your trousers?**' or '**What colour are they?**'

c Ask similar questions using the words **jacket, jumper, shoes, socks, shorts, skirt** and **T-shirt**.

d The negative forms of questions can also be introduced using the question '**Who isn't wearing a skirt?**'

Step 2 Colour

a Pupils colour the clothes in the second picture on AB page 8 using colours of their own choice. This is not a directed colouring exercise. Pupils should not copy one another as this will defeat the purpose of the exercise.

Step 3 Groupwork

a This is based on the pictures the pupils coloured in Step 2.

b In the left-hand column of the chart, pupils write the name of the clothing items in the picture. In the second column, labelled '**Me**', they should write the colour of these clothes in their pictures.

c Ask pupils about the colour of the clothes in their picture, e.g.
'*Andreas*, **what colour's the jumper in your picture?**'
'*Maria*, **what colour are the trousers in your picture?**'
Continue until pupils are familiar with the question forms.

d Divide the class into groups of three. Pupils ask and answer similar questions about the colour of the clothes in their pictures and record the answers in the third and fourth columns of their charts.

Step 4 Listen and circle

a Pupils listen to the tape and circle the appropriate word to indicate the colour of the clothes the boy and girl are wearing in the pictures at the top of AB page 9.

b Play the tape three times. Allow pupils to compare their answers before replaying the tape to focus their listening.

c Using the information from the listening, pupils colour the children's clothes.

Tapescript:

Look at the boy and girl. // She's wearing a pink T-shirt and a green skirt. // Her socks are blue and her shoes are black. // His shoes are grey and he's wearing a red jumper and brown trousers. //

Step 5 Trace and write

a Pupils trace through the 'wool' maze on AB page 9 to discover the colour of each item. Pupils then complete the sentences in writing and colour the wool and clothes appropriately.

Step 6 Count and write

a Pupils count the clothing items hidden in the picture and write the answers alongside the words.

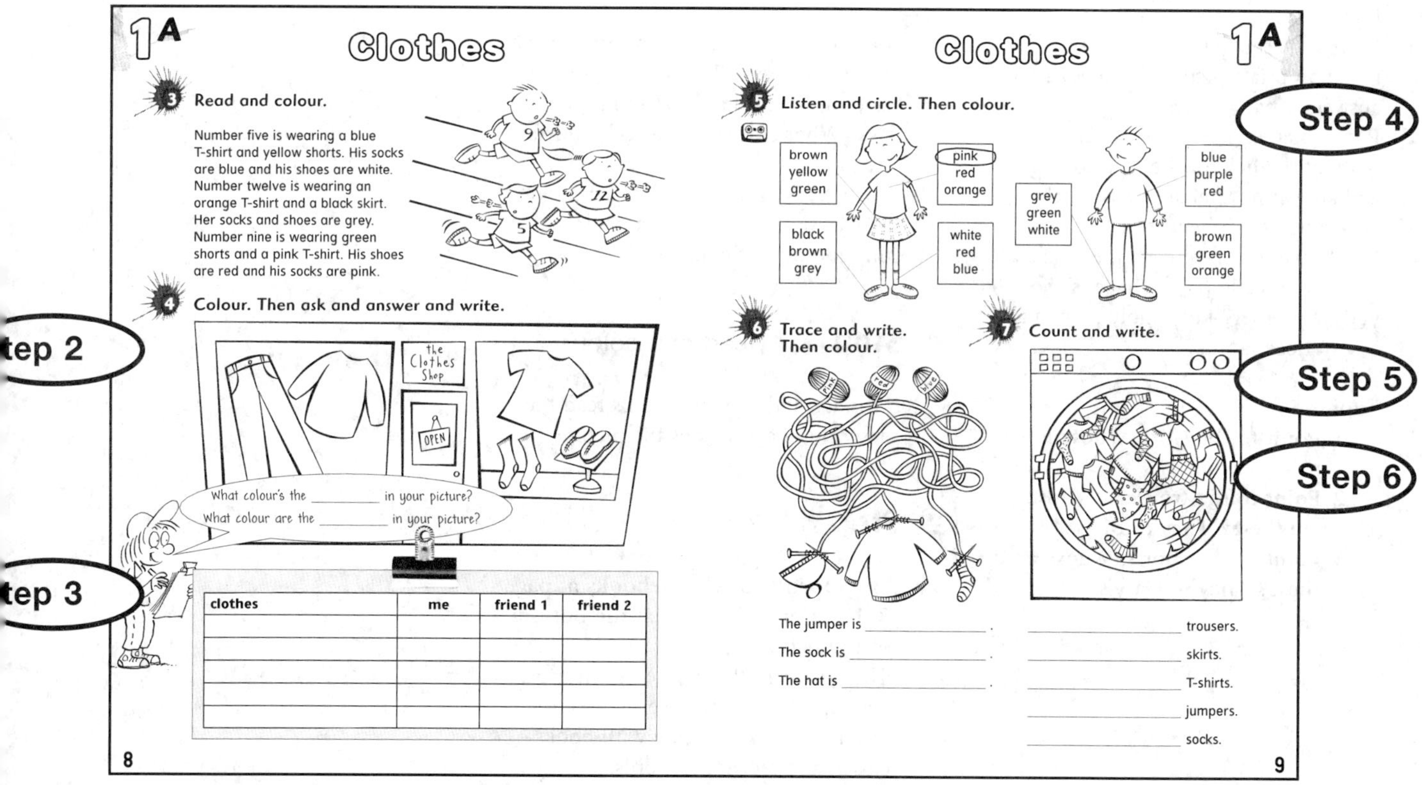

Step 2

Step 3

Step 4

Step 5

Step 6

1A

Clothes

3 Read and colour.

Number five is wearing a blue T-shirt and yellow shorts. His socks are blue and his shoes are white. Number twelve is wearing an orange T-shirt and a black skirt. Her socks and shoes are grey. Number nine is wearing green shorts and a pink T-shirt. His shoes are red and his socks are pink.

9
12
5

4 Colour. Then ask and answer and write.

The Clothes Shop
OPEN
What colour's the ________ in your picture?
What colour are the ________ in your picture?

clothes	me	friend 1	friend 2

8

Clothes

1A

5 Listen and circle. Then colour.

brown
yellow
green
pink
red
orange
black
brown
grey
white
red
blue
grey
green
white
blue
purple
red
brown
green
orange

6 Trace and write. Then colour.

The jumper is ________ .

The sock is ________ .

The hat is ________ .

7 Count and write.

________ trousers.

________ skirts.

________ T-shirts.

________ jumpers.

________ socks.

9

1B Lesson 1

Main Language Items		Resource File	Materials Needed
Whose is this?	son	27	coloured pencils
Whose are these?	went	33	cassette/cassette player
Possessive's	off		
	on		

Step 1 Pairwork

a Say '**Open your Coursebooks at page 8. Look at the picture of the clothes on the washing line.**' Hold up your book for the class. Quickly revise the names of the clothes items. Point to the clothes items and ask '**What's this?**' and '**What are these?**'

b Divide the class into pairs. All pairs work simultaneously. One CB between each pair should be open at page 8. Play the tape.

c P1 repeats the questions, pointing at the appropriate picture. P2 repeats the answers. Change roles.

d Pupils then continue the exercise without the help of the tape, asking and answering similar questions about all the items on the washing line. Pupils may either refer to the article of clothing directly (i.e. '**Whose is the yellow jumper?**') or simply point and ask '**Whose is this?**'

Tapescript:

1 **Point to the skirt. Whose is this? It's Suzy's.**
2 **Point to the trousers. Whose are these? They're Bill's.**
3 **Point to the shorts. Whose are these? They're Gary's.**

Step 2 Write. Then colour

a Pupils turn to the picture of the washing line on page 10 of their ABs and describe each item of clothing according to its owner and colour. The first one is given as an example.

b Faster pupils can colour the picture accordingly.

Step 3 Pairwork

a Briefly revise the question forms '**What colour is/are ...?**' relating to the clothing items on the washing line. Ask '**What colour are Gary's shorts?**' etc.

b Then working in pairs, pupils ask and answer similar questions about all of the clothes on the line.

Step 4 Read and colour

a Working individually, pupils read the description and colour the picture.

Step 5 Rhyme

a Say '**Open your Coursebooks at page 8. Look at the picture at the bottom of the page.**'

b Then listen to the rhyme on the tape, reading at the same time.

c Listen again line by line with books closed and repeat the words. Do each line in the same way. Play the rhyme again and chant along with the tape.

Step 1

Step 5

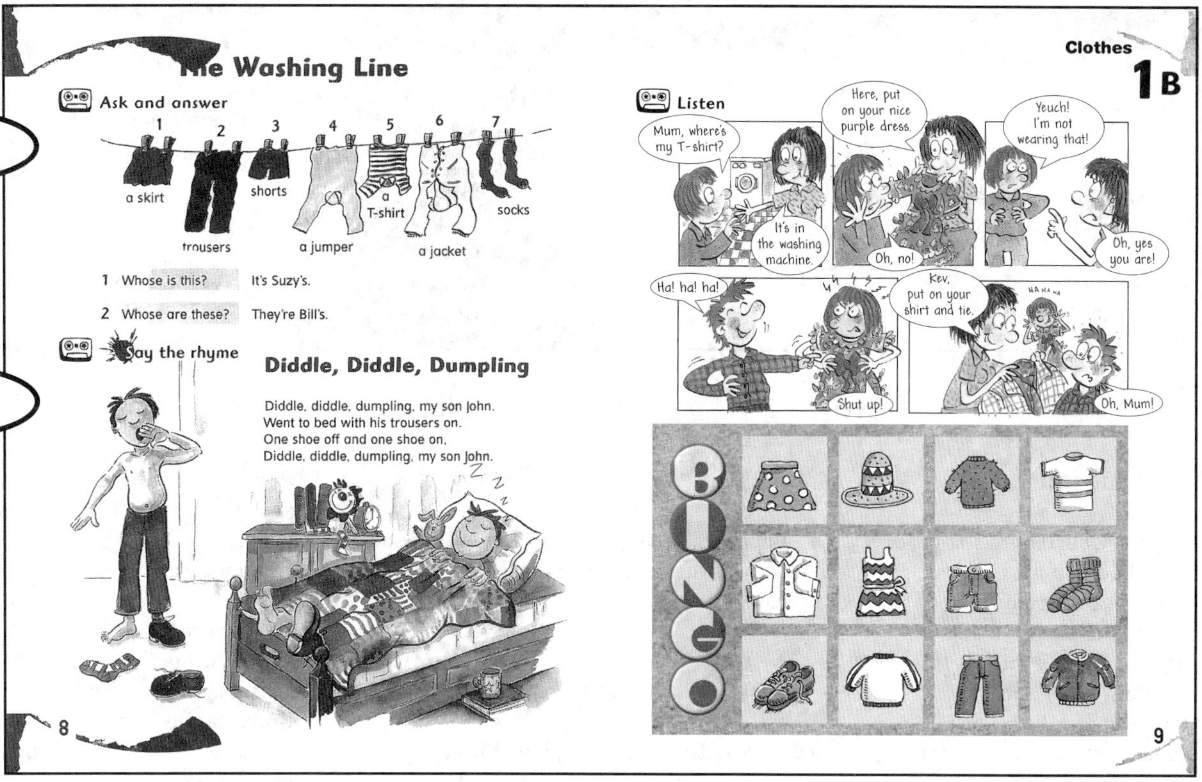

The Washing Line

Ask and answer

1 2 3 4 5 6 7
a skirt
trousers
shorts
a jumper
a T-shirt
a jacket
socks

1 Whose is this? It's Suzy's.

2 Whose are these? They're Bill's.

Say the rhyme

Diddle, Diddle, Dumpling

Diddle, diddle, dumpling, my son John.
Went to bed with his trousers on.
One shoe off and one shoe on.
Diddle, diddle, dumpling, my son John.

8

Clothes **1B**

Listen

Mum, where's my T-shirt?
It's in the washing machine.
Here, put on your nice purple dress.
Oh, no!
Yeuch! I'm not wearing that!
Oh, yes you are!
Ha! ha! ha!
Shut up!
Kev, put on your shirt and tie.
Oh, Mum!
BINGO

9

Step 2

Step 4

1B Clothes

1 Write. Then colour.

What's on the washing line?

1 2 3 4 5 6 7

1 Suzy's red skirt.
2 Bill's blue ______
3 Gary's ______
4 ______
5 ______
6 ______
7 ______

2 Read and colour.

This is a photograph of my mother and father. My mother has got black hair. She's wearing a red dress. My father has got black hair too. He's wearing a blue shirt and a green jumper. His tie is black and yellow.

Kev Brown

10

Clothes **1B**

3 Write.

1 Is Kate wearing her sweatshirt?
______
2 What is Kate wearing?
______
3 What colour is Kate's dress?
______
4 What's Kev wearing?
______

4 Make word stones.

hat
sock
socks
hats
dress
skirt
trousers

11

1B Lesson 2

Main Language Items		Resource File	Materials Needed
Is ... wearing ...?	dress	15	Bingo cover cards
She/He isn't ...	shirt		cassette/cassette player
They aren't ...	tie		
Shut up!	washing machine		

Step 1 Presentation

a Say **'Open your Coursebooks at page 9.'** Hold your book up for the class. Very quickly ask some preliminary questions about the pictures at the top of the page. Use **'Who's this? Is this ...? What colour's ...?'** etc.

b Play the tape. Pupils follow the dialogue looking at the pictures at the same time.

Step 2 Role play

a Divide the class into groups of three. Assign roles. One pupil in each group plays Kate's role, one pupil plays Kev's role and one pupil Mum's. Say **'Look at the pictures.'**

b Play the tape. Pupils repeat after the tape. Do this twice. Change roles and repeat the procedure. Then change roles again and repeat the procedure for a third time so that pupils have played all three characters' roles.

c Pupils act out the dialogue without the help of the tape.

d Then pupils practise the dialogue with actions, e.g. Kate with hands held up in horror saying **'Oh, no!'**

e Volunteers can be invited to act out the dialogue for the class if they wish.

Step 3 Write

a Pupils read the questions and write the answers in the spaces provided on AB page 11.

Step 4 Make Bingo cards

a To play Bingo each pupil will need to make twelve small cover cards. These should be approximately the same size as the squares on the Bingo card (CB page 9, 3cm x 3cm). They may be made from paper or thin card.

b Each card should have the same name of one of the items of clothing (shown in the Bingo card on CB page 9) clearly printed on it.

Step 5 Bingo

a Pupils will need their CBs open at page 9. Instruct them to cover any six squares on their Bingo card by placing the appropriate cover card face down over the picture. In this way, each pupil's card should now have six different pictures showing.

b The Bingo Caller (teacher) will also need a set of cover cards. Shuffle your cards. Lay them face down in front of you. Ask **'Are you ready?'**

c Encourage the answer **'Yes'** or **'No'**, as appropriate. Select a card. Read out the word on the card.

d Pupils cover the pictures on their card as the corresponding words are called out.

e Continue 'calling' until one of the pupils has covered all the squares on his/her card. The first player to do so shouts **'Bingo!'**

f This player must confirm that his/her Bingo card is correct by reading back the names from the cards that are face up. If correct, he or she is the winner.

g Divide the class into groups of 4–6 players. Pupils continue the game simultaneously in groups.

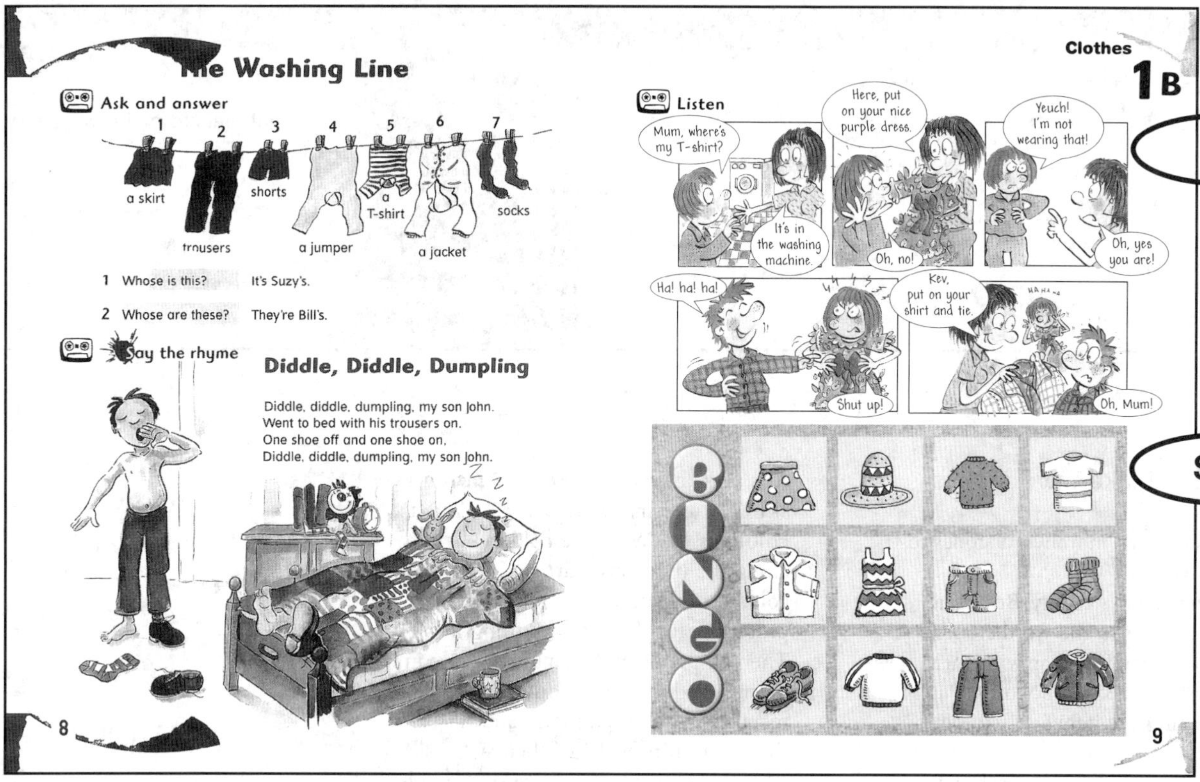

The Washing Line

Ask and answer

1 a skirt, 2 trousers, 3 shorts, 4 a jumper, 5 a T-shirt, 6 a jacket, 7 socks

1 Whose is this? It's Suzy's.

2 Whose are these? They're Bill's.

Say the rhyme

Diddle, Diddle, Dumpling

Diddle, diddle, dumpling, my son John.
Went to bed with his trousers on.
One shoe off and one shoe on,
Diddle, diddle, dumpling, my son John.

8

Clothes **1B**

Listen

Mum, where's my T-shirt?
It's in the washing machine.
Here, put on your nice purple dress.
Oh, no!
Yeuch! I'm not wearing that!
Oh, yes you are!
Ha! ha! ha!
Shut up!
Kev, put on your shirt and tie.
Oh, Mum!
BINGO

9

Step

Step 5

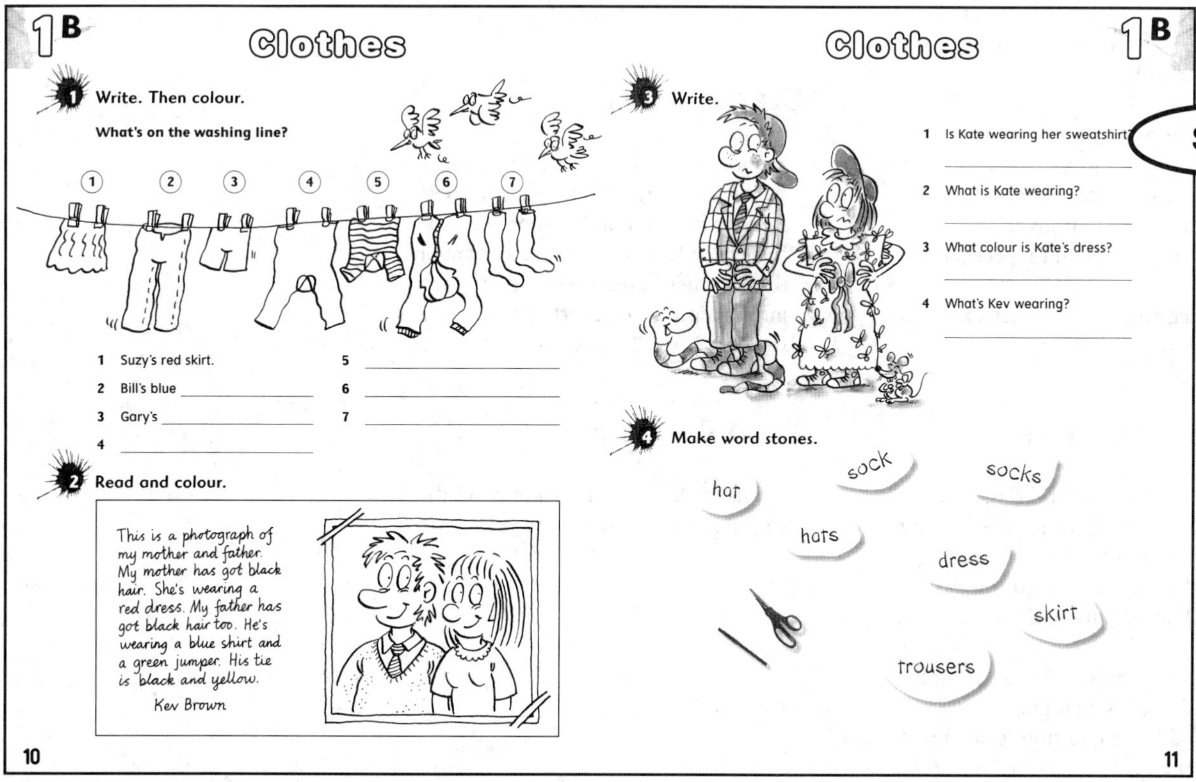

1B Clothes

1 Write. Then colour.

What's on the washing line?

1 Suzy's red skirt.
2 Bill's blue ______
3 Gary's ______
4 ______
5 ______
6 ______
7 ______

2 Read and colour.

This is a photograph of my mother and father. My mother has got black hair. She's wearing a red dress. My father has got black hair too. He's wearing a blue shirt and a green jumper. His tie is black and yellow.
Kev Brown

10

Clothes **1B**

3 Write.

1 Is Kate wearing her sweatshirt? ______
2 What is Kate wearing? ______
3 What colour is Kate's dress? ______
4 What's Kev wearing? ______

4 Make word stones.

hat
sock
socks
hats
dress
skirt
trousers

11

Step 3

1B Lesson 3

Main Language Items		Resource File	Materials Needed
What colour is your ...?	hat(s)		materials to make word stones
What colour are your ...?	sock(s)		
Are you wearing ...?	trousers		
... is wearing ...	skirt		
Plurals	dress		

Step 1 Make word stones

a Pupils add seven more word stones to their collection.

b Say **'Open your Activity Books at page 11.'** Point to the word stones. Check pupils are familiar with their meaning: say one of the words. Pupils mime putting the item(s) of clothing on.

c To make the word stones, each pupil requires seven 'stones' (either real stones or stone-shaped pieces of card, as before). Pupils write one word on each stone in felt-tip pen, as shown in the pictures.

d Working in pairs, pupils play a simple word-recognition game. Each pair uses one collection of stones, face up. P1 says a word and P2 finds the correct stone. Change roles and repeat the procedure.

e Pupils then store their stones for future use.

Step 2 Groupwork

a Ask various pupils in the class questions about what they are wearing. Use the structures: **'Are you wearing ...?'**, **'What colour are your trousers?'** and **'What colour's your T-shirt?'**

b Copy the grid from AB page 12 onto the blackboard. When pupils are familiar with the question form, direct them to the grid on page 12 of their ABs. Ask the class **'Is *Maria* wearing a skirt?'** If the answer is 'yes' ask **'What colour is it?'** Write the colour alongside the word **skirt** in the first column of your chart. Repeat the procedure for the other clothing items.

c Then all pupils work simultaneously in groups of three asking other group members similar questions, and fill in the chart on page 12 of their AB.

d Round up the exercise by asking pupils questions about other class members, i.e. **'What colour are *Maria's* socks?'**

Step 3 Write

a Demonstrate on the blackboard the sentences pupils should write in their exercise books. Pupils choose one of their friends and write sentences about their clothes based upon the information in the chart. e.g. **'*Enrique* is wearing *a red T-shirt.*'**

Step 4 Circle

a Pupils circle the words hidden on the washing line.

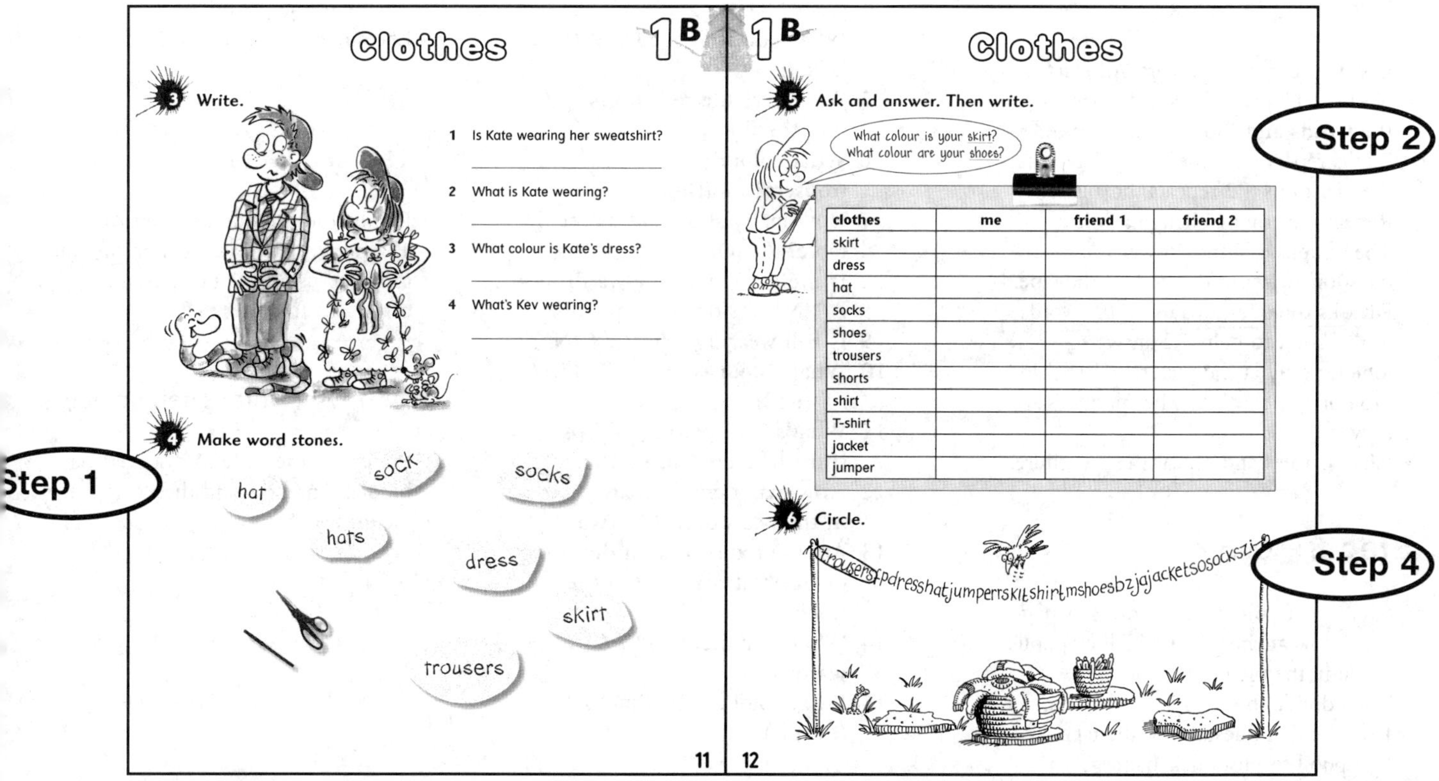
Clothes 1B

3 Write.

1 Is Kate wearing her sweatshirt?

2 What is Kate wearing?

3 What colour is Kate's dress?

4 What's Kev wearing?

4 Make word stones.

Step 1
hat
sock
socks
hats
dress
skirt
trousers

11

1B Clothes

5 Ask and answer. Then write.

What colour is your skirt?
What colour are your shoes?
Step 2

clothes	me	friend 1	friend 2
skirt			
dress			
hat			
socks			
shoes			
trousers			
shorts			
shirt			
T-shirt			
jacket			
jumper			

6 Circle.

trousersfpdresshatjumperrskitshirtmshoesbzjajacketsosocksz
Step 4

12

1c Lesson 1

Main Language Items			Resource File	Materials Needed
It's cold today *Question forms*	snow snowman boots coat	cardigan scarf	30 32	cassette/cassette player

Step 1 Presentation

a Say **'Look at the picture on page 10 of your Coursebook. Look at the children's clothes.'** Hold your book up for the class. Say **'It's very 'cold' in the picture.'** Mime the word 'cold' by shivering. Ask pupils **'Is it cold here?'**

b Then play the tape. Pupils listen to the description, reading at the same time.

Step 2 Pairwork

a Divide the class into pairs. All pairs work simultaneously. Say **'Cover all the words and look at the picture.'**

b Pupils repeat after the tape. P1 repeats the questions, P2 repeats the answers. Repeat four times, changing roles.

c Then pupils ask and answer the questions without the help of the tape. P1 asks the questions using the words in the book to help, P2 answers looking only at the picture. P1 should prompt and check his/her partner's answers.

d Change roles and repeat the procedure.

Step 3 Quiz

a Say **'Open your Coursebooks at page 11. Look at the picture.'** Allow pupils to study the picture briefly.

b Then divide the class into two teams. Play the first question on the tape. The first pupil to raise their hand gets a chance to answer, and if correct, wins two points for their team. If the answer is wrong, the opposing team may attempt the question for one point.

c Do all the questions in the same way.

Tapescript (with answers):

1 **Where's the purple hat? // (On the wardrobe)**
2 **Is there a pen on the table? // (Yes)**
3 **Is the pen on the table red or green? // (Red)**
4 **What's on Bill's bed? // (A jacket)**
5 **Where are the red shorts? // (On the floor)**
6 **What colour are Suzy's trousers? // (Blue)**
7 **How many shoes are under the table? // (One)**
8 **Is there a kite in the wardrobe? // (No, it's on the wardrobe)**
9 **Is Bill wearing a hat? // (No)**
10 **What colour is Suzy's T-shirt? // (Red)**
11 **What's Bill wearing? // (A shirt, trousers and socks)**
12 **How many children are there in the bedroom? // (Two)**
13 **Are the red shorts on the floor or on the bed? // (On the floor)**
14 **Where are the bags? // (In the wardrobe)**
15 **What colour is the hat? // (Purple)**

Step 4 Pairwork

a Elicit questions from pupils that they can ask about the picture on page 11. Pupils may use all the question forms they know, ranging from simple structures such as **'What's this?'**, to more complex forms such as **'Whose is the shoe under the table?'** Write the question forms on the blackboard.

b Divide the class into pairs. Pupils ask and answer as many questions as they can about the picture.

c Encourage pupils to help and prompt one another.

Step 5 Write

a Pupils read the questions on AB page 13 and write the answers on the lines provided using the picture on page 11 of the CB to help.

Step 6 Write. Then colour

a Pupils use the code to discover the hidden sentences and then colour the pictures accordingly.

tep 1

tep 2

Step 3

Step 4

Step 5

Step 6

It's Cold Today

Listen

It's cold today. The children are playing in the snow. Bill and Kate are making a snowman. The snowman is wearing a black hat and a scarf. Kate is wearing a big cardigan and boots, Bill is wearing a coat and an orange hat.

Ask and answer

What colour are Bill's boots?	Green.
What colour is Kate's cardigan?	Purple.
Is Kate wearing a coat?	No, she's wearing a cardigan.
What colour is Bill's coat?	Blue.

10

Clothes **1c**

Tell your friend

11

1B

Clothes

5 Ask and answer. Then write.

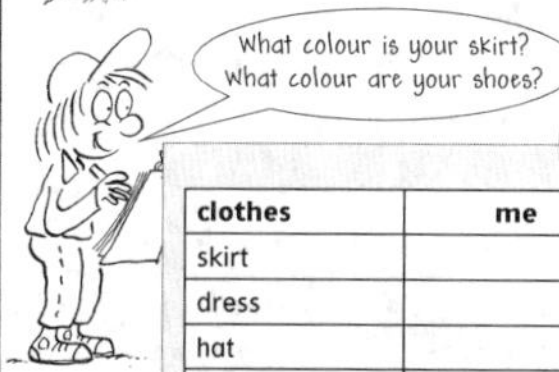
What colour is your skirt?
What colour are your shoes?

clothes	me	friend 1	friend 2
skirt			
dress			
hat			
socks			
shoes			
trousers			
shorts			
shirt			
T-shirt			
jacket			
jumper			

6 Circle.

trousersfpdresshatjumperrskitshirtmshoesbzjajacketsososockszi

12

Clothes

1c

1 Write.

Look at the picture on page 11 in your Coursebook.

1 Where are the red shorts? ____________
2 What colour are Suzy's trousers? ____________
3 What's on Bill's bed? ____________
4 Where's the yellow sock? ____________
5 What colour is the hat on the wardrobe? ____________

2 Write. Then colour.

a	b	c	d	e	f	g	h	i	j	k	l	m	n	o	p	q	r	s	t	u	v	w	x	y	z
1	2	3	4	5	6	7	8	9	10	11	12	13	14	15	16	17	18	19	20	21	22	23	24	25	

A 3 15 12 15 21 18 19 12 15 23' 19 8 1 20 15 18 1 14 7 5.
____

B 2 21 20 3 8 9 19 23 5 1 18 9 14 7 7 18 5 5 14 2 15 15 20 19.
____

C 19 1 13 9 19 23 5 1 18 9 14 7 1 7 18 5 25 8 1 20.
____

D 4 21 6 6 25' 19 19 8 15 5 19 1 18 5 2 18 15 23 14.
____

E 23 15 23' 19 8 1 20 9 19 18 5 4.
____

13

1c Lesson 2

Main Language Items		Resource File	Materials Needed
He's/She's wearing ...	in	33	coloured pencils
Who's wearing ...?	on		
There is ...	under		

Step 1 Presentation

a Instruct four or five pupils to come to the front of the classroom and stand in a line facing the class. (If necessary, pupils can stand on chairs to be seen more clearly.)
b Choose one pupil. Describe his/her clothes. The rest of the class must guess the identity of the pupil. Use the form: **(S)he's wearing a *red jumper*.** etc.
c Then ask one of the pupils to describe. Repeat the activity with other pupils.
d When pupils are comfortable with the structure, change the activity and ask the class questions about the pupils at the front. Use the structures: **Who's wearing ...?, Is *Maria* wearing a ...?**
e Encourage pupils to ask each other questions.
f Keep changing the pupils at the front of the classroom to allow for maximum permutations of questions and allow all pupils a turn.

Step 2 Colour

a Divide the class into pairs. P1 opens their CB on page 11 and P2 opens their AB on page 14.
b P1 describes the picture in front of him/her using the structure:
There is a (purple hat) in/on/under the ...
P2 colours the picture in the AB accordingly, without looking at the CB.
c Change roles and repeat the procedure.
d Finally pupils should compare their AB pictures with their CB, and check the colours of the clothes.

Step 3 Write

a Pupils look at the pictures they have coloured in their ABs and answer the questions in the spaces provided.

Step 4 Write

a Pupils unjumble the letters to find the name and colour of five items of clothing.

Homework

Pupils should find out what members of their family are wearing and write the answers in the grid provided at the top of page 15 in their AB. Then, using this information, they should draw a picture of a member of their family in the space provided and colour it accordingly.

It's Cold Today

Step 2

Listen

It's cold today. The children are playing in the snow. Bill and Kate are making a snowman. The snowman is wearing a black hat and a scarf. Kate is wearing a big cardigan and boots. Bill is wearing a coat and an orange hat.

Ask and answer

What colour are Bill's boots?	Green.
What colour is Kate's cardigan?	Purple.
Is Kate wearing a coat?	No, she's wearing a cardigan.
What colour is Bill's coat?	Blue.

Tell your friend

Step 2

Step 3

3 Listen to your friend and colour. Then write.

1 What colour's the hat? ______

2 Where's the jumper? ______

3 What colour are Suzy's shoes? ______

4 Where's the coat? ______

5 Where are the shorts? ______

Step 4

4 Write.

Pink socks

A ___ _____

_ _____ ____

_ _____ _______

_____ _____

Clothes 1c

5 Write. Then draw and colour.

Clothes	my ______	my ______

This is my ______.

6 Read and put the clothes on the boy and girl.

Look at the children on page 62 in your Coursebook.

You need

Clothes
Name:

1 The boy is wearing a red and white sweatshirt and grey trousers. His socks and shoes are red.

2 The girl is wearing an orange dress and a pink hat. She's wearing grey shoes and white socks.

1c Lesson 3

Main Language Items	Resource File	Materials Needed
Put a/the ... on ... Give ...	28 48 49	Clothes pieces (see AB cut-outs section) cassette/cassette player

Step 1 Presentation

This exercise is based upon the pictures pupils drew for homework.

a Select one of the pupil's ABs. Hold up the book so the class can see the picture he/she drew for homework. Point to the picture and ask the pupil **'Who's this?'** Then ask **'What's he/she wearing?'** Encourage all pupils to respond.

b Then divide the class into pairs. Pupils ask and answer similar questions about one another's pictures.

Step 2 Listening (Task)

For this exercise each pupil will need the cut-out section clothes pieces. The baseboard picture of the boy and girl on page 62 of the CB is also needed.

a Pupils listen to the description on the tape and place the clothes pieces in the appropriate place on their baseboard. After each complete description pupils should compare their answers with their partners'.

b To check that pupils have accurately followed the description, ask the class questions about their finished picture using the structure: **Is the boy/girl wearing a ...?**

Tapescript:

The boy is wearing red trousers and the girl is wearing grey trousers. // She is wearing a green and white jumper // and he is wearing a blue T-shirt. // His shoes are black // and her shoes are red.

Step 3 Reading (Task)

For this exercise each pupil will need the cut-out section clothes pieces and the boy and girl baseboard on CB page 62.

a Pupils read the instruction on page 15 of the AB and place the clothes pieces on their baseboard accordingly.

b When pupils have finished they should compare their completed picture with their partner's.

c Faster pupils can repeat the exercise, this time with one pupil giving the instructions.

Step 4 Pairwork

For this exercise each pupil will need the cut-out section clothes pieces and the baseboard on page 62 of the CB.

a Divide the class into pairs. Each pupil places their baseboard and clothes pieces in front of them. A book should be stood up on end between each pair of pupils, so that they cannot see one another's board.

b P1 dresses one or both of the children on their baseboard. Then using the structures:
Put a ... on the boy/girl.
Put the *red* ... on the boy/girl.
Give the boy/girl a/the ...
P1 describes his/her picture. P2 must try to reconstruct an identical picture following the instructions. (Write the structures on the blackboard to assist pupils.)

c P2 may ask questions in English to help if necessary. After each complete description pupils should compare their answers with their partners'.

d Then change roles and repeat the exercise.

Step 2

Step 3

Step 4

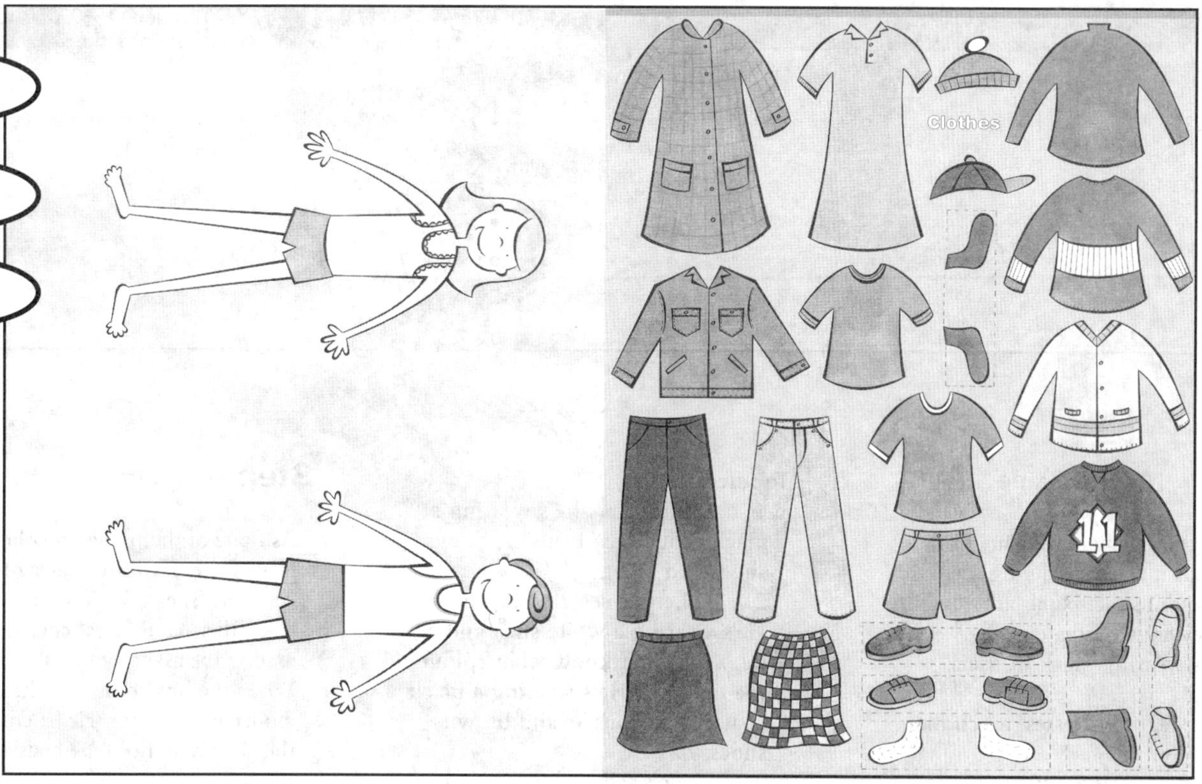
Clothes

1C **Clothes**

3 Listen to your friend and colour. Then write.

1 What colour's the hat?

____

2 Where's the jumper?

____

3 What colour are Suzy's shoes?

____

4 Where's the coat?

____

5 Where are the shorts?

____

4 Write.

Pink socks

A ___ _____

_ _____ ____

_ _____ ________

____ _____

Clothes 1C

5 Write. Then draw and colour.

Clothes	my ______	my ______

This is my

__________.

6 Read and put the clothes on the boy and girl.

Look at the children on page 62 in your Coursebook.

You need

1 The boy is wearing a red and white sweatshirt and grey trousers. His socks and shoes are red.

2 The girl is wearing an orange dress and a pink hat. She's wearing grey shoes and white socks.

Step 3

1D Lesson 1

Main Language Items		Resource File	Materials Needed
Is she/he wearing ...?	spy	32	cassette/cassette player
Has she/he got ...?	tie	33	
is/isn't	well		
I'm wearing ...			

Step 1 Action Game

a In this action game, revise any of the commands introduced during the course, and instruct pupils according to what they are wearing, e.g.
All boys wearing black trousers, stand up!
All girls wearing dresses, touch the floor!
Everybody wearing a jumper, put your hands on your head!

Step 2 Listen

a Say **'Look at the pictures at the top of page 12 of your Coursebooks.'** Pupils must listen to the three descriptions to decide which one of the four men is the spy.
b Write the four names on the blackboard with a box next to each name. Pupils copy the names onto a piece of paper.
c Play the tape. Pupils listen to the first description and decide which man does not fit the description. They should place a cross in the box by his name. Allow pupils to confer. Play the description twice.
d Repeat the procedure for the other descriptions.
e Pupils should then have eliminated three of the four men and the remaining character is the spy.

Tapescript:

1 Well, . . . he's wearing a black coat, black trousers, brown shoes and a hat. //
2 Let me see ... he's tall. He's wearing a white shirt and a tie. // I don't know what colour the tie is. // He's wearing a black coat, black trousers and brown shoes. //
3 He's tall and he's wearing a black coat, black trousers, a white shirt and a red tie. // Oh ... and his shoes are brown. //
Answer: Mr Green is the spy.

Step 3 Pairwork

a This exercise is again based upon the pictures on page 12. Say **'Look at the four men. Listen to the tape. Who is this?'** Play the tape. Then ask again **'Who is it? Who's the spy?'**
b Then divide the class into pairs. P1 decides which man is going to be the spy. P2 asks similar 'yes/no' type questions to determine which of the four men their partner has in mind.
c Pupils should use the model dialogue on page 12 as a guide to question types.

Step 4 Game (Whole class)

a Ask one of the pupils to volunteer to leave the room or turn away from the class. He/she is the 'policeman'.
b The other pupils must choose one among themselves to be the 'spy'.
c When the 'spy' has been chosen, the 'policeman' returns. He/she must ask the class **'yes/no'** type questions about the spy's appearance to determine his identity:
Is it a boy/girl?
Is he/she wearing trousers?
Has he/she got black hair?

Step 5 Words and pictures

a Say **'Open your Activity Books at page 16. Look at the pictures of the children and read the descriptions.'**
b Pupils must decide what each of the children is saying and connect the appropriate speech bubble to each character. The first one has been done as an example.

Homework

Ask pupils to bring a small item of their clothing to class with them next lesson. Ideal items might be a tie, a sock, a belt, a scarf, a glove, swimming trunks, but any item will suffice. Ask pupils not to show other pupils what they have brought.

Step 2

Step 3

What's He Wearing?

Listen

Who is the spy?

Mr Black
Mr White
Mr Grey
Mr Green

Ask and answer

Is he tall?
Yes, he is.
Is he wearing brown shoes?
Yes, he is.
Is he wearing a red tie?
No, he isn't.
It's Mr White.

12

Clothes **1D**

Ask and answer

Point to Bill.

Whose T-shirt is this?	Gary's.
Whose trousers are these?	Kev's.
Whose shoes are these?	Gary's.

HA HA HA

Listen

I'm wearing grey trousers, a brown jumper, a white shirt, white socks and brown shoes. My hat is red.

13

Step 5

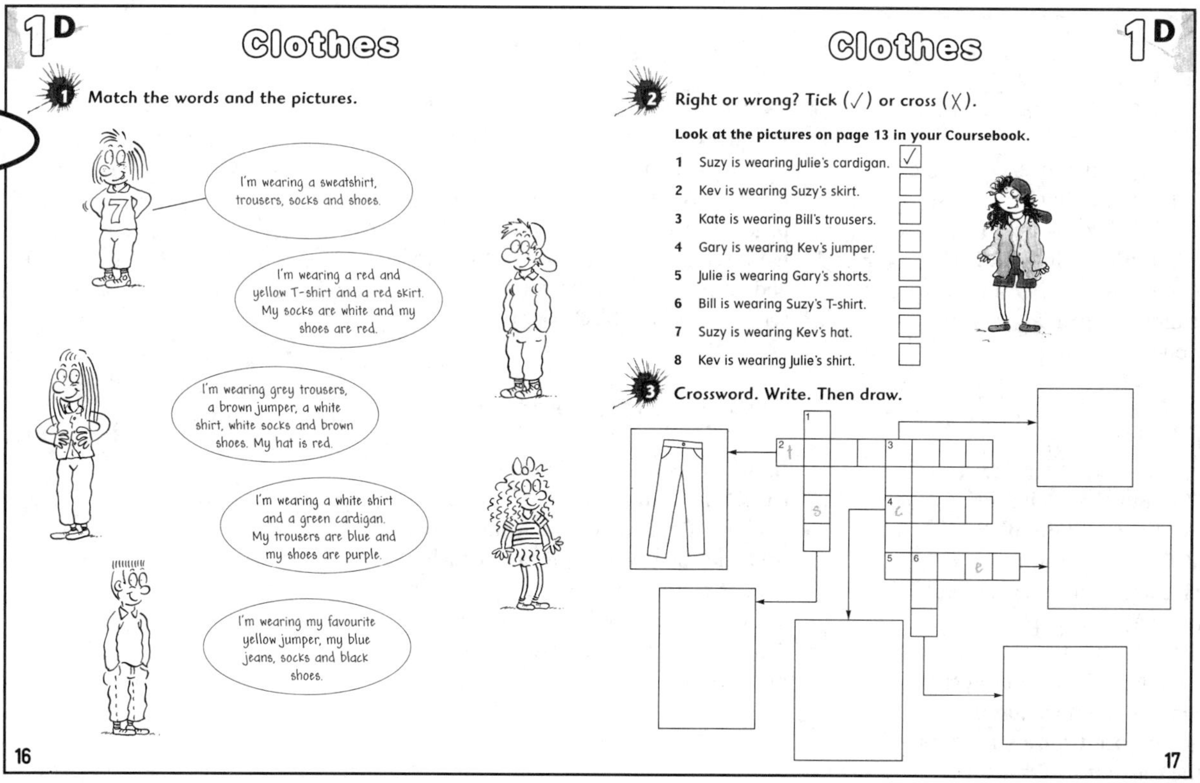

1D Clothes

1 Match the words and the pictures.

I'm wearing a sweatshirt, trousers, socks and shoes.
I'm wearing a red and yellow T-shirt and a red skirt. My socks are white and my shoes are red.
I'm wearing grey trousers, a brown jumper, a white shirt, white socks and brown shoes. My hat is red.
I'm wearing a white shirt and a green cardigan. My trousers are blue and my shoes are purple.
I'm wearing my favourite yellow jumper, my blue jeans, socks and black shoes.

16

Clothes **1D**

2 Right or wrong? Tick (✓) or cross (✗).

Look at the pictures on page 13 in your Coursebook.

1. Suzy is wearing Julie's cardigan. ✓
2. Kev is wearing Suzy's skirt. ☐
3. Kate is wearing Bill's trousers. ☐
4. Gary is wearing Kev's jumper. ☐
5. Julie is wearing Gary's shorts. ☐
6. Bill is wearing Suzy's T-shirt. ☐
7. Suzy is wearing Kev's hat. ☐
8. Kev is wearing Julie's shirt. ☐

3 Crossword. Write. Then draw.

17

1D Lesson 2

Main Language Items	Resource File	Materials Needed
Whose ... is this? Whose ... are these? *Possessive* 's (e.g. Gary's, Kev's)	31	items of clothing cassette/cassette player

Step 1 Game (Whole class)

a For homework, pupils were asked to find a small item of their own clothing and bring it to class. Begin the lesson by collecting these clothes items. Those pupils who do not bring an item of clothing should hand in a small object such as a pencil, etc.

b Select an item of clothing or object from those collected and hold it up for the class to see. Ask the class **'Whose is this?'** Pupils must guess the identity of the owner. The owner however should remain silent.

c Repeat the procedure for the remaining items.

d An element of competitiveness can be added to the game. Divide the class into two teams. Ask the questions to a pupil from each team in turn. If the pupil guesses correctly, he/she wins a point for his/her team. Players must not help one another.

Step 2 Pairwork

a Say **'Open your Coursebooks at page 13. Look at the picture of the children. They are wearing the wrong clothes.'** Hold up your book for the class. Ask the pupils if they know whose clothes the children are wearing. Point to the clothes items at random and ask **'Whose jumper is this?'** and **'Whose trousers are these?'**

b Divide the class into pairs. All pairs work simultaneously. One book between each pair should be open at page 13. Play the tape.

c P1 repeats the questions, pointing at the appropriate items of clothing that Bill is wearing. P2 repeats the answers. Change roles.

d Pupils then continue the exercise without the help of the tape, asking and answering similar questions about all the children.

Step 3 Right or wrong?

a Working individually, pupils read the sentences on page 17 of the AB and indicate whether they are true or false. Pupils must refer to the pictures on page 13 of the CB.

b Go through the answers with the class and let pupils write the correct sentences on the blackboard.

Step 4 Crossword

a In this crossword puzzle there are no clues, but all the words are items of clothing. Pupils write the words in the grid and then draw a picture of each item of clothing in the appropriate box, as indicated by the lines and arrows.

b This exercise may be finished for homework.

What's He Wearing?

Listen

Who is the spy?

Mr Black
Mr White
Mr Grey
Mr Green

Ask and answer

Is he tall?
Yes, he is.
Is he wearing brown shoes?
Yes, he is.
No, he isn't.
Is he wearing a red tie?
It's Mr White.

12

Clothes 1D

Ask and answer

Point to Bill.

Whose T-shirt is this?	Gary's.
Whose trousers are these?	Kev's.
Whose shoes are these?	Gary's.

HA HA HA

Listen

I'm wearing grey trousers, a brown jumper, a white shirt, white socks and brown shoes. My hat is red.

13

Step 2

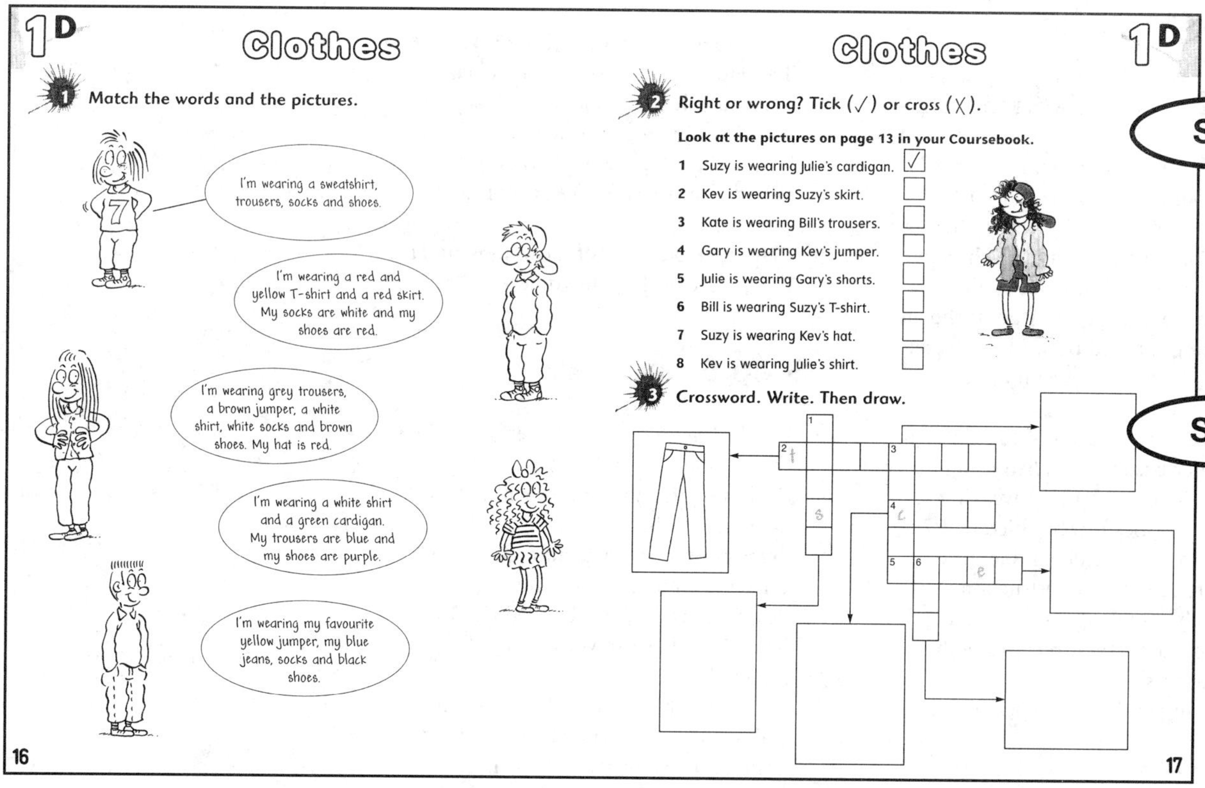

1D

Clothes

1 Match the words and the pictures.

I'm wearing a sweatshirt, trousers, socks and shoes.
I'm wearing a red and yellow T-shirt and a red skirt. My socks are white and my shoes are red.
I'm wearing grey trousers, a brown jumper, a white shirt, white socks and brown shoes. My hat is red.
I'm wearing a white shirt and a green cardigan. My trousers are blue and my shoes are purple.
I'm wearing my favourite yellow jumper, my blue jeans, socks and black shoes.

16

Clothes

1D

2 Right or wrong? Tick (✓) or cross (✗).

Look at the pictures on page 13 in your Coursebook.

1. Suzy is wearing Julie's cardigan. ✓
2. Kev is wearing Suzy's skirt.
3. Kate is wearing Bill's trousers.
4. Gary is wearing Kev's jumper.
5. Julie is wearing Gary's shorts.
6. Bill is wearing Suzy's T-shirt.
7. Suzy is wearing Kev's hat.
8. Kev is wearing Julie's shirt.

3 Crossword. Write. Then draw.

17

Step 3

Step 4

1D Lesson 3

Main Language Items	Resource File	Materials Needed
Bring me ... I'm wearing ...	1 8	clothes pieces (see AB cut-outs section) coloured pencils paper for display (optional) cassette/cassette player

Step 1 The Laundry Game

a Divide the class into two, three or four teams. Each team needs a set of cut-out clothes pieces. Alternatively, you could use the pupils' own clothes or bags of clothes.

b Each team selects a 'runner'. Say **'Bring me a black shoe.'** The first 'runner' to give the correct item to the teacher wins a point for their team.

c Repeat the instructions using other clothing items.

Step 2 Pairwork/Baseboard

For this exercise each pupil will need the cut-out clothes pieces and the baseboard on page 62 of their CB.

a Divide the class into pairs. Each pupil places their baseboard and clothes pieces in front of them. A book should be stood up on end between each pair of pupils so that they cannot see one another's board.

b P1 dresses one or both of the children on his/her baseboard. Then using the structure **The boy/girl is wearing ...** he/she describes his/her picture. P2 must try to reconstruct an identical picture following the instructions.

c After each complete description, pupils should compare their pictures with their partners'.

d Then change roles and repeat the exercise.

Step 3 Write

a When pupils have built up their own pictures in the above exercise, they should write a description of the boy and/or girl on AB page 18.

b Pupils should use the model from activity 6 on page 15 of their AB to help.

Step 4 Presentation

a Say **'Open your Coursebooks at page 13.'** Hold your book up for the class. Very quickly ask some preliminary questions about the picture at the bottom of the page. Use **'Who's this? What's he wearing? What colour is his hat?'**, etc.

b Play the tape. Pupils follow, looking at the picture at the same time.

Step 5 Personal file

a Pupils draw a picture of themselves in the box on AB page 18, either in the clothes they are wearing or in their favourite clothes, and write a description of their picture alongside. Encourage pupils to use the descriptions on page 16 of the AB to help. Provide extra vocabulary, if required.

b As before, this work makes excellent wall displays. Individual work can be done on loose paper and stuck into the AB when the display is dismantled.

What's He Wearing?

Listen

Who is the spy?

Mr Black
Mr White
Mr Grey
Mr Green

Ask and answer

Is he tall?
Yes, he is.
Is he wearing brown shoes?
Yes, he is.
Is he wearing a red tie?
No, he isn't.
It's Mr White.

12

Clothes **1D**

Ask and answer

Point to Bill.

Whose T-shirt is this?	Gary's.
Whose trousers are these?	Kev's.
Whose shoes are these?	Gary's.

HA HA HA

Listen

I'm wearing grey trousers, a brown jumper, a white shirt, white socks and brown shoes. My hat is red.

13

Step 4

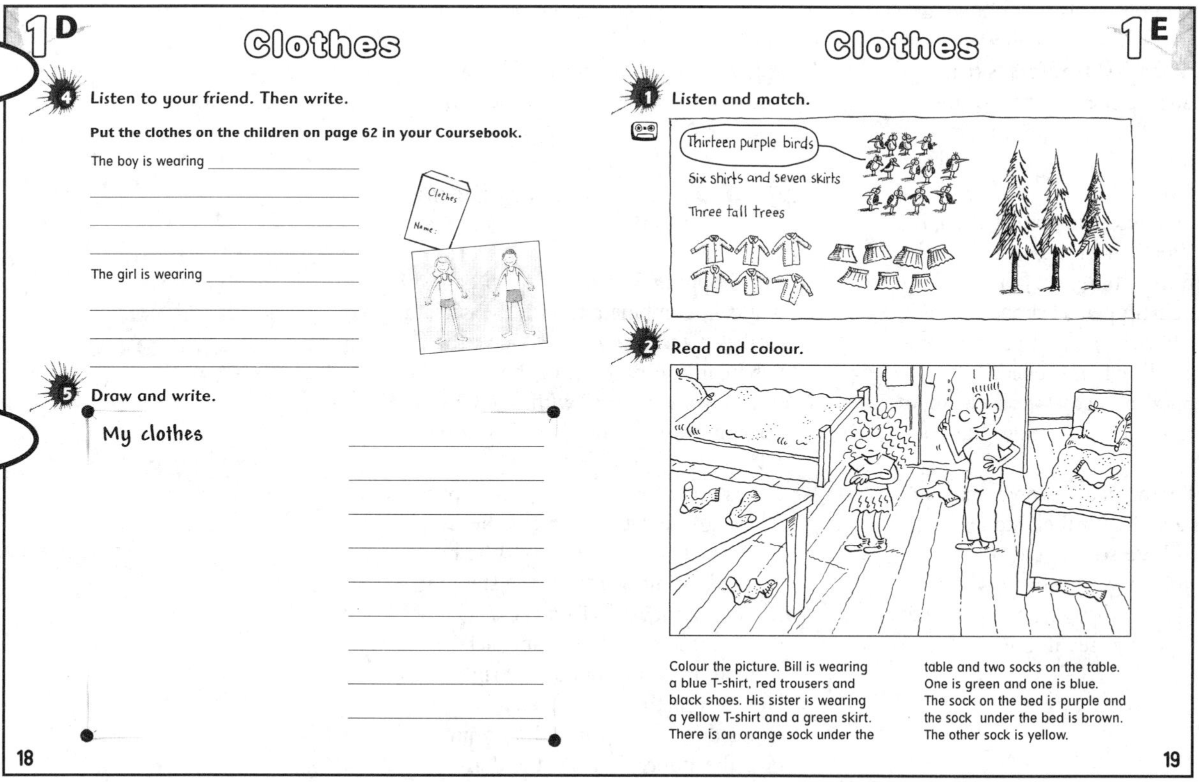

Step 3

1D Clothes

4 Listen to your friend. Then write.

Put the clothes on the children on page 62 in your Coursebook.

The boy is wearing ____________________

The girl is wearing ____________________

Clothes
Name:

Step 5

5 Draw and write.

My clothes

18

Clothes **1E**

1 Listen and match.

Thirteen purple birds
Six shirts and seven skirts
Three tall trees

2 Read and colour.

Colour the picture. Bill is wearing a blue T-shirt, red trousers and black shoes. His sister is wearing a yellow T-shirt and a green skirt. There is an orange sock under the table and two socks on the table. One is green and one is blue. The sock on the bed is purple and the sock under the bed is brown. The other sock is yellow.

19

1E Lesson 1

Main Language Items	Resource File	Materials Needed
Revision	31 32	materials to make word stones word stone collections cassette/cassette player

Step 1 Word stones

a From this point in the course, pupils use word stones they have made previously and make new word stones. Pupils should be familiar with the new vocabulary items. If pupils still have their collection of word stones from NEW STEPPING STONES 1, they will sometimes be able to reuse them rather than make new stones.

b Say **'Open your Coursebooks at page 14.'** Each pupil needs the following seven stones from their collection: **hat, hats, sock, socks, trousers, skirt, dress.** Listen to the first part of the tape. Pupils place the appropriate stones on their desks or on the pictures in their CBs.

c To make the word stones, each pupil requires eighteen 'stones'. Pupils write one word (**red**, **blue**, etc.) on each stone in felt-tip pen as shown in the pictures. Play the second part of the tape. Pupils listen and repeat.

d Each pupil also needs the seven stones shown from their collection (**hat**, **hats**, etc.).

e Pupils play the game shown, making nine sentences with their stones, **'a red hat'**, **'two blue socks'**, etc.

f When pupils have finished making their sentences, they can compare them with a friend's to see if any are the same.

Step 2 Listen and match

a Say **'Open your Activity Books at page 19.'** Point to the phrases and pictures.

b Play the tape, one phrase at a time. Pupils listen and draw a line to match the phrase and picture.

c Play the tape again, pausing for pupils to repeat.

d Play the tape again. Pupils repeat the phrases as quickly as they can.

e Pupils practise saying the phrases as quickly as they can.

f Ask volunteers to say the phrases as fast as they can in front of the class.

Step 3 The Stepping Stones Game

a The Stepping Stones Game on page 14 works in combination with the cut-out clothes pieces from the AB, and the baseboard on page 62 of the CB. Pupils work in pairs, with one CB open at page 14 and the other at page 62.

b Pupils dress the boy and girl on page 62 using the cut-out clothes pieces.

c Pupils make sentences about the boy and girl, using words on the stepping stones on page 14. To make a sentence, they choose one word from each column, moving from left to right. However, if their sentence ends with **shoes** or **trousers**, they should jump over the stones that say **a** and **an**.

d The pair that makes the most correct sentences about their picture are the winners.

Step 1

Step 3

Words and Sentences

Word Stones

Use hat hats sock socks trousers skirt dress

Make red blue yellow green pink purple white brown black

a x 5 two three four five

Play a red hat

two blue socks

The Stepping Stones Game

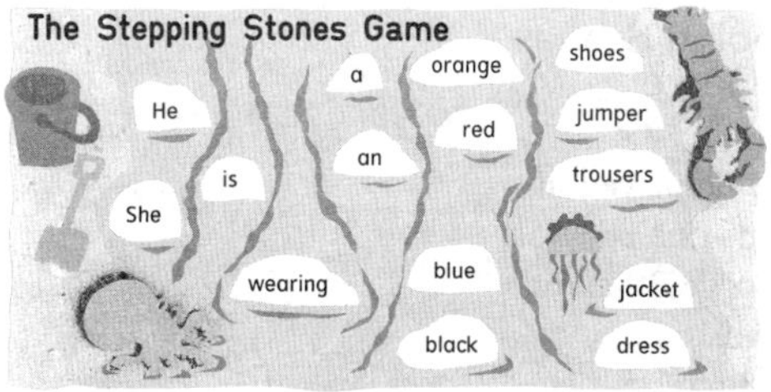

He
She
is
wearing
a
an
orange
red
blue
black
shoes
jumper
trousers
jacket
dress

Find more words

belt
glasses
zip
dungarees
jeans
necklace
earrings
button
sandals
trainers

4 Listen to your friend. Then write.

Put the clothes on the children on page 62 in your Coursebook.

The boy is wearing ____________________

____

____

____

The girl is wearing ____________________

____

____

____

Clothes
Name:

5 Draw and write.

My clothes

____

____

____

____

____

____

____

____

____

Step 2

1 Listen and match.

Thirteen purple birds
Six shirts and seven skirts
Three tall trees

2 Read and colour.

Colour the picture. Bill is wearing a blue T-shirt, red trousers and black shoes. His sister is wearing a yellow T-shirt and a green skirt. There is an orange sock under the table and two socks on the table. One is green and one is blue. The sock on the bed is purple and the sock under the bed is brown. The other sock is yellow.

1E Lesson 2

Main Language Items	Resource File	Materials Needed
Clothes (revision)	28 29	Story strips 1 (see AB cut-outs section) scissors (optional) coloured pencils cassette/cassette player dice/counters

Step 1 Jigsaw Reading/ Listening

a Play the introductory story again. Pupils listen.
b The cut-out 'Story strips 1' in the centre of the AB form the text to the introductory story on page 4 of the CB. Pupils should cut them out and jumble them up.
c Pupils then try to put their story strips in the correct order, without looking at their CB.
d When pupils have finished the jigsaw reading task, they should look at a partner's story strips to check the order.
e Finally, play the complete story again on tape to confirm the correct order.

Tapescript:

What a Mess!
There are socks under the table,
There are shoes under the bed,
There's a coat on the cupboard,
And a hat on Rover's head.
There are skirts and trousers on the floor,
And there's a jacket on the chair,
But when I open the wardrobe
I've got no clothes to wear.

Step 2 Read and colour

a Pupils read the description and colour the picture on AB page 19 accordingly.

Step 3 The Stepping Stones Spelling Game 1

a Ideally the game should be played in groups. Each group needs one copy of the board game on AB page 20 and a dice. (If no dice is available, the numbers 1–6 can be written on each side of a six-sided pencil.)
Each group nominates a referee. The referee's job is to check the answers and adjudicate. The rest of the group are the players. Each player needs a coloured counter (or small coloured piece of paper), a pencil and a sheet of paper.
b The object of the game is to make your way from the start to the finish.
c Players take it in turns to throw the dice and move around the board. When they land on a letter they must say a word beginning with that letter, write the word and say each letter as they write. When they land on a picture they must say the word, write the word and say each letter as they write.
d Encourage pupils to use English as they play. They should count in English and use phrases such as **'Your/My turn.'**
e In addition ask pupils questions about the game as you monitor their progress, e.g. **'Is it your turn?' 'What's your colour?'**

Step 1

1 Clothes
STORY
What a Mess!
There are socks under the table.
There are shoes under the bed.
There's a coat on the cupboard.
And a hat on Rover's head.
There are skirts and trousers on the floor.
And there's a jacket on the chair.
But when I open the wardrobe,
I've got no clothes to wear.
GET THIS!
4
5

Step 2

Clothes
1E
1 Listen and match.
Thirteen purple birds
Six shirts and seven skirts
Three tall trees
2 Read and colour.
Colour the picture. Bill is wearing a blue T-shirt, red trousers and black shoes. His sister is wearing a yellow T-shirt and a green skirt. There is an orange sock under the table and two socks on the table. One is green and one is blue. The sock on the bed is purple and the sock under the bed is brown. The other sock is yellow.
19

Step 3

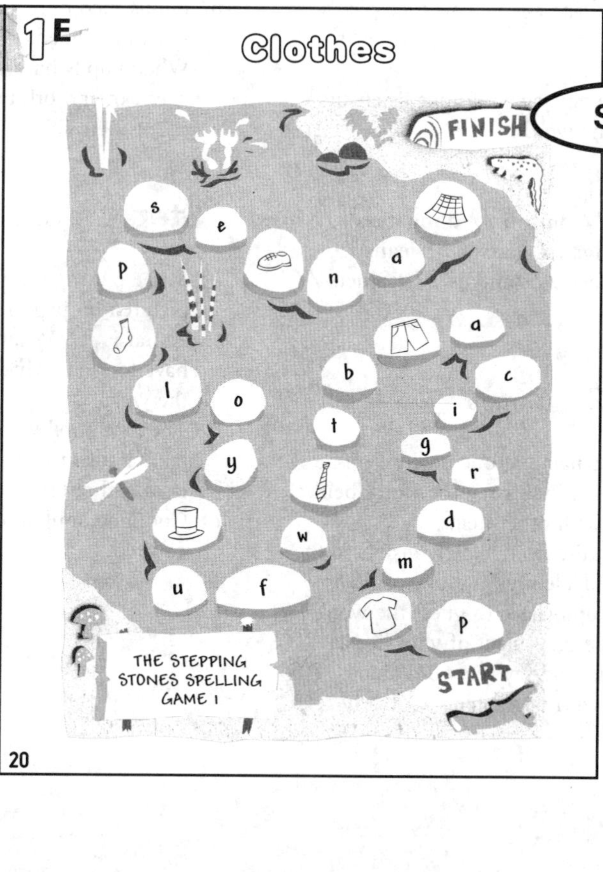
1E
Clothes
FINISH
THE STEPPING STONES SPELLING GAME 1
START
20

1E Lesson 3

Main Language Items		Resource File	Materials Needed
dungarees sandals jeans trainers earrings necklace	glasses belt button zip	33	cassette/cassette player

Step 1 Find more words

a Say **'Open your Coursebooks at page 15'** and look at the photos. Ask pupils in their L1 if any of them can see anything they are wearing at the moment. Then ask them to find something they would not wear to school. Ask them if they can name any of the items in English.
b Play the tape and listen to the words while looking at the pictures.
c Play the tape again. This time pupils point to the appropriate place as they hear the word.
d Play the tape again. Pupils listen and repeat the words.

Tapescript:
belt // button // dungarees // earrings // glasses // jeans // necklace // sandals // trainers // zip //

Step 2 Games

a Spell the name of one of the items, e.g. **'B-E-L-T'**. Pupils say the word **'belt'**. Repeat with other items.
b Stand at the front, clearly visible to the class, and silently 'say' one of the items. Pupils have to guess the word, using the movement of your lips as their cue, and say the word aloud. Repeat with other items.
c Ask 'What this?' and indicate the appropriate number of letters on the blackboard, e.g. _ _ _ _ _ _. Pupils say the word (**button**). Repeat with other items.

Step 3 Write. Then draw

a Pupils solve the anagrams on AB page 21 and write the words in the spaces provided.
b Pupils then draw the items in the spaces provided.
c When pupils have finished, they can check their work by looking at page 15 of their CB.

Step 4 Guess

a Mime putting on one of the items pictured on page 15 of the CB and ask **'What is it?/What are they?'** Pupils have to guess which item it is and say the word.
b The first pupil who guesses correctly takes a turn to come to the front of the class and mime.
c Continue until all the items have been covered.

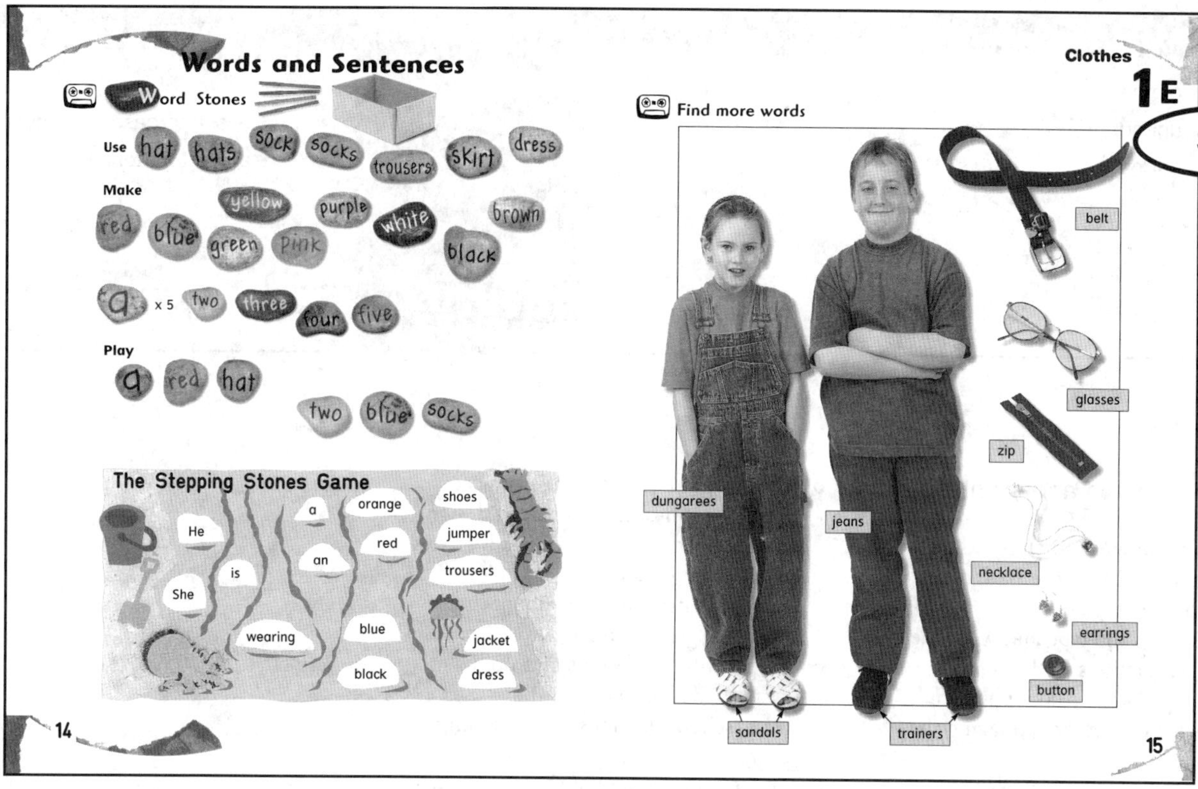
Words and Sentences
Word Stones
Use hat hats sock socks trousers skirt dress
Make yellow purple white brown red blue green pink black
a x 5 two three four five
Play
a red hat
two blue socks
The Stepping Stones Game
He She is a an orange red shoes jumper trousers wearing blue black jacket dress
14
Clothes
1E
Find more words
belt
glasses
zip
dungarees
jeans
necklace
earrings
button
sandals
trainers
15

Step 1

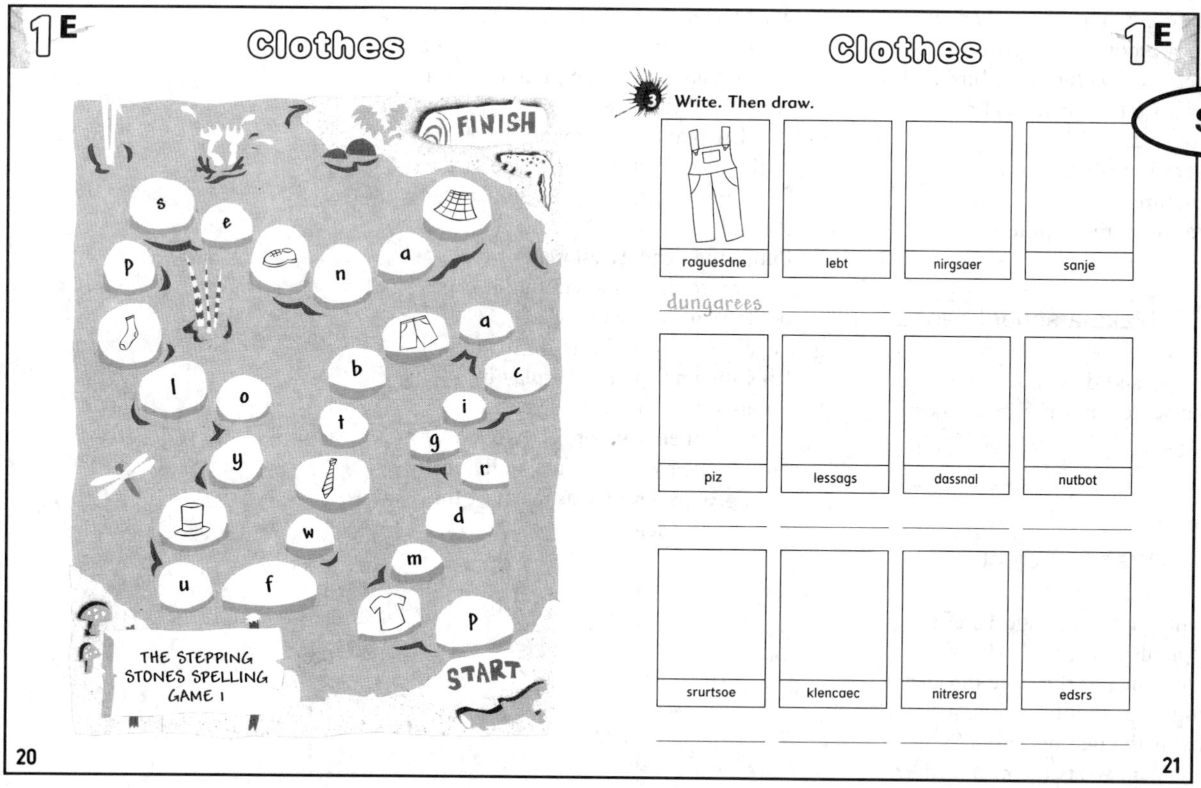
1E
Clothes
FINISH
s e p n a a b c l o i t g y r d w m u f p
THE STEPPING STONES SPELLING GAME 1
START
20
Clothes
1E
Write. Then draw.
raguesdne
lebt
nirgsaer
sanje
dungarees
piz
lessags
dassnal
nutbot
srurtsoe
klencaec
nitresra
edsrs
21

Step 3

1F Lesson 1 - Project

Main Language Items		Resource File	Materials Needed
There is ...	clothes		cassette/cassette player
There are ...	uniform		project materials
	badge		

Step 1 Listen and number

a Say '**Open your Activity Books at page 22 and look at the badges at the top of the page.**'

a Pupils listen to the tape and write the appropriate numbers in the boxes.

a Play the tape twice. Allow pupils to compare answers before replaying the tape.

Tapescript:

1 **There is a tree on the badge and a picture of a girl.**

2 **There is a picture of a bird and a picture of a snake. There are two trees.**

3 **There is a picture of a boy and a picture of a girl. There are two birds and a house.**

Step 2 Make a school badge

a Pupils design and draw a school badge.

b They then write a description of their badge, beginning *There is ...* or *There are ...* .

Step 3 Start a project

a Look at the photos on page 16 of the CB. Ask pupils in their L1 what they can see. Ask them if they like the idea of wearing a uniform to school. Ask them what is the purpose of uniforms in general. Who wears them, and why?

b Encourage pupils to start a project based on uniforms. Pupils can design and draw their own uniforms for boys and girls and label the picture in English. They can write about their choice of design in L1.

c Display all the designs and hold a secret ballot of pupils in the class/school to choose one winning design.

d Discuss the winning design in L1: why is it the best/most popular? Discuss what materials are needed to make it.

e Pupils work in groups. One pupil lies on the floor on a large piece of paper (a roll of wallpaper is ideal for this). Another pupil draws round the shape of the body. Cut out the shape of the body and pin the life-size model on the wall.

f Pupils then choose an item of the uniform to draw and cut out in paper or cloth, to fit the model.

g Finally, pin the uniform on the model, label the uniform and display it.

h Pupils should be encouraged to continue their own project work outside their English class, individually or in groups. Display as much of the work as possible.

Step 3

START A PROJECT

KUS
KUS

16

Clothes **1F**

SUPERSNAKE
What are these?
They look like trousers. But whose are they?
Snail, are these your trousers?
No, I haven't got any legs.
Centipede, are these your trousers?
Don't be silly! I've got a hundred legs.
Fly, are these your trousers?
How many legs have they got?
Eight.
I've only got six legs. Spider's got eight legs.
Here are your trousers, Spider. Come on, Fly. Let's go!

17

1F Clothes

Step 1

1 Listen and number the badges.

Step 2

2 Draw a school badge. Then write.

22

Clothes **1F**

3 Right or wrong? Listen and tick (✓) or (✗).

4 Write.

socks

1 Is she wearing a skirt? ______
2 Is he wearing a hat? ______
3 What's she wearing? ______
4 What's he wearing? ______

23

1F Lesson 2 - Evaluation

Main Language Items		Resource File	Materials Needed
Are these your trousers? I've got ... I haven't got ...	centipede fly snail spider		Test cards 1F (see photocopy master on TG p.174) Supersnake puppets cassette/cassette player scissors (optional)

Step 1 Listening (Test)

a Look at the pictures on page 23 of the AB. There is a short dialogue or sentence about each picture on the tape. Pupils must decide if the dialogue or sentence is appropriate to the picture. If it is appropriate, they should put a tick in the corresponding box, if not, they should put a cross. Play each sentence three times.

Tapescript (with answers):

1 **Is that a jumper or a jacket? // It's a jacket. (✓)**
2 **What are these? // Shoes. (✗)**
3 **Where are the shoes? // They're under the bed. (✗)**
4 **Well ... he's wearing a hat, a coat, a shirt and a tie. // (✓)**
5 **He's wearing a jumper and trousers. // (✓)**
6 **Where's the sock? // It's on the table. No, it isn't. It's under the table. (✓)**
7 **She's wearing a T-shirt and trousers. // (✗)**
8 **Bill is wearing a hat. // (✗)**
9 **He's wearing a jumper and trousers. // (✗)**
10 **She's wearing a hat and a dress. // (✓)**

Step 2 Write (Test)

a Working individually, pupils look at the pictures and label the items of clothing in the spaces provided.

b Pupils then read the questions and write the answers.

c Credit should be given for answers which show that pupils have understood the meaning of the questions and where their answers are comprehensible and appropriate.

Step 3 Test yourself

a Photocopy one set of test cards 1F for each pupil (see TG page 174).

b Say **'Open your Activity Books at page 24 and look at the pictures.'** Pupils colour the items on their test cards according to the written description, e.g. **'White socks'**. Pupils then cut out the cards. Alternatively, give each pupil a set of cards already cut out for them to colour. Pupils then fold the ten cards along the dotted line, as shown in the picture.

c To do the first self-test, pupils place all their cards in front of them with the pictures showing, following the instructions. Demonstrate.

d Pupils then read the first sentence in the left-hand list, **'White socks'**. Pupils must find the card with the picture of the white socks, pick it up and read the words on the card. They then put a tick or cross in the box in their AB. Repeat for the other cards.

e To do the second self-test, pupils first cover the words in the left-hand list and then place all their cards in front of them again with the pictures showing. Demonstrate.

f Pupils then look at the first question and picture in the right-hand list (**'What's this?'**). Pupils must write the appropriate answer in the space provided (**'A grey T-shirt'**). They then find the card with the appropriate picture, pick it up and look at the words to check. They put a tick or a cross in the box accordingly. Repeat.

g Pupils add up their scores out of ten for each test and total them. Finally, they circle the appropriate comment.

h Pupils can create other cards to test themselves or their friends, using other clothes vocabulary they have met in the topic and project work, e.g. scarf, boots, etc.

Step 4 Supersnake

a Look at the Supersnake cartoon on page 17 of the CB. Pupils listen to the dialogue, reading at the same time.

b As in CB1, the dialogue may be used as a basis for role play. Divide the class into groups of five. One pupil needs a Supersnake puppet, or he can mimic a snake using his hand and arm. A fist and a thumb can be used for Snail, a finger for Centipede, two hands together with two thumbs for Fly and eight fingers for Spider.

START A PROJECT

KUS
KUS

Step 4

SUPERSNAKE
What are these?
They look like trousers. But whose are they?
Snail, are these your trousers?
No, I haven't got any legs.
Centipede, are these your trousers?
Don't be silly! I've got a hundred legs.
Fly, are these your trousers?
How many legs have they got?
Eight.
I've only got six legs. Spider's got eight legs.
Here are your trousers, Spider. Come on, Fly. Let's go!

Clothes 1F

Step 1

3 Right or wrong? Listen and tick (✓) or (✗).

4 Write.

socks

1 Is she wearing a skirt? ____
2 Is he wearing a hat? ____
3 What's she wearing? ____
4 What's he wearing? ____

1F Clothes

Step 3

5 Test yourself. Right (✓) or wrong (✗).

You need

Colour the cards.
Cut and fold.

TEST 1

* ***Put the cards like this.***
* ***Read these words.***
* ***Find the pictures.***
* ***Check. Right (✓) or wrong (✗)?***

White socks. ☐
A blue sweatshirt. ☐
Yellow trousers. ☐
A grey T-shirt. ☐
An orange jumper. ☐
A purple dress. ☐
Black shoes. ☐
A pink skirt. ☐
Green shorts. ☐
A brown shirt. ☐

SCORE /10

TEST 2

* ***Put the cards like this.***
* ***Read these questions.***
* ***Write the answers.***
* ***Check. Right (✓) or wrong (✗)?***

What's this? ____
What are these? ____
What's this? ____
What are these? ____
What's this? ____
What's this? ____
What are these? ____
What's this? ____
What are these? ____
What's this? ____

SCORE /10

TOTAL /20

Circle your total score

20 Excellent **19–18** Very good **17–16** Good
15–13 Quite good **12–0** Do it again!

2 Story lesson

Main Language Items		Resource File	Materials Needed
Days of the week	shop		
week	peanuts		cassette/cassette player
morning	chocolate		
afternoon	crisps		
	sweets		
	biscuits		
	ice-cream		

Step 1 Topic warm-up

a Tell pupils in their L1 that they are going to continue their English lessons by looking at food and drink. Introduce the words **'food'** and **'drink'** at this point.
b Then ask pupils what words they think they might learn.
c Ask pupils what they have eaten and drunk so far today. Can they name anything in English? Ask if they always have the same things for breakfast or if they sometimes have different things. If so, why?
d Discuss what they can eat and drink and what they can't and why/why not.
e Ask pupils if they think food and drink in other countries are the same. Why do they think they are/aren't?

Step 2 Story warm-up

a Say **'Open your Coursebooks at page 18. Look at the pictures.'** Demonstrate what you mean by holding up your CB and pointing to the pictures.
b Ask pupils in their L1 what they can see. Where did Jemimah go? What did she buy?
c Ask pupils if they can see anything in the pictures they can name in English.

Step 3 Story listening

a Say **'Listen to the tape.'** Pupils cover the words, look at the pictures and listen to the tape at the same time.
b Play the tape again.
c Ask questions in the pupils' L1 to check they have understood the story.

Tapescript:

Story Jemimah's Week //
On Monday, Jemimah went to the shop // and bought a packet of peanuts. //
On Tuesday, Jemimah went to the shop // and bought a bar of chocolate. //
On Wednesday, Jemimah went to the shop // and bought a packet of crisps. //
On Thursday, Jemimah went to the shop // and bought a bag of sweets. //
On Friday, Jemimah went to the shop // and bought a packet of biscuits. //
On Saturday, Jemimah went to the shop // and bought a tub of ice-cream. //
On Sunday morning, the shop was closed. // Jemimah ate a packet of peanuts, // a bar of chocolate, // a packet of crisps, // a bag of sweets, // a packet of biscuits // and a tub of ice-cream … //
and on Sunday afternoon, she was sick. //

Step 4 Story listen and repeat

a Play the complete story again. Pupils listen and look at the pictures. Pupils can also mouth the words as they listen to the tape.
b Then play the story pausing after each line for pupils to repeat.

Step 5 Story task

a Tell pupils to close their CBs. Then write or draw the items Jemimah bought (a packet of peanuts, a bar of chocolate, a packet of crisps, a bag of sweets, a packet of biscuits and a tub of ice-cream) on the blackboard, in a random order.
b Say each word for pupils to repeat two or three times.
c Pupils now have to say in what order the items were bought. Say **'Monday'**. Pupils say what Jemimah bought on Monday, etc. Write the appropriate day of the week next to each item on the blackboard.
d Listen to the tape again to confirm the correct order.
e Finally listen to the tape again, or say the story, leaving gaps for the nouns (**Monday, shop, a packet of peanuts,** etc.). Pupils try to join in and say the story.

Step 2

Step 3

Step 4

2 Food

STORY

Jemimah's Week

SHOP
CRISPS
On Monday, Jemimah went to the shop and bought a packet of peanuts.
On Tuesday, Jemimah went to the shop and bought a bar of chocolate.
On Wednesday, Jemimah went to the shop and bought a packet of crisps.
On Thursday, Jemimah went to the shop and bought a bag of sweets.
On Friday, Jemimah went to the shop and bought a packet of biscuits.
On Saturday, Jemimah went to the shop and bought a tub of ice-cream.
On Sunday morning, the shop was closed. Jemimah ate a packet of peanuts, a bar of chocolate, a packet of crisps, a bag of sweets, a packet of biscuits and a tub of ice-cream...
and on Sunday afternoon, she was sick.

18 19

2A Lesson 1

Main Language Items			Resource File	Materials Needed
What's ... eating?	apple	chicken	18 18a	cassette/cassette player
Does ... like ...?	biscuit	cake		
Do you like ...?	banana	lemonade		
I like ...	sausage			
I don't like ...	cheese			

Step 1 Presentation

a Say **'Open your Coursebooks at page 20. Look at the pictures.'** Hold up your book and ask some questions about who pupils can see in the pictures. Use the question forms **'Who's this? What's his/her name? What's he/she called? Is this ...?'**

b Play the tape. Pupils follow looking at the pictures. It is not intended that pupils understand every word of the dialogue.

Tapescript:

KEV: **Can I have the lemonade?**
BILL: **Yes, here you are. Who's got the biscuits?**
SUZY: **Gary has. Gary, Bill wants the biscuits.**
JULIE: **Stop it Butch ... Get off. Suzy do you want an apple?**
SUZY: **Yes please. I love apples.**
JULIE: **Who wants some cake?**
BILL: } KEV: } KATE: } **ME!**
ALL: **GO AWAY!**
GARY: **Bill, Suzy! Look! The pets are in the kitchen. There's food everywhere! There are sausages, bananas and a chicken on the floor. There's a hamburger and a cake on the table and Duffy's sitting on the table eating a fish!**

Step 2 Pairwork

a Divide the class into pairs (P1 and P2). All pairs work simultaneously. Say **'Look at the pictures at the bottom of page 20. Cover the words underneath the pictures.'**

b Pupils repeat after the tape. P1 repeats the questions, P2 repeats the answers. Repeat four times changing roles.

c Then pupils ask and answer the questions without the help of the tape. P1 asks the questions using the words in the book to help, P2 answers using only the pictures. P1 should prompt and check P2's answers.

d Change roles and repeat the procedure.

e Continue until pupils can ask and answer the questions without the help of the words.

Step 3 Listen and read

a The first passage is on the tape to allow pupils to hear the new words. Play the tape. Pupils follow, reading at the same time on page 25 of their ABs.

b Ask some questions about the passage, e.g. **'Does Butch like chicken?'** Pupils answer **'yes'** or **'no'**.

c When they understand the meaning of **like**, they complete the chart about Butch. Write the names of the foods that Butch likes in the left-hand column and draw a picture. Do the same in the right-hand column for the foods Butch doesn't like. An example is given in each column.

d Repeat step **c** for the passage about Slow.

Step 4 Groupwork

a Ask various pupils in the class the question **'Do you like biscuits?'** Then ask about the other food items introduced in this lesson. You can also revise various vocabulary items using the same structure, e.g. **boys, girls, snakes, English.**

b When pupils are familiar with the question form, direct them to the grid on page 25 of their ABs. Copy the grid onto the blackboard. Select one pupil. Ask the questions and write the answers in the grid.

c Divide the class into groups of three. Then all groups work simultaneously asking each other similar questions and filling in the chart in their ABs.

d Finish the exercise by asking pupils questions about other class members, e.g. **'Does *Alex* like *chicken*?'**

Step 1

Step 2

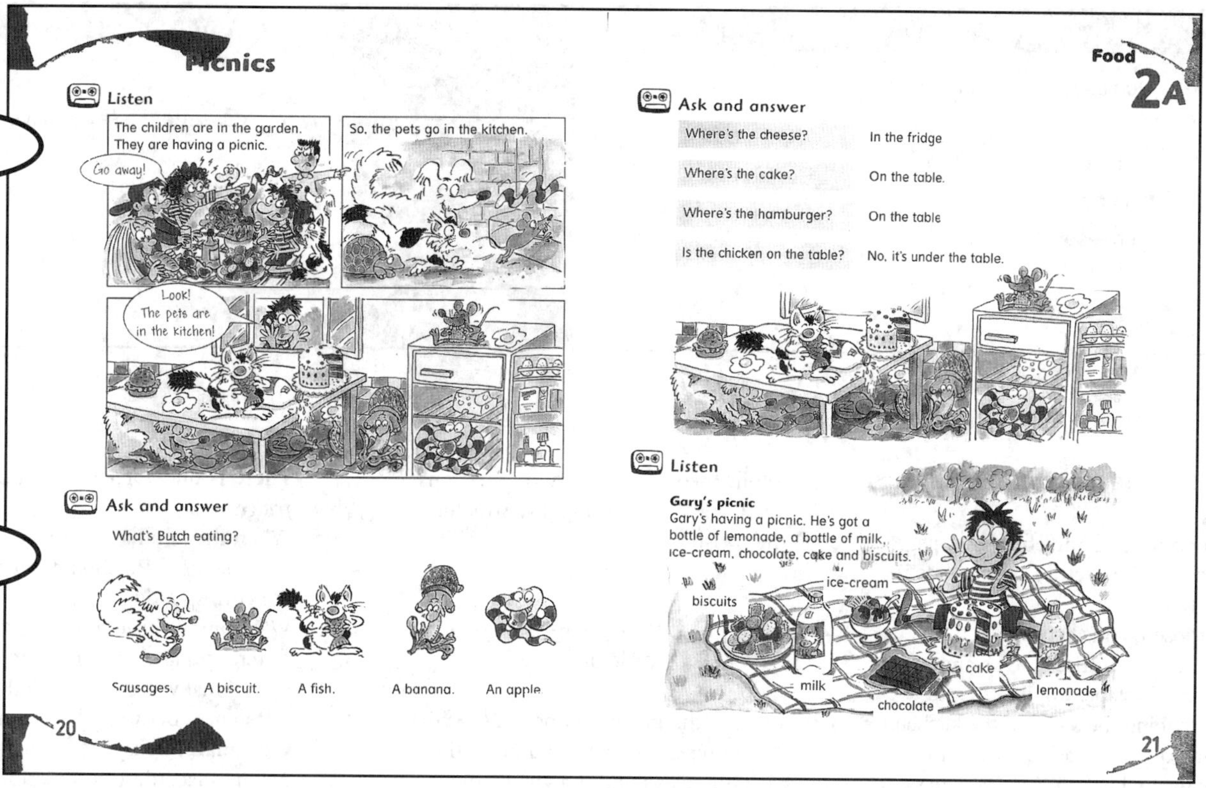

Picnics

Listen

The children are in the garden. They are having a picnic.

Go away!

So, the pets go in the kitchen.

Look! The pets are in the kitchen!

Ask and answer

What's Butch eating?

Sausages. A biscuit. A fish. A banana. An apple

20

Food

2A

Ask and answer

Where's the cheese?	In the fridge
Where's the cake?	On the table.
Where's the hamburger?	On the table
Is the chicken on the table?	No, it's under the table.

Listen

Gary's picnic

Gary's having a picnic. He's got a bottle of lemonade, a bottle of milk, ice-cream, chocolate, cake and biscuits.

biscuits
ice-cream
milk
cake
chocolate
lemonade

21

Step 3

Step 4

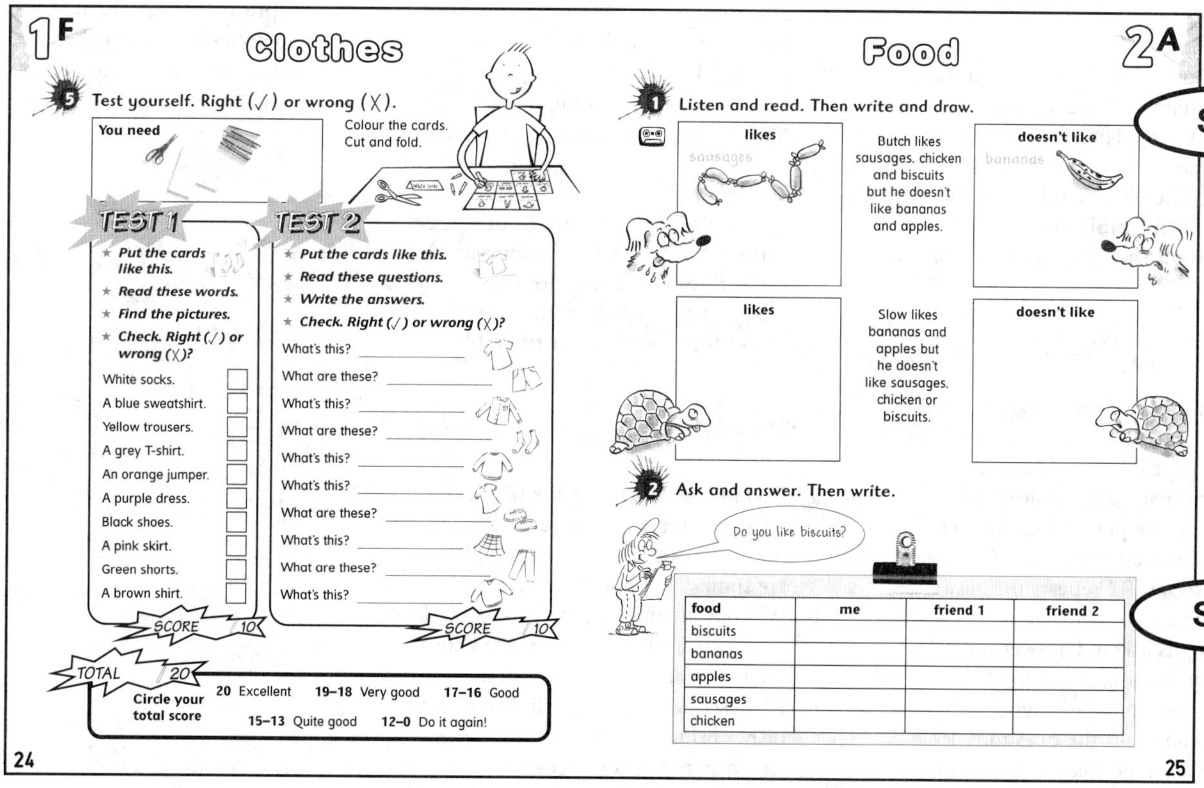

1F

Clothes

5 Test yourself. Right (✓) or wrong (✗).

You need

Colour the cards. Cut and fold.

TEST 1

- *Put the cards like this.*
- *Read these words.*
- *Find the pictures.*
- *Check. Right (✓) or wrong (✗)?*

White socks. ☐
A blue sweatshirt. ☐
Yellow trousers. ☐
A grey T-shirt. ☐
An orange jumper. ☐
A purple dress. ☐
Black shoes. ☐
A pink skirt. ☐
Green shorts. ☐
A brown shirt. ☐

SCORE /10

TEST 2

- *Put the cards like this.*
- *Read these questions.*
- *Write the answers.*
- *Check. Right (✓) or wrong (✗)?*

What's this? ______
What are these? ______
What's this? ______
What are these? ______
What's this? ______
What's this? ______
What are these? ______
What's this? ______
What are these? ______
What's this? ______

SCORE /10

TOTAL /20

Circle your total score

20 Excellent 19–18 Very good 17–16 Good 15–13 Quite good 12–0 Do it again!

24

Food

2A

1 Listen and read. Then write and draw.

likes		doesn't like
sausages	Butch likes sausages, chicken and biscuits but he doesn't like bananas and apples.	bananas
likes	Slow likes bananas and apples but he doesn't like sausages, chicken or biscuits.	doesn't like

2 Ask and answer. Then write.

Do you like biscuits?

food	me	friend 1	friend 2
biscuits			
bananas			
apples			
sausages			
chicken			

25

2A Lesson 2

Main Language Items			Resource File	Materials Needed
There is/are ...	chicken	in	13	cassette/cassette player
... is eating ...	cake	on	26	
Where is/are ...?	fridge	under		
	hamburger			
	cheese			

Step 1 Presentation

a Say **'Open your Coursebooks at page 21. Look at the picture of the pets in the kitchen.'**

b The purpose of this activity is to present the prepositions *in*, *on* and *under*. Play the tape. Pupils listen to Gary describing the scene in the kitchen.

c Ask some questions about where the pets are in the kitchen, e.g. **'Where's *Slow*?'** and **'Is *Slow* under the *table*?'**

Tapescript:
Bill, Suzy! Look! The pets are in the kitchen. There's food everywhere! There are sausages, bananas and a chicken on the floor. There's a hamburger and a cake on the table and Duffy's sitting on the table eating a fish.

Step 2 Pairwork

a Divide the class into pairs (P1 and P2), with only one book between each pair open at page 21. Say **'Cover the words on page 21. Look at the picture of the pets in the kitchen.'**

b Pupils repeat after the tape. P1 repeats the questions, P2 repeats the answers. Repeat twice then change roles.

c Then pupils ask and answer the questions without the help of the tape. P1 uses the words on page 21 as prompts and asks the questions, P2 answers. Change roles and repeat the procedure.

d Pupils then ask a variety of questions about the picture using any structures they wish.

Step 3 Listen, draw and colour

a Look at the picture on page 26 of the AB. Listen to the description on the tape. Pupils should draw and colour the food items in their picture according to the description.

b First play the whole description straight through. Then play it again a line at a time, giving pupils sufficient time to draw and colour their pictures.

Tapescript:
There's a cake on the floor under the table // and a hamburger on the floor. // There are two green apples and a fish in the fridge // and four bananas on the table.

Step 4 Pairwork

a Divide the class into pairs (P1 and P2). P1 opens the CB at page 21 and P2 opens the AB at page 26. The pictures are similar, but not identical.

b Without looking at each other's books, pupils must find the difference between the two pictures.

c P1 describes the picture in front of him or her using the structures:
Butch is eating sausages.
There is a *cake* in/on/under the *table*.
There is one *apple* in/on/under the *fridge*, etc.

d When they find a difference between their pictures, P2 should put a cross in the corresponding area.

e When pupils have found as many differences as they can, they change roles. Finally they compare the differences between the pictures.

f **Optional** Pupils can colour their pictures according to descriptions given by their partners.

g **Optional** When pupils have completed the exercise, elicit the differences and write them on the blackboard.

Picnics

Listen

The children are in the garden. They are having a picnic.

Go away!

So, the pets go in the kitchen.

Look! The pets are in the kitchen!

Ask and answer

What's Butch eating?

Sausages. A biscuit. A fish. A banana. An apple

20

Food 2A

Ask and answer

Where's the cheese?	In the fridge
Where's the cake?	On the table.
Where's the hamburger?	On the table
Is the chicken on the table?	No, it's under the table.

Listen

Gary's picnic
Gary's having a picnic. He's got a bottle of lemonade, a bottle of milk, ice-cream, chocolate, cake and biscuits.

ice-cream
biscuits
cake
milk
lemonade
chocolate

21

Step 1

Step 2

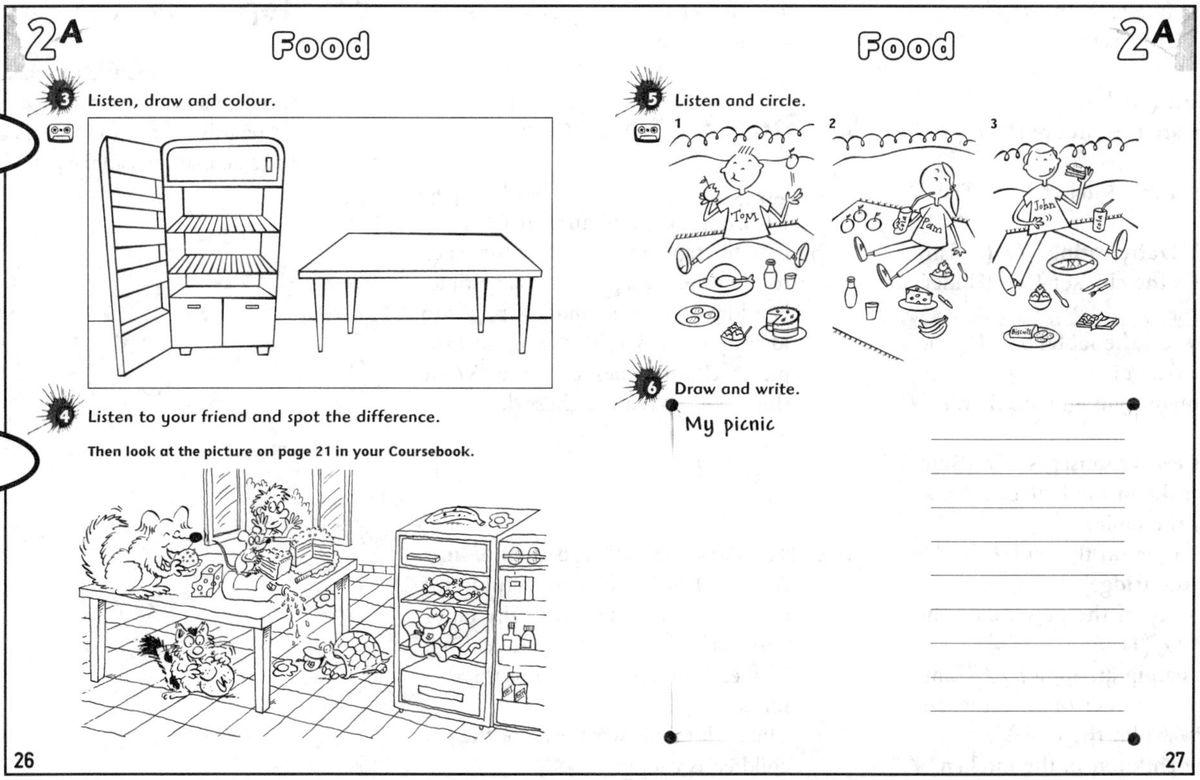

2A Food

3 Listen, draw and colour.

4 Listen to your friend and spot the difference.

Then look at the picture on page 21 in your Coursebook.

26

Food 2A

5 Listen and circle.

1 2 3

Tom
Pam
John

6 Draw and write.

My picnic

27

Step 3

Step 4

2A Lesson 3

Main Language Items			Resource File	Materials Needed
Revision of question forms	picnic	lemonade		
What's this?	ice-cream	cake	1	coloured pencils
What are these?	chocolate	biscuits	9	paper for display (optional)
	milk		26	cassette/cassette player

Step 1 Quiz

a Divide the class into two teams.
b Say **'Open your Coursebooks at page 20. Look at the picture.'** Play the first question on the tape. The first pupil to raise their hand gets a chance to answer, and if correct, wins two points for their team. If the answer is wrong, the opposing team may attempt the question for one point.
c Do all the questions in the same way pausing before each answer to give pupils time to answer.

Tapescript (with answers):

1 **Where are the children? // (In the garden)**
2 **Who's in the kitchen? // (The pets)**
3 **What's Duffy eating? // (A fish)**
4 **Where's the chicken? // (Under the table)**
5 **Is Wow on the table? // (No, he's on the fridge)**
6 **How many sausages are there? // (Five)**
7 **Who's eating sausages? // (Butch)**
8 **Is the cake in the fridge? // (No, it's on the table)**
9 **Is the apple on the table? // (No, it's in the fridge)**
10 **How many of the pets are on the floor? // (Two)**
11 **Who's eating an apple? // (Sam)**
12 **Is the hamburger on or under the table? // (On the table)**
13 **Are the children in the kitchen? // (No)**
14 **Who's eating a banana? // (Slow)**
15 **Who finds the pets in the kitchen? // (Gary)**

Step 2 Pairwork

a Elicit questions from pupils that they can ask about the picture at the top of page 21. Write the question forms on the blackboard.
b Divide the class into pairs. Pupils ask and answer as many questions as they can about the picture.

Step 3 Presentation

a Say **'Open your Coursebook at page 21. Look at the picture of Gary.'**
b Play the tape. Pupils follow the tape, reading the passage at the same time. Hold up your book and ask pupils to identify what Gary is having for his picnic. Use the question forms **'What's this?'** and **'What are these?'**.

Step 4 Listen and circle

a Say **'Now turn to page 27 of your Activity Book. The three children are having a picnic. Listen to the tape and circle the food they are eating.'**
b Play each description two or three times.
c Then ask pupils what each of the children is eating.

Tapescript:

1 **Tom's having a picnic. He's got two apples, a bottle of milk and some biscuits. //**
2 **Pam's having cola and ice-cream for her picnic. //**
3 **John's going to have a big picnic. He's got a hamburger, biscuits, chocolate and ice-cream // and cola to drink.**

Step 5 Personal file

a Pupils draw a picture of what they would like to take on a picnic and write a list of the food items alongside. Provide extra vocabulary if required.

Step 1

Step 2

Step 3

Picnics

Listen

The children are in the garden. They are having a picnic.

Go away!

So, the pets go in the kitchen.

Look! The pets are in the kitchen!

Ask and answer

What's Butch eating?

Sausages. A biscuit. A fish. A banana. An apple

20

Food

2A

Ask and answer

Where's the cheese?	In the fridge
Where's the cake?	On the table.
Where's the hamburger?	On the table
Is the chicken on the table?	No, it's under the table.

Listen

Gary's picnic

Gary's having a picnic. He's got a bottle of lemonade, a bottle of milk, ice-cream, chocolate, cake and biscuits.

biscuits
ice-cream
cake
milk
chocolate
lemonade

21

Step 4

Step 5

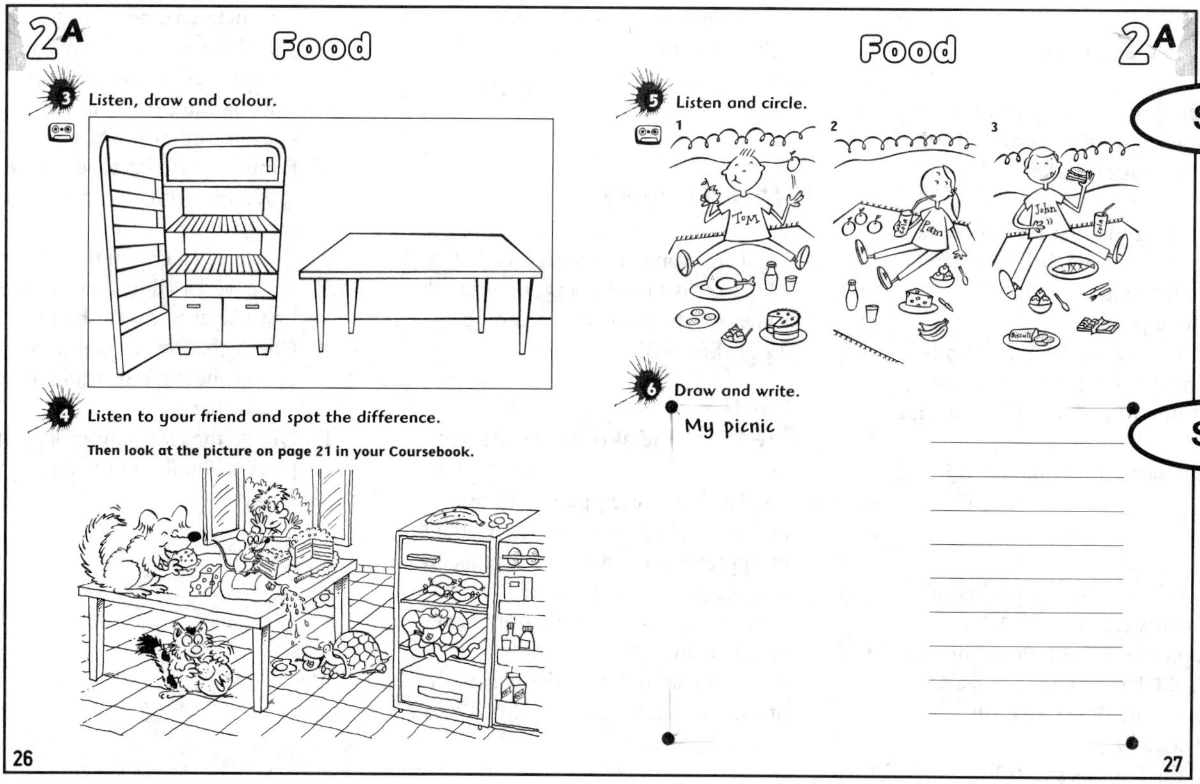
2A Food

3 Listen, draw and colour.

4 Listen to your friend and spot the difference.

Then look at the picture on page 21 in your Coursebook.

26

Food 2A

5 Listen and circle.

1
Tom
2
Pam
3
John

6 Draw and write.

My picnic

27

2B Lesson 1

Main Language Items		Resource File	Materials Needed
I like ...	eggs	23	cassette/cassette player
I don't like ...	meat	39	Bingo cover cards
40p (pence)	bread		
£1.20 (pound)	custard		

Step 1 Say the rhyme

a Pupils listen to the rhymes on the tape and read at the same time from page 22 of their CBs.
b Listen to the first rhyme again, line by line, and repeat the words. Do each line in the same way.
c Finally, chant the rhyme along with the tape.
d Do the second rhyme in the same way.

Step 2 Listen and circle

a Say **'Open your Activity Book at page 28. Look at the picture of Julie. She's in the supermarket. What is she buying?'**
b Before playing the first part of the tape teach pupils about English currency. p=pence, £=pound, one hundred pence = one pound.
c Play the first part of the tape. Pupils look at the conveyor belt and circle any food items they hear. Play the tape two or three times.
d Repeat the same procedure for Bill and Suzy.

Tapescript:

CASHIER: **Good morning. A packet of biscuits ... 40p // A kilo of apples ... £1.20 // A chicken ... £3.15 // and ... chocolate. That's £6.00 please. //**

CASHIER: **Hello. Sausages ... 90p // Milk ... 40p // Six eggs ... 95p // and ... bananas. That's £3.10 please. //**

CASHIER: **Good morning. A cake ... £1.50 // A bottle of lemonade ... 85p // A kilo of apples ... £1.95 // and cheese ... That's £5.60 please. //**

Step 3 Write

a Pupils write shopping lists for Julie, Bill and Suzy in the spaces provided, according to the items they circled in Step 2.

Step 4 Write

a Pupils rearrange the letters to find the names of five food items and write the names on the lines provided on page 29 of their ABs.

Step 5 Make Bingo cards

a To play Bingo each pupil will need twelve small cover cards. These should be approximately the same size as the Bingo squares (CB page 22, 3cm x 3cm). They may be made from paper or thin card.
b Each card should have the name of one of the food items clearly printed on it.

Step 6 Bingo

a Tell pupils to look at the Bingo card on page 22 of their CBs. Instruct pupils to cover any six squares on their Bingo card by placing the appropriate cover card face down over the picture. In this way, each pupil's card should now have six different pictures showing.
b The Bingo Caller (teacher) will need a set of word cards. Shuffle your cards. Lay them face down in front of you. Ask **'Are you ready?'** Encourage the answer 'Yes' or 'No', as appropriate.
c Select a card, read out the word and put the card down face up.
d Pupils cover each food item that is called out with the appropriate cover card face up.
e Continue calling until one of the pupils has covered all of their squares. The first player to do so shouts **'Bingo!'** Check that the winner is correct by asking the pupil to read back the words that are now face up.
f Divide the class into groups of 4–6 players. Pupils continue the game in groups.

I Like Fish

Step 1

Say the rhyme

I Like ...

I like fish,
I like eggs,
I like cheese and meat,
I like cake and biscuits,
In fact, I like to eat.

I Don't Like ...

I don't like milk,
I don't like bread,
I don't like custard
On my head!

MILK

Step 6

BINGO
MILK
LEMONADE

What do the pets like?

✓ = Likes
X = doesn't Like

	Butch	Wow	Slow	Duffy	Sam
chocolate	✓	✓	✗	✗	✗
cake	✓	✓	✗	✗	
cabbage	✗	✗	✓	✗	✗
carrots	✗	✗	✓	✗	✗
apples		✓	✓	✗	✓
oranges	✗	✗		✗	
grapes	✗	✓	✓	✗	✓
milk	✓			✓	✓

Ask and answer

Does Butch like chocolate? Yes, he does.

Does Wow like oranges? No, he doesn't.

What does Slow like? Cabbage, carrots, apples and grapes.

Ask and answer

Fruit and vegetables
What's number one?
Is it an orange?

potatoes
cauliflower
beans
onions
tomatoes

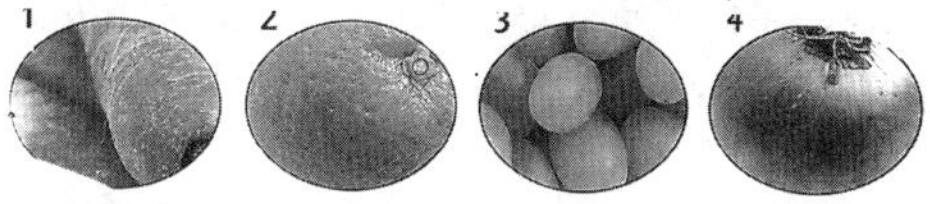
1
2
3
4

1 Listen and circle. Then write.

Step 2

Step 3

biscuits

£3

2 Write.

Step 4

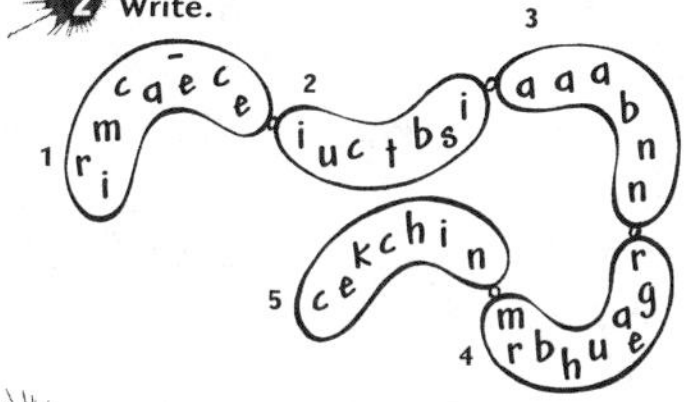
1
2
3
4
5

1 ______________
2 ______________
3 ______________
4 ______________
5 ______________

3 Listen and tick (✓) or cross (X).

What do the children like?

	Bill	Suzy	Julie	Kev	Kate
cheese	X				
biscuits	✓				
milk					
fish	✓				
cake	✓				

Who is it?

Is it a boy?
Yes.
Does he like fish?
Yes.
Is it Bill?
Yes!

4 Write.

Bill likes ____________, ____________ and ____________

but he doesn't like ______________________________.

Suzy likes ______________________________

____

______________________________.

2B Lesson 2

Main Language Items		Resource File	Materials Needed
What does … like? Does he/she like …? Is it a boy/girl? does/doesn't	carrots grapes cabbages oranges	17 18	cassette/cassette player

Step 1 Presentation

a Ask various pupils in the class what foods they like. Use the question form: **'Do you like …?'**

b Then ask pupils what drinks they like, using the same form.

Step 2 Pairwork

a Say **'Open your Coursebooks at page 23.'** Point to the chart at the top of the page and ask questions about what the pets like, e.g. **'Does Butch like chocolate?'**, **'Does Sam like carrots?'** Pupils answer **'yes/no'**, using the information in the chart.

b Divide the class into pairs. Only one CB is used for each pair, open at page 23. Say **'Cover the words on page 23 and look at the chart at the top of the page.'**

c Play the tape. P1 repeats the question, P2 answers using the information in the chart to help. Repeat twice, then change roles.

d Finally, pupils ask and answer questions without the help of the tape, using the chart only. Pupils should ask questions about all the pets.

Step 3 Listen and tick or cross

a Tell pupils to look at the chart on page 29 of their ABs. Pupils place a tick on the chart to indicate the food items each of the characters like and a cross for those they dislike.

b Play the tape two or three times.

c Check the answers by asking **'What does *Bill* like? Does *Suzy* like *cheese*?'** etc.

Tapescript:

BILL: **I like biscuits, cake and fish, // but I don't like cheese. //**

SUZY: **I like cheese, fish and milk, // but I don't like biscuits. //**

JULIE: **I like cheese, biscuits and cake, // but I don't like milk. //**

KEV: **I don't like fish or cheese, // but I do like cake and biscuits. //**

KATE: **I like everything. // I like cheese, biscuits, milk, fish and cakes. //**

Step 4 Pairwork

a This exercise is based on the chart completed in Step 3 above.

b Divide the class into pairs. All pairs work simultaneously.

c P1 thinks of one of the characters. P2 asks **'yes/no'** questions to determine who his or her partner is thinking of.

d Pupils should use the model questions on page 29 as a guide to the types of question.

Step 5 Write

a Using the information in the chart, pupils complete the sentence about Bill in their ABs and then write a similar description of the foods that Suzy likes.

I Like Fish

Say the rhyme

I Like ...

I like fish.
I like eggs.
I like cheese and meat.
I like cake and biscuits.
In fact, I like to eat.

I Don't Like ...

I don't like milk.
I don't like bread.
I don't like custard
On my head!

MILK

BINGO
LEMONADE

What do the pets like?

✓= Likes
X = doesn't Like

	Butch	Wow	Slow	Duffy	Sam
chocolate	✓	✓	✗	✗	✗
cake	✓	✓	✗	✗	
cabbage	✗	✗	✓	✗	✗
carrots	✗	✗	✓	✗	✗
apples		✓	✓	✗	✓
oranges	✗	✗		✗	
grapes	✗	✓	✓	✗	✓
milk	✓			✓	✓

Step 2

Ask and answer

Does Butch like chocolate? Yes, he does.

Does Wow like oranges? No, he doesn't.

What does Slow like? Cabbage, carrots, apples and grapes.

Ask and answer

Fruit and vegetables
What's number one?
Is it an orange?

potatoes
cauliflower
beans
onions
tomatoes

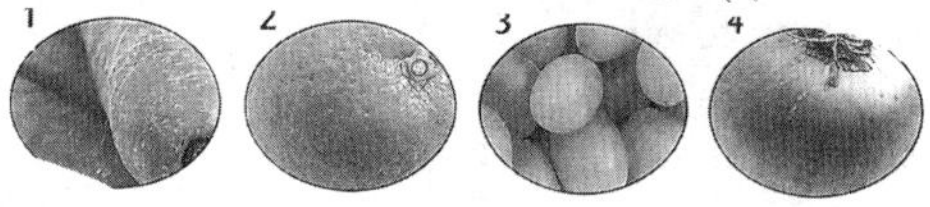
1
2
3
4

1 Listen and circle. Then write.

biscuits

2 Write.

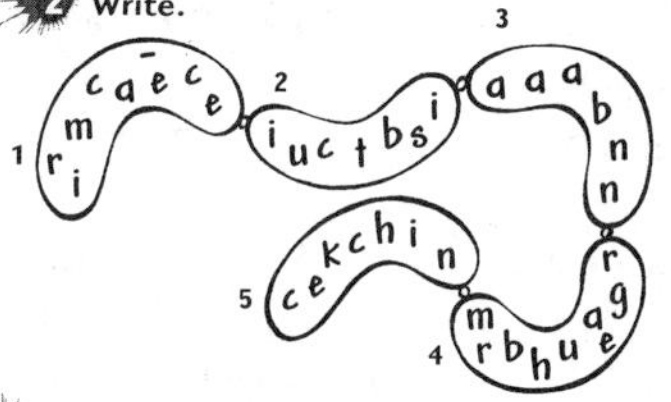
1 rimcaece
2 iuctbsi
3 aaabnn
4 rgaehubrm
5 nihkcec

1 ____________
2 ____________
3 ____________
4 ____________
5 ____________

3 Listen and tick (✓) or cross (X).

What do the children like?

	Bill	Suzy	Julie	Kev	Kate
cheese	X				
biscuits	✓				
milk					
fish	✓				
cake	✓				

Who is it?

Is it a boy?
Yes.
Does he like fish?
Yes.
Is it Bill?
Yes!

Step 3

Step 4

4 Write.

Bill likes ____________, ____________ and ____________
but he doesn't like ____________.
Suzy likes ____________
____
____________.

Step 5

2B Lesson 3

Main Language Items		Resource File	Materials Needed
Is it ... or ...?	fruit	1	cassette/cassette player
What's number 1?	tomato(es)	8	
a/an	potato(es)	9	
	onion		
	vegetables		
	beans		
	cauliflower		

Step 1 Pairwork

a Say **'Open your Coursebook at page 23. Look at the photographs of the fruit and vegetables.'** Hold up your book for the class. Point to one or two of the fruits and vegetables that pupils know and ask **'What's this? What are these?'** etc.

b Divide the class into pairs, with only one CB between each pair, open at page 23.

c Pupils repeat after the tape. P1 repeats the questions, P2 answers. Then change roles.

d Most of the pupils should have worked out the meaning of the words **fruit** and **vegetable**. Hold up your book, point to one or two of the fruits and vegetables and ask **'Is this a fruit or a vegetable?'**

e Then pupils ask and answer similar questions in pairs.

Tapescript:

Is an apple a fruit or a vegetable?
A fruit.
Is a carrot a fruit or a vegetable? A vegetable.
Is an onion a fruit or a vegetable?
A vegetable.
Is a potato a fruit or a vegetable?
A vegetable.
Is a tomato a fruit or a vegetable?
A fruit.

Step 2 Pairwork

a Say '**Look at the photographs at the bottom of the page.**'

b Pupils work in pairs and try to identify the fruits and vegetables in each of the four ovals. Encourage pupils to discuss in English and ask questions such as **'What's number one? Is it an orange? Are they apples?'**.

Step 3 Write

a Read the questions on page 30 of the AB and write the answers in the spaces provided.

b Encourage pupils to check each other's work.

c Ask '**Is an orange a fruit or a vegetable?** Write '**Fruit**' and '**Vegetable**' on the blackboard. Write '**orange**' under '**Fruit**'.

d Pupils then make a list of fruits and vegetables in their notebooks. Go over this list on the blackboard and add the English names of any other common local fruits and vegetables.

Step 4 Crossword

a Pupils read the clues and fill in the answers in the crossword.

Step 5 Personal file

a Pupils make a list of the food they like and don't like on page 30 of their ABs, using the words presented to date.

b Complete the exercise by asking pupils orally around the class '**Do you like *biscuits*?**' etc.

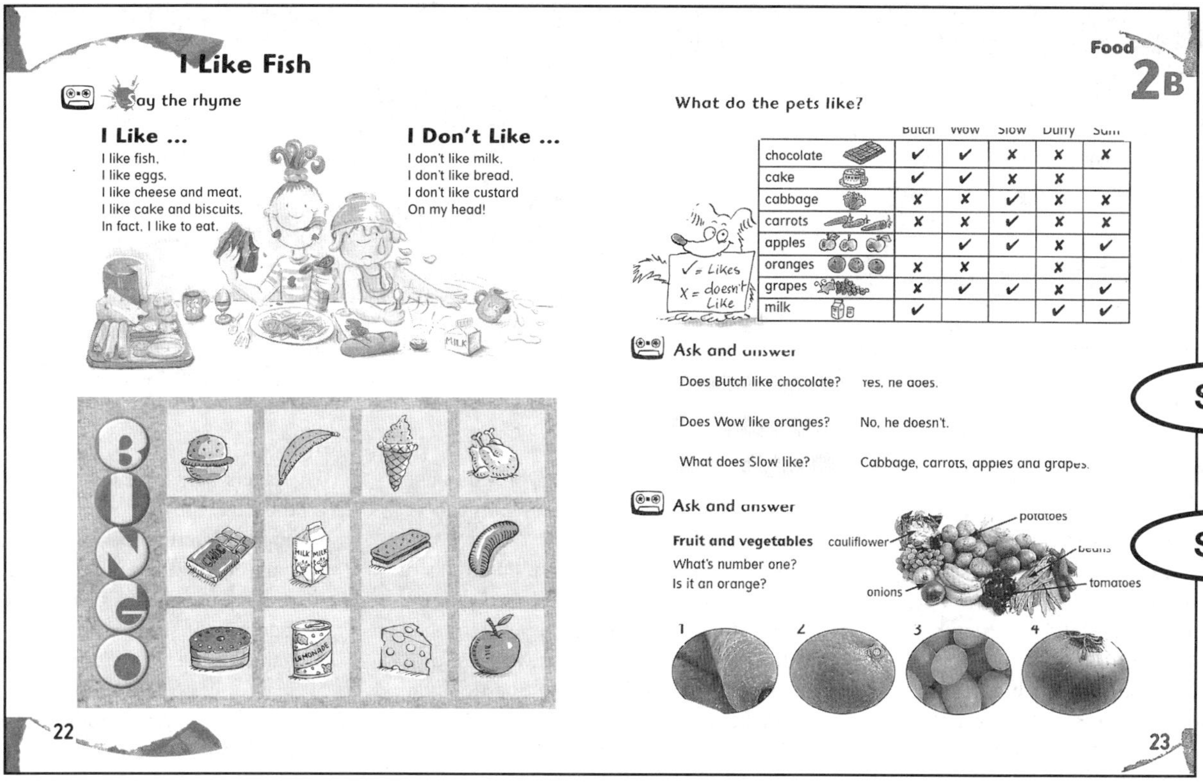

I Like Fish

Say the rhyme

I Like ...

I like fish.
I like eggs.
I like cheese and meat.
I like cake and biscuits.
In fact, I like to eat.

I Don't Like ...

I don't like milk.
I don't like bread.
I don't like custard
On my head!

MILK
BINGO
CHOC
MILK
LEMONADE

22

Food
2B

What do the pets like?

	Butch	Wow	Slow	Duffy	Sam
chocolate	✔	✔	✘	✘	✘
cake	✔	✔	✘	✘	
cabbage	✘	✘	✔	✘	✘
carrots	✘	✘	✔	✘	✘
apples		✔	✔	✘	✔
oranges	✘	✘		✘	
grapes	✘	✔	✔	✘	✔
milk	✔			✔	✔

✔ = Likes
✘ = doesn't Like

Ask and answer

Does Butch like chocolate? Yes, he does.

Does Wow like oranges? No, he doesn't.

What does Slow like? Cabbage, carrots, apples and grapes.

Ask and answer

Fruit and vegetables

What's number one?

Is it an orange?

cauliflower
potatoes
beans
onions
tomatoes
1
2
3
4

23

Step 1

Step 2

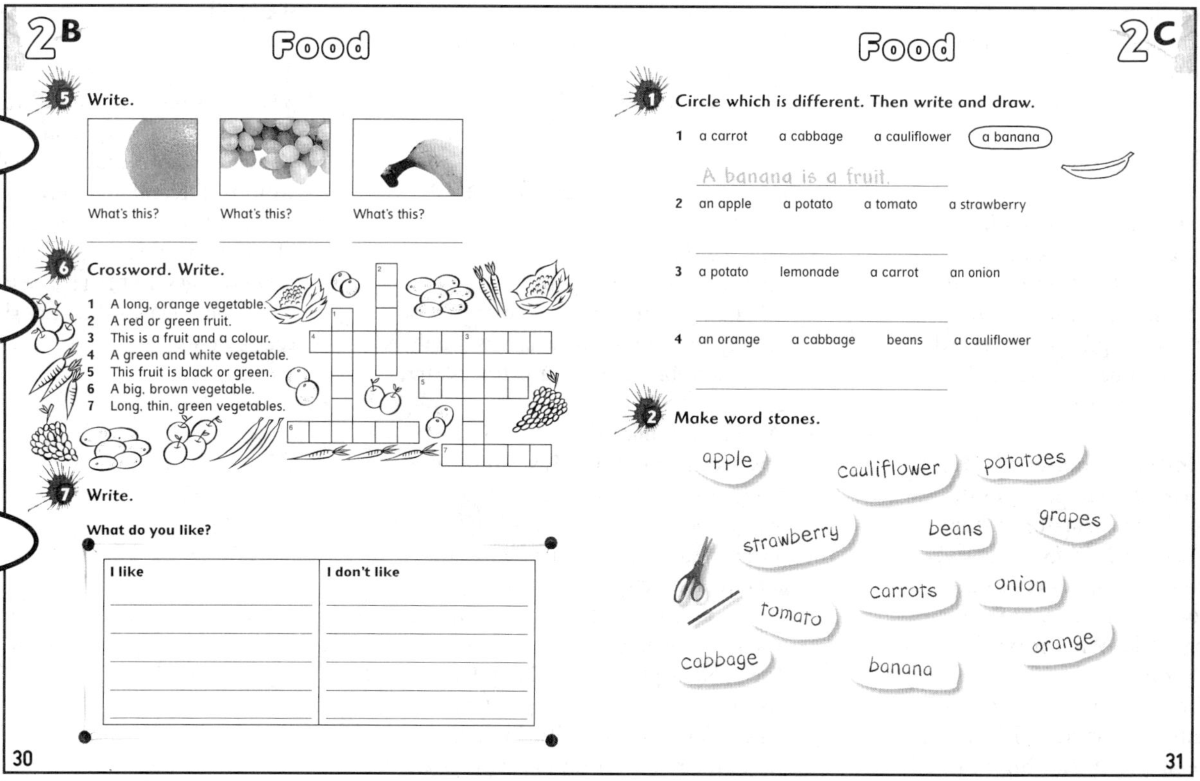

2B

Food

5 Write.

What's this? What's this? What's this?

6 Crossword. Write.

1 A long, orange vegetable.
2 A red or green fruit.
3 This is a fruit and a colour.
4 A green and white vegetable.
5 This fruit is black or green.
6 A big, brown vegetable.
7 Long, thin, green vegetables.

7 Write.

What do you like?

I like	I don't like

30

Food

2C

1 Circle which is different. Then write and draw.

1 a carrot a cabbage a cauliflower a banana

A banana is a fruit.

2 an apple a potato a tomato a strawberry

3 a potato lemonade a carrot an onion

4 an orange a cabbage beans a cauliflower

2 Make word stones.

apple
cauliflower
potatoes
strawberry
beans
grapes
carrots
onion
tomato
cabbage
banana
orange

31

tep 3

tep 4

tep 5

2c Lesson 1

Main Language Items			Resource File	Materials Needed
Is it big/small?	water	strawberry	23a	dice/counters
How many letters?	chips		42	cassette/cassette player
	orange juice			
	milk shake			
	lemonade			
	hot-dog			
	cheeseburger			

Step 1 Presentation

a Write an English word on the blackboard, e.g. **carrot**. Say **'There are six letters in carrot.'** Circle each letter in turn and count aloud along with the class.

b Write more words on the board and ask pupils, **'How many letters are there in this word?'**

c Make the exercise a little more challenging by asking pupils similar questions without writing the words on the blackboard, e.g. **'How many letters in sausage?'**

Step 2 Pairwork

a Say **'Open your Coursebooks at pages 24 and 25. Look at the pictures of the food. Listen to the tape and guess the food or drink.'**

b Play the tape. Pupils must guess what kind of food is being described. Do all three in the same way.

Tapescript (with answers):

1 **There are ten letters in the word. It's a small red fruit. What is it? // (Strawberry)**

2 **There are six letters in this word. It's a long, orange vegetable. What is it? // (Carrot)**

3 **There are five letters in the name of this fruit. It's red or green and it isn't big or small. What is it? // (Apple)**

c Teach any new vocabulary at this stage (hot-dog, strawberry, cheeseburger, milk shake, water, chips).

d Divide the class into pairs. P1 thinks of a fruit or vegetable, P2 asks questions and tries to determine the mystery food. P1 should only answer **'Yes'** or **'No'**. Write the following questions on the board to help pupils if necessary:
Is it a fruit/vegetable?
Is it red/green/brown?
Is it big/small?
How many letters?

d P2 is only allowed one guess at the name of the food. If correct, then players change roles.

Step 3 The Food Game

a This is a dice game to be played in groups of four. Each pupil needs a coloured counter and a piece of paper. Each group needs a dice and uses only one Coursebook, open at pages 24 and 25.

b Quickly introduce the names of the new foods and drinks. Say **'Point to a *can of lemonade*. Point to a *can of orange juice*. Point to a *packet of biscuits*,'** etc. Pupils must point to the appropriate picture on the board. If further practice is required, continue briefly in small groups.

c The game is played as follows. Each player selects a food category (**fruit, vegetables, drinks** or **fast food**) and places their counter on the appropriate picture in the centre of the board.

d Players then take turns to throw the dice and move around the board the appropriate number of squares. Players may move in any direction. The aim is to land on squares of their own food category. If successful, they write the name of the given item(s). Each item may only be written once.

e The first player to collect six different items is the winner.

Step 4 Circle which is different

a Tell pupils to open their ABs at page 31. Pupils select the word which is different in each group in activity 1, write a sentence explaining why the word is different and draw the item.

b You can continue the exercise on the blackboard, revising vocabulary from NEW STEPPING STONES 1, e.g. pencil, pen, blue, ruler clothes, e.g. shoes, hat, socks, boots.

tep 2

tep 3

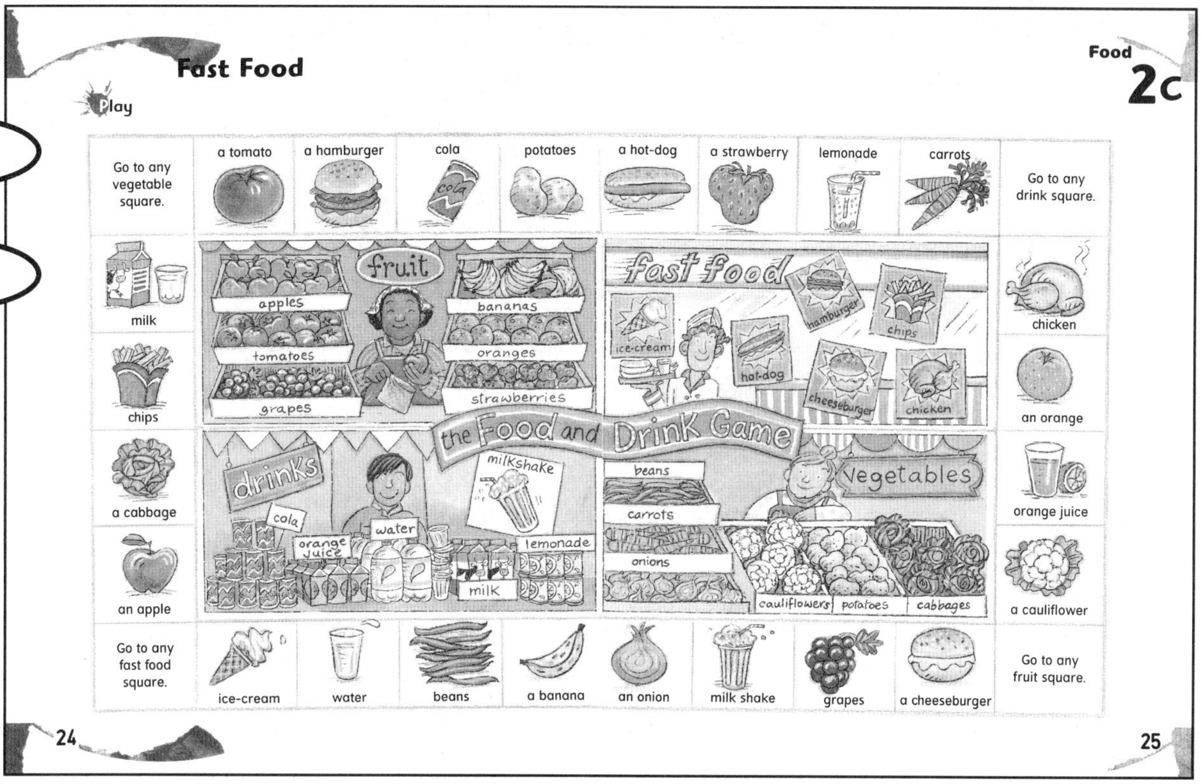
Fast Food

Food

2c

Play

Go to any vegetable square.	a tomato	a hamburger	cola	potatoes	a hot-dog	a strawberry	lemonade	carrots	Go to any drink square.

milk
chips
a cabbage
an apple
chicken
an orange
orange juice
a cauliflower
fruit
apples
tomatoes
grapes
bananas
oranges
strawberries
fast food
ice-cream
hamburger
chips
hot-dog
cheeseburger
chicken
the Food and Drink Game
drinks
cola
orange juice
water
milkshake
lemonade
milk
Vegetables
beans
carrots
onions
cauliflowers
potatoes
cabbages

Go to any fast food square.	ice-cream	water	beans	a banana	an onion	milk shake	grapes	a cheeseburger	Go to any fruit square.

24

25

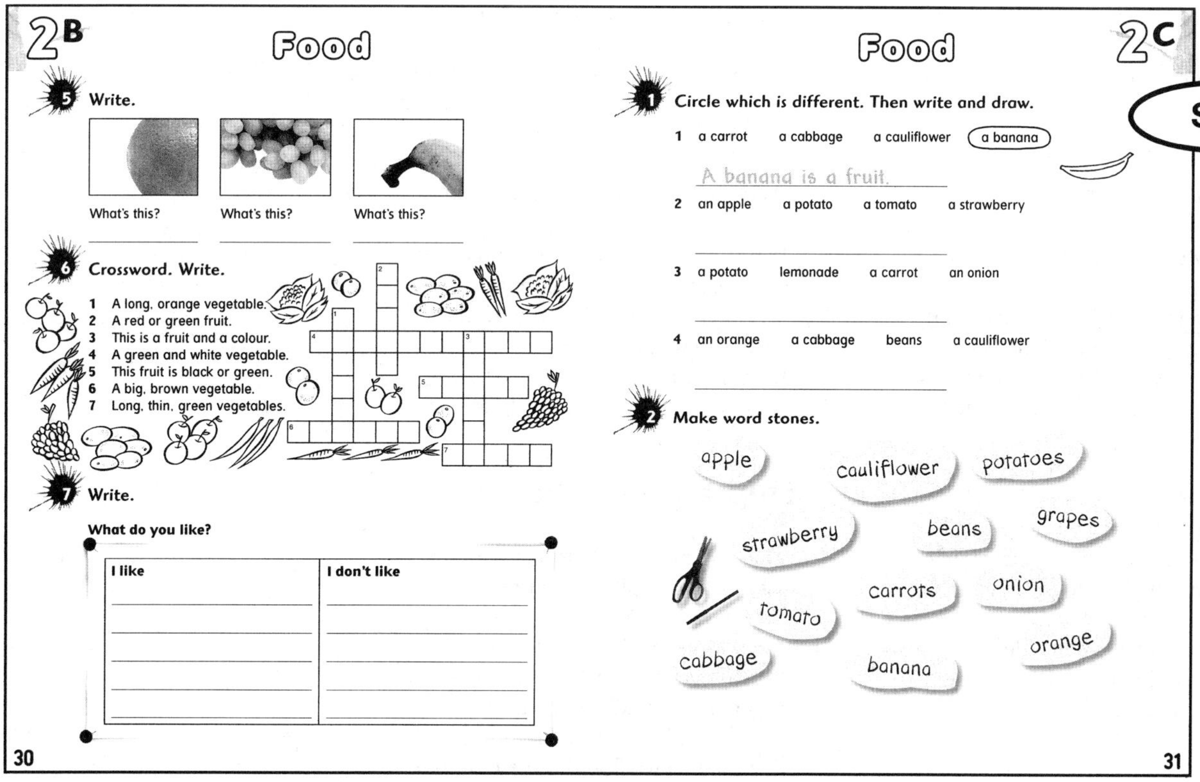
2B

Food

5 Write.

What's this? ______ What's this? ______ What's this? ______

6 Crossword. Write.

1 A long, orange vegetable.
2 A red or green fruit.
3 This is a fruit and a colour.
4 A green and white vegetable.
5 This fruit is black or green.
6 A big, brown vegetable.
7 Long, thin, green vegetables.

7 Write.

What do you like?

I like	I don't like

30

Food

2C

1 Circle which is different. Then write and draw.

1 a carrot a cabbage a cauliflower (a banana)

A banana is a fruit.

2 an apple a potato a tomato a strawberry

3 a potato lemonade a carrot an onion

4 an orange a cabbage beans a cauliflower

2 Make word stones.

apple
cauliflower
potatoes
strawberry
beans
grapes
carrots
onion
tomato
cabbage
banana
orange

31

Step 4

2c Lesson 2

Main Language Items		Resource File	Materials Needed
What's your favourite ...? My favourite ... is ...	drink	1 3 9	materials to make word stones cassette/cassette player

Step 1 Make word stones

a Pupils add twelve more word stones to their collection.

b Say **'Open your Activity Books at page 31.'** Point to the word stones. Check pupils are familiar with their meaning.

c To make the word stones, each pupil requires twelve 'stones' (either real stones or stone-shaped pieces of card, as before). Pupils write one word on each stone in felt-tip pen, as shown in the pictures.

d Pupils then store their stones for future use.

Step 2 Listen and write

a Write **'My favourite fruit is ...'** on the blackboard and ask pupils about their own favourite food and drink, using the questions **'What's your favourite fruit/vegetable/drink?'** Use the board game on pages 24 and 25 of the CB for reference.

b Pupils listen to the tape and complete the sentences on AB page 32. The first two words are given as an example.

c Play each passage two or three times and pause the tape to give pupils a chance to write.

d Pupils then draw and colour the appropriate food and drink in the spaces provided.

Tapescript:

GARY: **My favourite fruit is grapes, // my favourite vegetable is carrots // and my favourite drink is lemonade. //**

SUZY: **My favourite fruit is oranges // and er ... my favourite vegetable is green beans. // I like orange juice, milk and cola but my favourite drink is orange juice. //**

BILL: **My favourite fruit is strawberries. They're great. // I don't like vegetables but I suppose my favourite is potatoes because I like chips. // My favourite drink is cola.**

Step 3 Personal file

a Pupils draw a picture of their favourite fruit, vegetable and drink in the space provided on page 32 of the AB and write a description alongside. Encourage pupils to use the exercise above as a model for their descriptions.

Step 4 Game (Groups)

a This is a memory game, based on the information pupils have just written in the above Personal File exercise.

b Ask various pupils the question: **'What's your favourite fruit/ vegetable/drink?'** When pupils are familiar with the question form tell them they must find out the favourite fruit, vegetable and drink of four other pupils.

c Then make sure that all ABs are closed. See how much pupils can remember about their friends' favourite food and drink. Ask **'What's *Maria's* favourite fruit?'** etc.

Step 2

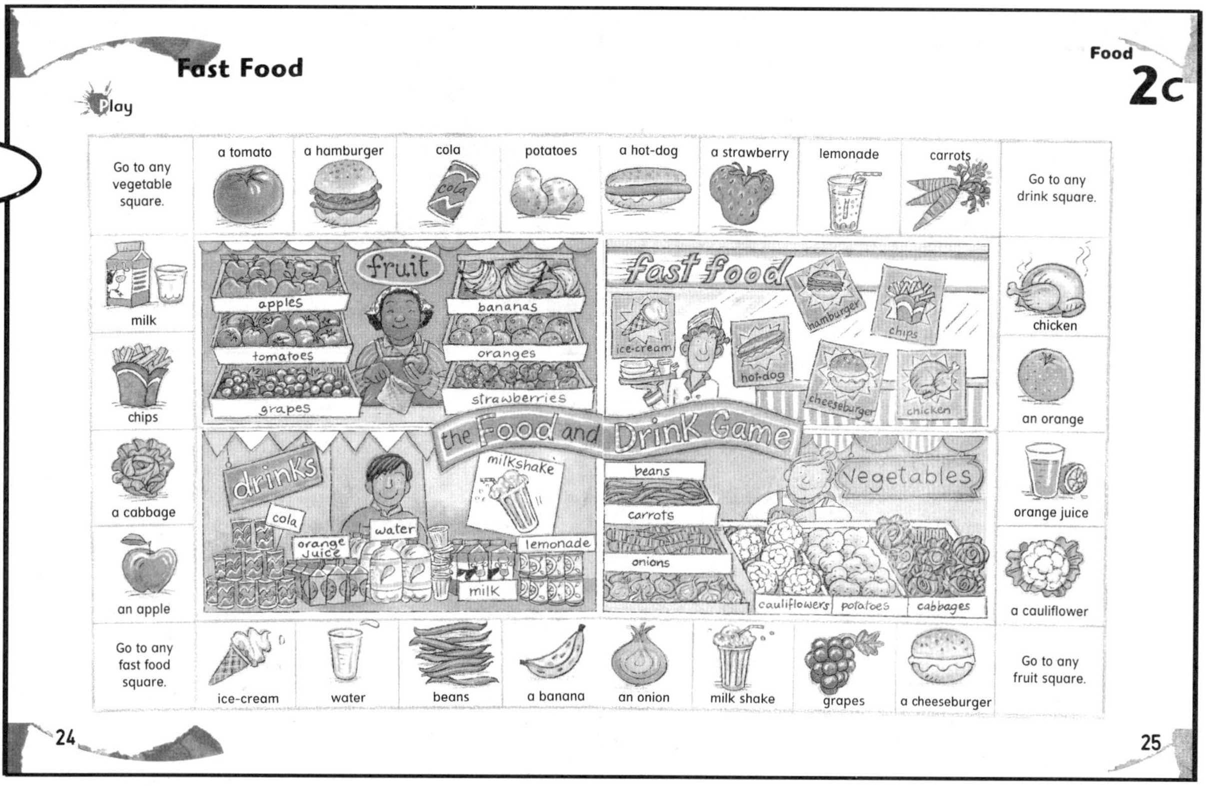

Fast Food
Play
Food
2c
Go to any vegetable square.
a tomato
a hamburger
cola
potatoes
a hot-dog
a strawberry
lemonade
carrots
Go to any drink square.
milk
chips
a cabbage
an apple
chicken
an orange
orange juice
a cauliflower
fruit
apples
bananas
tomatoes
oranges
grapes
strawberries
fast food
hamburger
chips
ice-cream
hot-dog
cheeseburger
chicken
the Food and Drink Game
drinks
milkshake
cola
orange juice
water
lemonade
milk
beans
carrots
onions
Vegetables
cauliflowers
potatoes
cabbages
Go to any fast food square.
ice-cream
water
beans
a banana
an onion
milk shake
grapes
a cheeseburger
Go to any fruit square.
24
25

Food 2c

1 Circle which is different. Then write and draw.

1 a carrot a cabbage a cauliflower (a banana)

A banana is a fruit.

2 an apple a potato a tomato a strawberry

3 a potato lemonade a carrot an onion

4 an orange a cabbage beans a cauliflower

Step 1

2 Make word stones.

apple cauliflower potatoes strawberry beans grapes carrots onion tomato cabbage banana orange

31

2c Food

3 Listen and write. Then draw and colour.

What are their favourites?

Step 2

1 My favourite fruit is grapes.
2 My favourite vegetable is carrots.
3 My favourite drink is ______.

1 My favourite fruit is ______.
2 My favourite vegetable is ______.
3 My favourite drink is ______.

1 My favourite fruit is ______.
2 My favourite vegetable is ______.
3 My favourite drink is ______.

4 Draw and write.

Step 3

My favourites

1 ______
2 ______
3 ______

32

2C Lesson 3

Main Language Items	Resource File	Materials Needed
Miss a turn. Hard luck. Do you like ...? If you like ..., ...!	4 5	dice/counters

Step 1 Action Game

a Bring four chairs to the front of the classroom. Bring four pupils to the front. Say **'Sit on the chairs.'**

b Say **'If you like cheese, stand up! If you like tomatoes, put your finger on your ear! If you like chocolate, put your hand on your head!'** As a check on pupils' understanding of the instructions it may be useful to write some of their likes and dislikes on the blackboard before you start.

c Then practise the same commands with the whole class using other food items. Revise other commands such as:
Pick up ...
Open ...
Touch ...
Close ...
(Parts of the body, classroom objects, clothes, etc.)

Step 2 The Food Game

a This game is similar to that played in 2C Lesson 1 but not exactly the same. (Pupils play in groups of four using counters, a dice and one Coursebook open at page 24.)

b Each player writes down the name of six items of food or drink that they like on a sheet of paper. On another sheet of paper, they write down six items that they don't like, e.g.:

I like	I don't like
apples	oranges
milk	orange juice
beans	cauliflower
ice-cream	bananas
chips	carrots
cola	chicken

c Players take turns throwing the dice and moving around the board on CB pages and 25 in any direction. The aim is to land on food squares from their 'like' list. Each time they do so, they tick that food item on their list.

d If any pupil lands on a 'don't like' food, they miss their next turn.

e The first player to collect five items from his or her 'like' list, is the winner.

f Pupils must count in English and should use phrases such as **'Your turn'**, **'My turn'**, **'Miss a turn'**, **'Yes I like ...'**, **'Hard luck. You don't like ...'** etc.

Step 3 Groupwork

a Ask various pupils in the class what foods they like. Use the question form: **'Do you like ...?'**

b Then copy the grid on page 33 of the AB onto the blackboard. Select one pupil to draw any food item in the left-hand column of the grid and write the names of two pupils in the top row. If the pupil draws **'cheese'**, he or she should ask other pupils **'Do you like cheese?'**, and record their answers in the grid using ticks and crosses.

c Pupils then work in groups of three. Each pupil chooses the food and drink that they want to ask about and writes and draws them in their grid.

d Pupils ask each other similar questions and fill in their charts.

e Finish off the exercise by asking pupils questions about other class members, e.g. **'Does *Alex* like *chicken*?' 'What does *Maria* like?'** etc. Pupils should answer **'I don't know'** if the appropriate answers are not on their chart.

Step 4 Write

a Using the information in the chart to help, pupils write sentences about themselves and their friends in the second table on AB page 33.

b Faster pupils can continue in their exercise books.

Step 2

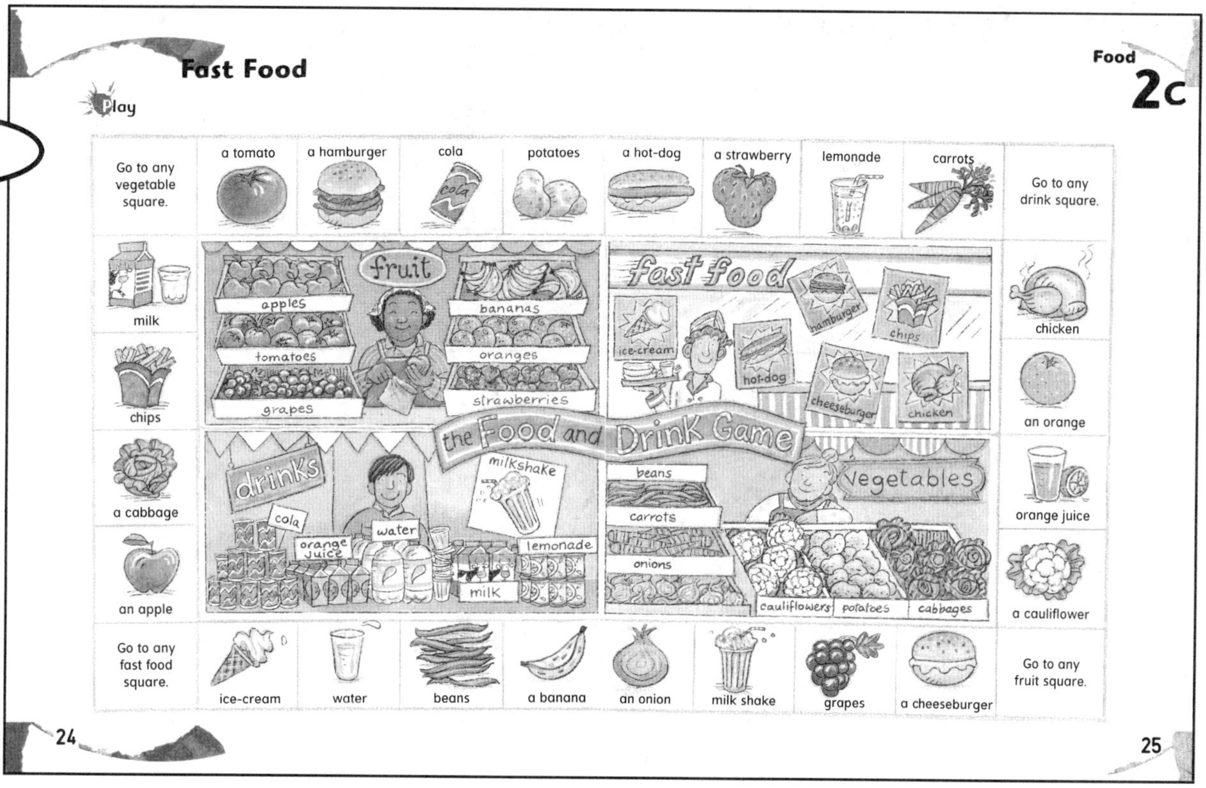

Fast Food
Food
2c
Play
Go to any vegetable square.
a tomato
a hamburger
cola
potatoes
a hot-dog
a strawberry
lemonade
carrots
Go to any drink square.
milk
chips
a cabbage
an apple
chicken
an orange
orange juice
a cauliflower
fruit
apples
tomatoes
grapes
bananas
oranges
strawberries
fast food
ice-cream
hamburger
chips
hot-dog
cheeseburger
chicken
the Food and Drink Game
drinks
cola
orange juice
water
milkshake
lemonade
milk
beans
carrots
onions
vegetables
cauliflowers
potatoes
cabbages
Go to any fast food square.
ice-cream
water
beans
a banana
an onion
milk shake
grapes
a cheeseburger
Go to any fruit square.
24
25

2c

Food

3 Listen and write. Then draw and colour.

What are their favourites?

1 My favourite fruit is grapes.
2 My favourite vegetable is carrots.
3 My favourite drink is ______.

1 My favourite fruit is ______.
2 My favourite vegetable is ______.
3 My favourite drink is ______.

1 My favourite fruit is ______.
2 My favourite vegetable is ______.
3 My favourite drink is ______.

4 Draw and write.

My favourites

1 ______
2 ______
3 ______

32

Food

2c

5 Ask and answer. Then write.

Do you like ice-cream?

Step 3

food and drink	me	friend 1	friend 2
ice-cream			

6 Write.

Step 4

I like ______	My friend ______ likes

33

2D Lesson 1

Main Language Items		Resource File	Materials Needed
How many ...?	vanilla	3a	coloured pencils
Find ...	strawberry		
good for you	banana		
bad for you	chocolate		

Step 1 Pairwork

a Elicit questions from pupils that they can ask about the photographs on page 26 of the CB. Pupils may use any question forms they know ranging from simple structures such as **'What's this?'** to more complex forms such as **'How many apples are there in the picture?'** Write the question forms on the blackboard.

b Divide the class into pairs. Use one book between each pair of pupils. Pupils ask and answer as many questions as they can about the photographs.

Step 2 Look and find

a The instructions on page 26 tell pupils to look carefully at the photographs and find specific things.

b Give an example. Say **'Find three vegetables.'** and ask a number of pupils. Write the answers on the blackboard. Pupils then work in pairs and complete the other tasks.

c Complete the activity by writing the answers on the blackboard.

d The exercise can be done more competitively by turning it into a team race. Do not set a time limit, but instead the first pair or group to complete the tasks successfully, wins.

Step 3 Write. Then colour

a Introduce the names of different ice-cream flavours: vanilla, strawberry, banana and chocolate. Ask pupils **'Do you like ice-cream?'** Then ask **'Do you like *chocolate* ice-cream?'**

b Pupils look at the puzzle on page 34 of the AB. They trace through the maze to discover which ice-cream each of the pets is eating and complete the sentences.

c Pupils then colour the maze appropriately.

Step 4 Write

a Write the headings 'Good for you' and 'Bad for you' on the blackboard. Ask pupils to think of an item of food and drink for each heading. Discuss with them why they chose these items. Can they add any other items to the list?

b Pupils look at the pictures of food and drink and write the words in the appropriate list, 'Good for you' or 'Bad for you'.

Step 1

Step 2

Oh No! More Monsters!

Food

2D

Look and find

1 Find six things that you like.
2 Find two things that you don't like.
3 Find Gary's favourite drink.
4 Find four seven-letter words.
5 Find three red fruits.
6 Find three things that Sam likes.

Lemonade
Digestive

Listen

This is Cruncher Monster and his sister Muncher. They love eating. Cruncher has got big, yellow teeth and green hair. He likes trees, tables and rulers. His favourite food is red chairs. He hates cakes, chocolate, biscuits and ice-cream. Muncher has got small, green teeth and red hair. She hates fruit and vegetables.She likes sausages, chicken and meat. Her favourite food is little boys!

Listen

In the café

Man: Yes, please?
Suzy: A hamburger, please.
Man: Anything else?
Suzy: Er ... some chips.
Man: Do you want a drink?
Suzy: Yes, a cola, please.
Man: Thank you.

MENU

26

27

Step 3

Step 4

2D Food

1 Write. Then colour.

Toni's Ice-cream
Vanilla Strawberry Banana Chocolate

1 Butch is eating ______ ice-cream.
2 Wow is eating ______
3 Slow is ______
4 Duffy ______

2 Write.

good for you
milk
bad for you
COLA

Food 2D

3 Listen and tick (✓) or cross (✗).

What do the monsters like?

1 2 3

4 Draw. Then write.

My monster

34

35

2D Lesson 2

Main Language Items		Resource File	Materials Needed
Who's got ...?	love	1	coloured pencils
Who likes ...?	sister	9	paper for display (optional)
(he, she, his, her)	teeth	36	cassette/cassette player
	hate		
	hair		

Step 1 Presentation

a Say '**Look at the picture of the monsters at the top of page 27 in your Coursebooks.**' Pupils listen to the tape and read at the same time.

Step 2 Pairwork

a Divide the class into pairs. Only one book between each pair should be open at page 27.

b Pupils repeat after the tape. P1 repeats the questions and P2 repeats the answers. They then change roles.

c Then pupils ask and answer their own questions about the two monsters in terms of both their physical appearance and their likes and dislikes.

Tapescript:

What is Cruncher's sister called?
Muncher.
What colour is Muncher's hair?
Red.
Who's got big yellow teeth?
Cruncher.
Who like sausages and chicken?
Muncher.
Who's got big teeth? Cruncher.

Step 3 Listen and tick or cross

a Say '**Now turn to page 35 in your Activity Books. The three monsters are friends of Cruncher and Muncher. They all like eating. Listen to the tape to find out what they like eating.**'

b Pupils place a tick in the box beside the food that the monsters like and a cross beside those they don't like.

c Play each description two or three times.

d Finish the exercise by asking pupils what each monster likes eating.

Tapescript:

1 **This is Swallow monster. He eats vegetables. He loves cabbage and beans and he likes cauliflower. // He doesn't like potatoes or carrots and he hates tomatoes. //**

2 **This is Nibble. She eats pencil sharpeners and rubbers and her favourite food is hats. // She doesn't like pencils or socks and she hates books. //**

3 **This monster is called Chew. He's very dangerous. He doesn't like fruit or vegetables and he hates chips. // Chew likes to eat boys and girls but his favourite food is teachers! //**

Step 4 Personal file

a Pupils invent a monster of their own. They draw a picture of it in the box in the place where it lives. Then they write a description alongside. They should think of a name for their monster and write about what it eats. Its size, build, teeth, etc. should be appropriate to the type of food it eats.

b Tell pupils to use the descriptions of Cruncher and Muncher on page 27 in the CBs to help.

c Expect differences in terms of accuracy and length of the descriptions according to individual ability.

Oh No! More Monsters!

Look and find

1 Find six things that you like.
2 Find two things that you don't like.
3 Find Gary's favourite drink.
4 Find four seven-letter words.
5 Find three red fruits.
6 Find three things that Sam likes.

Food
2D

Listen

This is Cruncher Monster and his sister Muncher. They love eating. Cruncher has got big, yellow teeth and green hair. He likes trees, tables and rulers. His favourite food is red chairs. He hates cakes, chocolate, biscuits and ice-cream. Muncher has got small, green teeth and red hair. She hates fruit and vegetables. She likes sausages, chicken and meat. Her favourite food is little boys!

Listen

In the café

Man: Yes, please?
Suzy: A hamburger, please.
Man: Anything else?
Suzy: Er ... some chips.
Man: Do you want a drink?
Suzy: Yes, a cola, please.
Man: Thank you.

26

27

Lemonade
MENU
Digestive

Step 1

Step 2

2D Food

1 Write. Then colour.

Toni's Ice-cream
Vanilla Strawberry Banana Chocolate

1 Butch is eating ______ ice-cream.
2 Wow is eating ______
3 Slow is ______
4 Duffy ______

2 Write.

good for you	bad for you
milk	

Food 2D

3 Listen and tick (✓) or cross (✗).

What do the monsters like?

1 2 3

4 Draw. Then write.

My monster

34

35

COLA
CHOC

Step 3

Step 4

2D Lesson 3

Main Language Items		Resource File	Materials Needed
Do you want …?	please	46	Menu cards (see AB cut-outs section)
Anything else?	tea	55	cassette/cassette player
	pizza		
	menu		
	thank you		
	coffee		
	spaghetti		

Step 1 Listen and write

a Tell pupils to open their Activity Books at page 36. Pupils listen to the tape and write down the order on each of the three menus.

b Play the first restaurant scene once. Then ask the class **'What do the children want?' 'How many colas do they want?'** Play the first scene again.

c Pupils then complete the order for scenes 2 and 3. Play the tape three times for each scene. Allow pupils time to compare their answers between each listening.

Tapescript:

1

WOMAN: **Yes, please.**
KATE: **We'd like two colas, two lemonades and a milk shake. //**
WOMAN: **Would you like ice-cream?**
KATE: **Yes, please. Three vanilla and one chocolate.**
WOMAN: **Thank you. //**

2

BILL: **Hello.**
MAN: **Hello, Bill. What do you want?**
BILL: **Three beefburgers, two cheeseburgers and an eggburger.**
MAN: **OK. Three beefburgers, two cheeseburgers and an eggburger. Thank you. //**

3

WAITER: **Your menu, sir, We've got soup or fruit, chicken or fish with vegetables, and ice-cream or chocolate cake.**
MR KAY: **I want soup. Who wants soup? One, two, three, four soups and Suzy?**
SUZY: **Fruit, please.**
MR KAY: **Four soups and one fruit. //**
WAITER: **Four soups … and one … fruit. Chicken or fish?**
MR KAY: **Chicken? One, two, three. Three chicken and two fish.**
WAITER: **Ice-cream or chocolate cake?**
CHILDREN: **Ice-cream.**
MR KAY: **Five ice-creams, please.**

Step 2 Role play

a Divide the class into pairs. One pupil in each pair plays the part of the waiter and one pupil plays the part of Suzy. Say **'Look at the picture of Suzy on page 27 of your Coursebook and listen to the tape.'**

b Play the dialogue. Pupils read at the same time.

c Then play Part 1. Pupils repeat after the tape, twice.

d Pupils act out the dialogue without the help of the tape.

e Repeat steps b–d for the second part of the dialogue.

f Then pupils practise the whole dialogue. Insist upon actions to make the role play realistic.

Step 3 Role plays

Pupils will need the four menu cards from the AB cut-outs section.

a Divide the class into pairs or groups. Pupils act out dialogues using the menu cards as prompts and the above role play as a guide.

b Pupils practise all four skills. One pupil from each pair or group plays the part of the waiter and writes down the order. The other pupil(s) decide what they would like to eat.

c All pupils should take a turn at playing the waiter.

d Teach extra vocabulary and phrases if required, e.g. **'What would you like?' 'Excuse me,' 'I'd/We'd like …' 'That's all.'**

NOTE The prices on the menus are for use with role plays and games later in the book and should be ignored at this stage.

Oh No! More Monsters!

Look and find

1 Find six things that you like.
2 Find two things that you don't like.
3 Find Gary's favourite drink.
4 Find four seven-letter words.
5 Find three red fruits.
6 Find three things that Sam likes.

Lemonade
Digestive

Food

2D

Listen

This is Cruncher Monster and his sister Muncher. They love eating. Cruncher has got big, yellow teeth and green hair. He likes trees, tables and rulers. His favourite food is red chairs. He hates cakes, chocolate, biscuits and ice-cream. Muncher has got small, green teeth and red hair. She hates fruit and vegetables.She likes sausages, chicken and meat. Her favourite food is little boys!

Listen

In the café

Man: Yes, please?
Suzy: A hamburger, please.
Man: Anything else?
Suzy: Er ... some chips.
Man: Do you want a drink?
Suzy: Yes, a cola, please.
Man: Thank you.

MENU

26 27

Step 2

Step 1

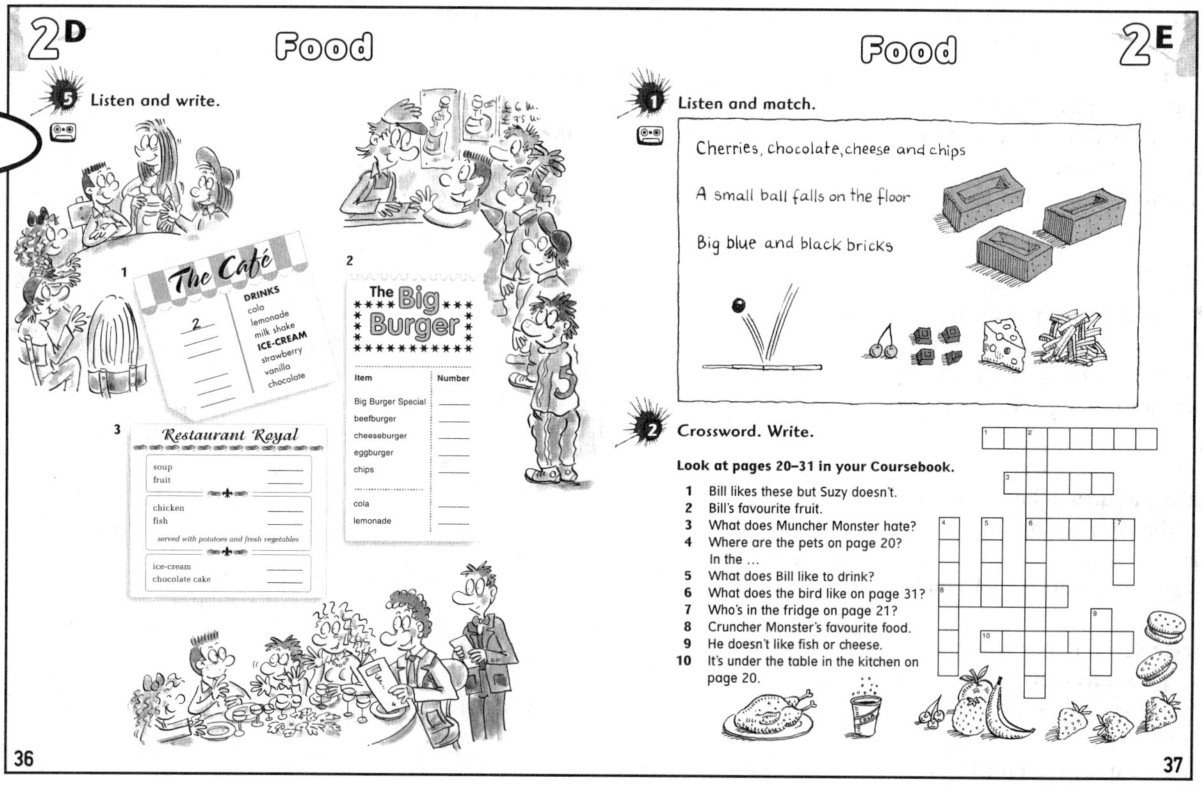

2D Food

5 Listen and write.

1

The Café

2

DRINKS
cola
lemonade
milk shake
ICE-CREAM
strawberry
vanilla
chocolate

2

The Big Burger

Item	Number
Big Burger Special	______
beefburger	______
cheeseburger	______
eggburger	______
chips	______
cola	______
lemonade	______

3

Restaurant Royal

soup ______
fruit ______

chicken ______
fish ______
served with potatoes and fresh vegetables

ice-cream ______
chocolate cake ______

Food **2E**

1 Listen and match.

Cherries, chocolate, cheese and chips

A small ball falls on the floor

Big blue and black bricks

2 Crossword. Write.

Look at pages 20–31 in your Coursebook.

1 Bill likes these but Suzy doesn't.
2 Bill's favourite fruit.
3 What does Muncher Monster hate?
4 Where are the pets on page 20? In the ...
5 What does Bill like to drink?
6 What does the bird like on page 31?
7 Who's in the fridge on page 21?
8 Cruncher Monster's favourite food.
9 He doesn't like fish or cheese.
10 It's under the table in the kitchen on page 20.

36 37

2E Lesson 1

Main Language Items	Resource File	Materials Needed
Revision of singular/plural nouns a/an	5 6	materials to make word stones word stone collections cassette/cassette player

Step 1 Word stones

a Say **'Open your books at page 28.'** To make the word stones, each pupil requires seven 'stones'. Pupils write the word **'an'** on three stones in felt-tip pen, as shown in the picture, and leave four stones blank.
b Each pupil also needs the seventeen stones shown from their collection (**apple, potatoes,** etc.).
c Pupils play the game shown, putting the appropriate stones together, '**a banana**', '**an orange**', '(blank) **potatoes**', etc.
d When pupils have finished, they can compare their stones with a friend's to see if they are the same.
e Pupils then store their stones for future use.

Step 2 Listen and match

a Say **'Open your Activity Books at page 37.'** Point to the phrases and pictures.
b Play the tape, one phrase at a time. Pupils listen and draw a line to match the phrase they hear with the appropriate picture.
c Play the tape again, pausing for pupils to repeat.
d Play the tape again. Pupils repeat the phrases as quickly as they can.
e Pupils practise saying the phrases as quickly as they can.
f Ask volunteers to say the phrases as fast as they can in front of the class.

Step 3 The Stepping Stones Game

a The Stepping Stones Game refers to the chart at the top of page 23 and to pupils' own preferences. Pupils make sentences going from left to right across the stepping stones. They must begin in the first column and take one word from each column.
b Divide the class into pairs. Give the class ten minutes to make as many sentences as possible from the words on the stones.
c Check the answers with the whole class. The pair to get the most correct and true sentences are the winners.

Step 1

Step 3

Words and Sentences

Word Stones

Use

apple potatoes strawberry grapes carrots cabbage a x 5 cauliflower orange beans tomato onion banana

Make

an x 3 x 4

Play

a banana an orange potatoes

The Stepping Stones Game

I
like
chocolate
Butch
cakes
carrots
Slow
don't
likes
doesn't
cabbage
apples

Find more words

roller skates
ball
bike
crisps
sweets
pizza
salad
computer game

5 Listen and write.

1
The Café
DRINKS
cola
lemonade
milk shake
ICE-CREAM
strawberry
vanilla
chocolate
2
The Big Burger
Item
Number
Big Burger Special
beefburger
cheeseburger
eggburger
chips
cola
lemonade
3
Restaurant Royal
soup
fruit
chicken
fish
served with potatoes and fresh vegetables
ice-cream
chocolate cake

Step 2

1 Listen and match.

Cherries, chocolate, cheese and chips

A small ball falls on the floor

Big blue and black bricks

2 Crossword. Write.

Look at pages 20–31 in your Coursebook.

1 Bill likes these but Suzy doesn't.
2 Bill's favourite fruit.
3 What does Muncher Monster hate?
4 Where are the pets on page 20? In the …
5 What does Bill like to drink?
6 What does the bird like on page 31?
7 Who's in the fridge on page 21?
8 Cruncher Monster's favourite food.
9 He doesn't like fish or cheese.
10 It's under the table in the kitchen on page 20.

2E Lesson 2

Main Language Items	Resource File	Materials Needed
Food (revision)	8 17	Story strips 2 (see AB cut-outs section) scissors (optional) cassette/cassette player dice/counters

Step 1 Jigsaw Reading/ Listening

a Play again the introductory story on pages 18 and 19 of the CB. Pupils listen.

b The cut-outs 'Story strips 2' in the centre of the AB form the text to the story. Pupils should cut them out and jumble them up.

c Pupils then try to put their story strips in the correct order, without looking at their CB.

d When pupils have finished the jigsaw reading task, they should look at the pictures on pages 18 and 19 of their CB to check the order.

e Finally, play the complete story again on tape, to confirm the correct order.

Tapescript:

Jemimah's Week

On Monday, Jemimah went to the shop and bought a packet of peanuts.

On Tuesday, Jemimah went to the shop and bought a bar of chocolate.

On Wednesday, Jemimah went to the shop and bought a packet of crisps.

On Thursday, Jemimah went to the shop and bought a bag of sweets.

On Friday, Jemimah went to the shop and bought a packet of biscuits.

On Saturday, Jemimah went to the shop and bought a tub of ice-cream.

On Sunday morning, the shop was closed.

Jemimah ate a packet of peanuts, a bar of chocolate, a packet of crisps, a bag of sweets, a packet of biscuits and a tub of ice-cream … and on Sunday afternoon, she was sick.

Step 2 Crossword

a The clues in the crossword on AB page 37 are all about the Food topic.

b Pupils read the clues, find the answers on pages 20–31 of their Coursebook and then write the words in the crossword grid.

Step 3 The Stepping Stones Spelling Game 2

a Ideally the game should be played in groups. Each group needs one copy of the board game on AB page 38 and a dice. (If no dice is available, the numbers 1–6 can be written on each side of a six-sided pencil.) Each group nominates a referee. The referee's job is to check the answers and adjudicate. The rest of the group are the players. Each player needs a coloured counter (or small coloured piece of paper), a pencil and a sheet of paper.

b The object of the game is to make your way from the start to the finish.

c Players take it in turns to throw the dice and move around the board. When they land on a letter they must say a word beginning with that letter. Then they write the word and say each letter as they write. When they land on a picture they must say the word, write the word and say each letter as they write.

d Encourage pupils to use English as they play. They should count in English and use phrases such as **'Your/My turn.'**

e In addition, ask pupils questions about the game as you monitor their progress, e.g. **'Is it your turn?'**, **'What's your colour?'**

Step 1

2 Food

STORY

Jemimah's Week

On Monday, Jemimah went to the shop and bought a packet of peanuts.

On Tuesday, Jemimah went to the shop and bought a bar of chocolate.

On Wednesday, Jemimah went to the shop and bought a packet of crisps.

On Thursday, Jemimah went to the shop and bought a bag of sweets.

On Friday, Jemimah went to the shop and bought a packet of biscuits.

On Saturday, Jemimah went to the shop and bought a tub of ice-cream.

On Sunday morning, the shop was closed. Jemimah ate a packet of peanuts, a bar of chocolate, a packet of crisps, a bag of sweets, a packet of biscuits and a tub of ice-cream...

and on Sunday afternoon, she was sick.

SHOP
CRISPS
ICE CRE

18 19

Step 2

Step 3

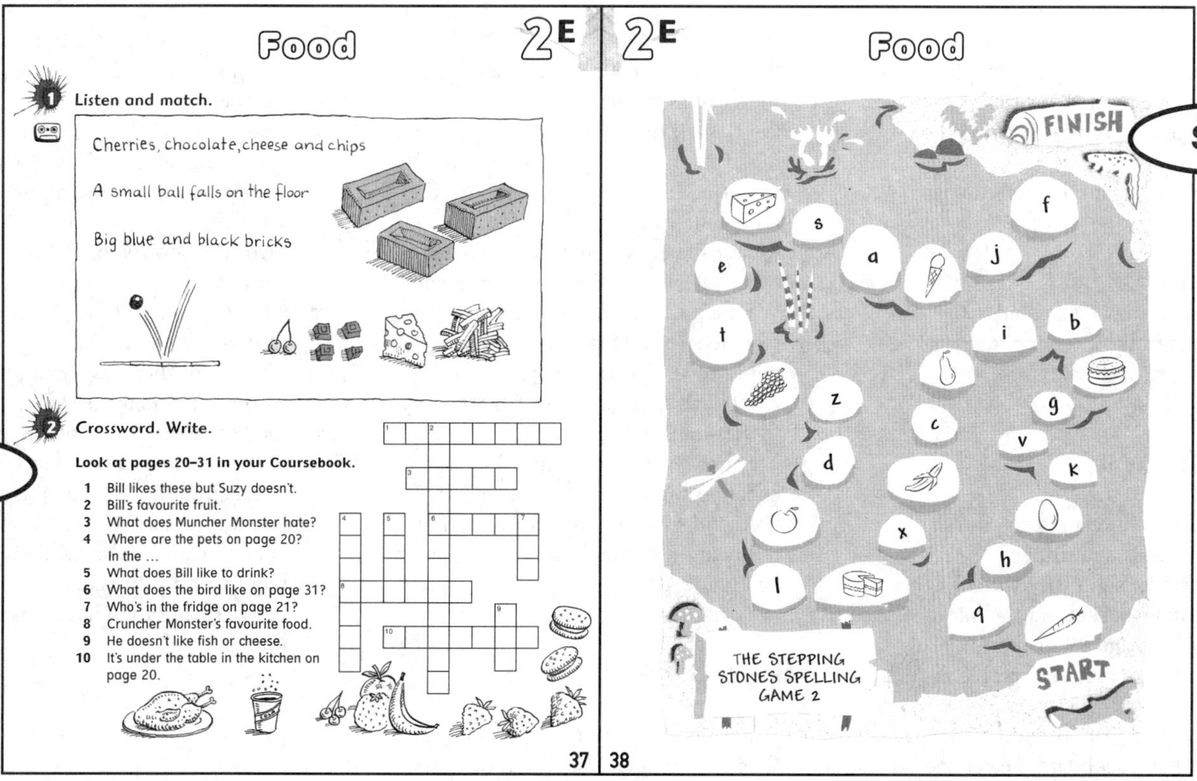

Food 2E

1 Listen and match.

Cherries, chocolate, cheese and chips

A small ball falls on the floor

Big blue and black bricks

2 Crossword. Write.

Look at pages 20–31 in your Coursebook.

1 Bill likes these but Suzy doesn't.
2 Bill's favourite fruit.
3 What does Muncher Monster hate?
4 Where are the pets on page 20? In the ...
5 What does Bill like to drink?
6 What does the bird like on page 31?
7 Who's in the fridge on page 21?
8 Cruncher Monster's favourite food.
9 He doesn't like fish or cheese.
10 It's under the table in the kitchen on page 20.

37

2E Food

FINISH
s
f
e
a
j
t
i
b
z
g
c
v
d
k
x
h
l
q
THE STEPPING STONES SPELLING GAME 2
START

38

2E Lesson 3

Main Language Items			Resource File	Materials Needed
favourite	crisps	ball	18	cassette/cassette player
pizza	ice-cream	bike	18a	card for menus
spaghetti	vanilla	computer game		
chicken	strawberry	roller skates		
salad	banana			
hot-dog	chocolate			

Step 1 Find more words

a Say **'Open your Coursebooks at page 29 and look at the photograph.'** Ask pupils in their L1 if any of them can see something they like to eat or drink. Then ask them to find something they would not eat or drink. Ask them if they can name any of the items in English. What occasion do they think it is? Do they have similar food/drink for their birthday parties? Talk about 'favourite' food and drink.

b Play the tape and listen to the words while looking at the photograph.

c Play the tape again. This time pupils point to the appropriate item as they hear the word.

d Play the tape again. Pupils listen and repeat the words.

Tapescript:
crisps // pizza // salad // sweets // bike // computer game // ball // roller skates

Step 2 Write

a This is a survey relating to pupils' favourite foods and drinks.

b Before pupils begin they should write their own 'favourites' on the lines provided on page 39 of the AB. (This will avoid organisational problems later.)

c Copy the grid from the top of AB page 39 onto the blackboard. Select one pupil and ask **'What's your favourite food?'** Write the answer on the blackboard. Then find out how many other pupils have the same favourite food. Ask **'Who's favourite food is ...? Put up your hand!'** Count aloud along with the class or nominate a pupil to keep the score. Ask for a volunteer to write the number alongside the food on the blackboard.

d Then find out another pupil's favourite food. Repeat the procedure. Continue until all the pupils have been included in the count. When you have finished, the total on the blackboard should be the same as the number of pupils in the class. If not, someone has either not raised their hand or has more than one favourite! (Encourage pupils to do the arithmetic in English.)

e Repeat the above procedure for the other categories; **drink** and **ice-cream**.

f When all the figures have been recorded on the blackboard, direct pupils to the grids on page 39 of their AB. Pupils transfer the words and figures into their books.

g The activity can be extended by collating the information separately for boys and girls and/or displaying the information in the form of a wall chart and graphs.

Step 3 Personal file

a Pupils draw a picture of their favourite food and write a description of it in the space provided.

b Pupils need not limit their descriptions: individuals should be encouraged to write as much as they can. Expect differences according to individual abilities.

Step 4 My favourite food game

a This game involves pupils successively adding to the length of a sentence by repeating what previous pupils have said and then adding something themselves.

b P1 says, e.g., **'My favourite food is pizza.'** P2 adds to the list, e.g., **'My favourite food is pizza and biscuits.'** P3 adds to the list again, e.g., **'My favourite food is pizza, biscuits and ice-cream.'**

c Continue until all the pupils have had a turn.

d The rest of the class should help pupils who cannot remember all the items in the list. Alternatively one pupil can draw each item on the blackboard as it is added to the list. The pictures on the board can then be used as a memory aid and emphasis is taken away from remembering the sequence to simply remembering the English name for things.

Words and Sentences

Word Stones

Use

apple potatoes strawberry grapes carrots a x 5 cabbage orange cauliflower beans tomato onion banana

Make

an x 3 x 4

Play

a banana an orange potatoes

The Stepping Stones Game

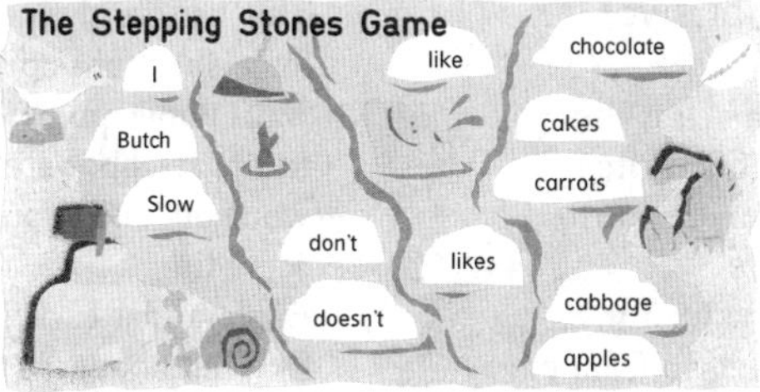

I
Butch
Slow
don't
doesn't
like
likes
chocolate
cakes
carrots
cabbage
apples

Find more words

roller skates
ball
bike
crisps
sweets
pizza
salad
computer game

Step 1

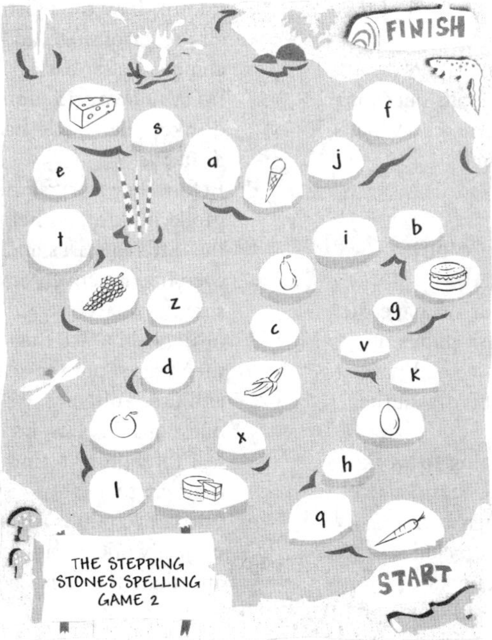

FINISH
s
f
e
a
j
t
i
b
z
g
c
v
d
k
x
h
l
q
START
THE STEPPING STONES SPELLING GAME 2

3 Write.

What's your favourite food?

me		
food	drink	ice-cream

Step 2

my class		
food	drink	ice-cream

4 Draw and write.

My favourite food

Step 3

2F Lesson 1 - Project

Main Language Items			Resource File	Materials Needed
What's your favourite ...?	food drink games colours	toys teams places countries		cassette/cassette player project materials

Step 1 Listen and circle

a Say **'Open your Activity Book at page 40, and look at the chart at the top of the page.'**

b Pupils listen to the tape and circle the appropriate favourite colour and toy for each of the characters.

c Play the tape three times. Allow pupils to compare answers before replaying the tape.

Tapescript:

BILL: **Favourite colour ... er ... that's red and my favourite toy is my yo-yo. // Suzy, what's your favourite colour? //**

SUZY: **Yellow. //**

BILL: **And what's your favourite toy? //**

SUZY: **My kite ... no, no ... my computer game. //**

BILL: **Kev. Kate. Come here. What's your favourite colour? //**

KEV: **My favourite colour's brown and Kate's is pink. //**

KATE: **Yeuch! No, it isn't. It's blue. //**

BILL: **Oh. And your favourite toys? //**

KEV: **Oh ... I don't know. My computer games or my bike. Er ... er ... no, I don't know. //**

BILL: **OK. I'll put down two favourites. Bike and computer games. // And what's your favourite toy, Kate? //**

KATE: **My xylophone. //**

BILL: **Thanks. I've finished. //**

Step 2 Ask and answer

a Ask various pupils in the class the question **'What's your favourite colour?'** or **'What's your favourite toy?'**

b When pupils are familiar with the question form, copy the grid from page 40 of the AB onto the blackboard. Ask one pupil the questions **'What's your name?'** and **'What's your favourite colour/toy?'** Write the responses in the grid.

c All pupils work simultaneously, asking other class members similar questions, and fill in the chart on page 40 of their AB.

d When pupils have finished, end the exercise by asking the pupils questions about other class members, i.e. **'What's *Maria's* favourite colour?'**

Step 3 Start a project

a Say **'Look at the photos on page 30 of the Coursebook'**. Ask pupils in their L1 what they can see and have a class discussion about their favourite games, toys, etc.

b Explain that they are going to work together in small groups in order to make a scrapbook of their own 'favourites'. These could include food/(wild) animals/fictional characters/insects/football teams or any other heading they wish to include on the list. Encourage originality. This list can then be written up on a large sheet of paper and stuck to the wall. Pupils put their names down next to the scrapbook page they want to work on, and groups can be formed accordingly.

c Explain that each group will have to find out about everyone's 'favourites' for their particular topic. After interviewing their classmates, preferably in English, and writing down the answers, the groups can plan the necessary pages for the scrapbook. This in turn will depend on how varied the answers are. Pupils will have to find or draw the illustrations to show all the 'favourites', adding a short comment after each name and picture: **'*María's* favourite animal is the donkey; her uncle has got three grey donkeys.'**

d Before they start, sit down with each group in turn and help pupils organise the different tasks and materials so that everyone is actively involved. Make sure they have the necessary vocabulary in English. Once they have completed their pages, put the scrapbook together and use it often to ask 'real-life questions' in class. Encourage pupils to leaf through it to find out more about their classmates.

e Encourage pupils to continue their project work outside their English class and share their discoveries with friends.

Step 3

START A PROJECT

My favourites
My favourite game is Donkey Kong.
My favourite colour is yellow.
My favourite place is Edinburgh.
My favourite toy is my kite.
My favourite food is pizza.
My favourite football team is Liverpool.

SUPERSNAKE
I'm hungry!
Dinner time!
I like slugs.
I like snails!
And I like worms.
Supersnake, HELP!
I like worms too! But I don't like birds!
Aagh!
Thank you Supersnake.
I hate Supersnake!
I love Supersnake!

Food

Step 1

1 Listen and circle.

name	favourite colour			favourite toy		
Bill	blue	green	red	yo-yo	plane	ball
Suzy	orange	yellow	grey	kite	doll	computer game
Kev	pink	black	brown	computer game	roller skates	bike
Kate	blue	pink	white	bike	xylophone	ball

Step 2

2 Ask and answer. Then write.

	favourite colour	favourite toy
me		
friend 1		
friend 2		
friend 3		

What's your favourite colour?
What's your favourite toy?

3 Listen and number the picture.

1
P Q R T S U
A O X Z

4 Write.

1 What's Slow eating? ______
2 What's Duffy eating? ______
3 Is there a cauliflower on the table? ______
4 Where's the cake? ______
5 How many apples are there? ______
6 Where are the carrots?
______
7 Is a banana a fruit or a vegetable?
______
8 What colour is milk? ______
9 What is your favourite drink?
______
10 Do you like ice-cream? ______

2F Lesson 2 - Evaluation

Main Language Items		Resource File	Materials Needed
I'm hungry I love ... I hate ...	dinner time slugs snails		Test cards 2F (see photocopy master on TG p.174) scissors (optional) cassette/cassette player

Step 1 Listen and number

a Look at the pictures at the top of page 41 in the AB. There is a short dialogue or sentence referring to each of the pictures on the tape. Pupils must decide which dialogue refers to which picture, and then write the appropriate numbers in the boxes.

Tapescript:

1 **These are small red fruits. //**
2 **The carrots are under the table. //**
3 **Slow is eating a vegetable. //**
4 **Can I have two ice-creams please? ~ Yes, here you are. ~ Thanks. //**
5 **There are six letters in the picture. P, Q, R, S, T and U. //**
6 **It's an ice-cream. //**
7 **How many letters can you see in the picture? ~ One ... two ... three ... four. Yes, four. //**
8 **Is this a fruit or a vegetable? ~ It's a fruit, of course. //**
9 **Where are the vegetables? ~ They're on the table. //**
10 **What's Slow doing now? ~ He's drinking milk. //**

Step 2 Write (Test)

a Working individually, pupils read the questions and write the answers in their AB or on a sheet of paper.

b The tests are designed to test communication as much as accuracy. Credit should be given for answers which show that pupils have understood the meaning of the questions, and where their answers are comprehensible and appropriate to the question.

Step 3 Test yourself

a Photocopy one set of test cards 2F for each pupil (see photocopy master on TG page 174).

b Say '**Open your Activity Books at page 42 and look at the pictures.**' Hand out the test card sheets and ask pupils to cut out the cards. Alternatively, give each pupil a set of cards already cut out. Pupils then fold the ten cards along the dotted line as shown in the picture.

c To do the first self-test, pupils place all their cards in front of them with the pictures showing, following the visual instructions. Demonstrate.

d Pupils then read the first sentence in the left-hand list, '**Biscuits**'. Pupils must find the card with the picture of '**biscuits**', pick it up and read the word on the card. They then put a tick or a cross in the box in their AB if they were right or wrong. Repeat for the other cards.

e To do the second self-test, pupils first cover the words in the left-hand list and then place all their cards in front of them again with the pictures showing, following the visual instructions. Demonstrate.

f Pupils then look at the first question and picture in the right-hand list ('**What's this?**'). Pupils must write the appropriate answer in the space provided ('An ice-cream.'). They then find the card with the appropriate picture, pick it up and look at the words to check. They put a tick or a cross in the box accordingly. Repeat for the other pictures.

g Pupils add up their scores out of ten for each test and total them. Finally, they circle the appropriate comment.

h Pupils can create other cards to test themselves or their friends, using the food vocabulary they have met in the topic and project work. The photocopy master includes some blank cards for this purpose.

Step 4 Supersnake

a Look at the Supersnake cartoon on page 31 of the CB. Pupils listen to the dialogue, reading at the same time.

b The cartoon may be used as a basis for role play. Divide the class into groups of three. Pupils can use their whole arms and a finger to play the worms.

c Play the tape again. This time pupils repeat.

d Pupils practise the puppet show without the help of the tape.

e Ask for one group to volunteer to act out the puppet show for the rest of the class.

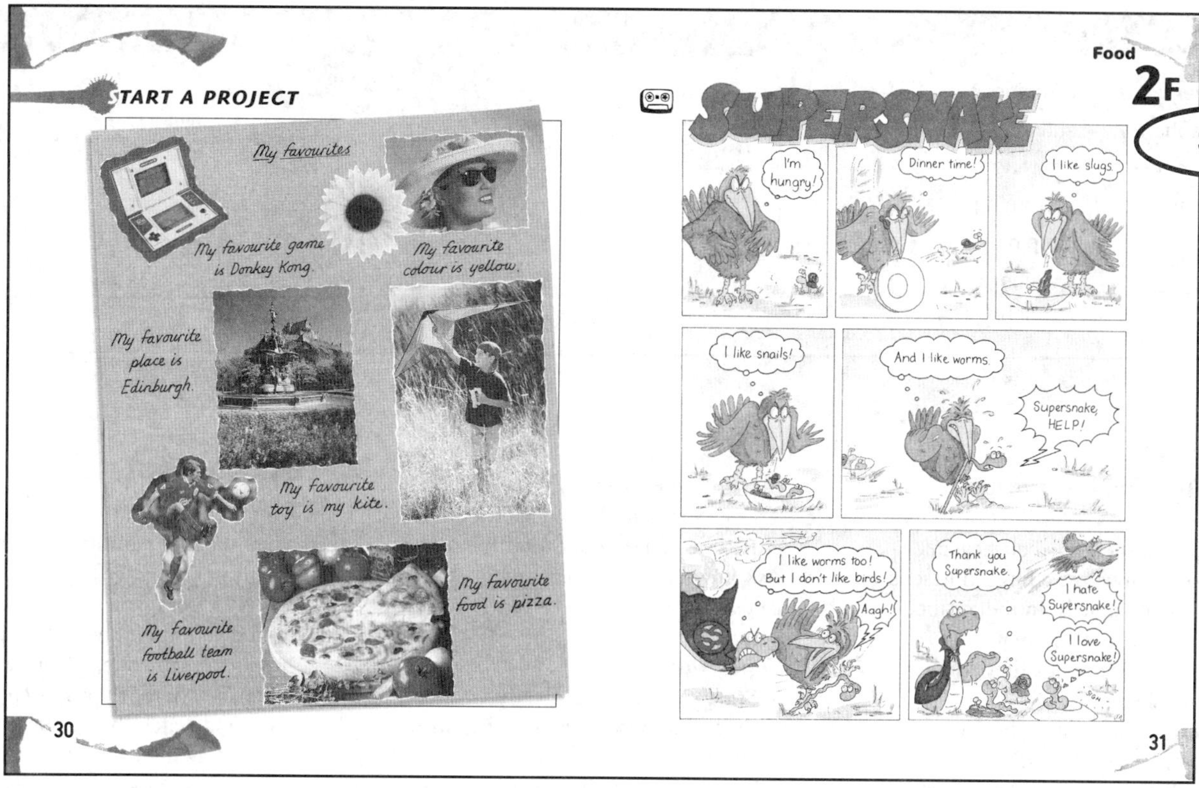
START A PROJECT
My favourites
My favourite game is Donkey Kong.
My favourite colour is yellow.
My favourite place is Edinburgh.
My favourite toy is my kite.
My favourite food is pizza.
My favourite football team is Liverpool.
30
Food
2F
SUPERSNAKE
I'm hungry!
Dinner time!
I like slugs.
I like snails!
And I like worms.
Supersnake, HELP!
I like worms too! But I don't like birds!
Aagh!
Thank you Supersnake.
I hate Supersnake!
I love Supersnake!
31

Step 4

Food 2F

3 Listen and number the picture.

Step 1

1
P Q R T S U
A O X Z

4 Write.

Step 2

1 What's Slow eating? ____________
2 What's Duffy eating? ____________
3 Is there a cauliflower on the table? ____
4 Where's the cake? ____________
5 How many apples are there? ________
6 Where are the carrots?
____
7 Is a banana a fruit or a vegetable?
____
8 What colour is milk? ____________
9 What is your favourite drink?
____
10 Do you like ice-cream? ____

41 | 42

2F Food

5 Test yourself. Right (✓) or wrong (✗)?

Step 3

You need

TEST 1

- *Put the cards like this.*
- *Read these words.*
- *Find the pictures.*
- *Check. Right (✓) or wrong (✗)?*

Biscuits. ☐
Bananas. ☐
A hamburger. ☐
An ice-cream. ☐
Cheese. ☐
Cola. ☐
A cake. ☐
An apple. ☐
Chocolate. ☐
Sausages. ☐

SCORE /10

TEST 2

- *Put the cards like this.*
- *Read these questions.*
- *Write the answers.*
- *Check. Right (✓) or wrong (✗)?*

What's this? ____________
What are these? ____________
What's this? ____________
What's this? ____________
What's this? ____________
What are these? ____________
What's this? ____________
What's this? ____________
What are these? ____________
What's this? ____________

SCORE /10

TOTAL /20

Circle your total score

20 Excellent 19–18 Very good 17–16 Good
15–13 Quite good 12–0 Do it again!

3 Story lesson

Main Language Items			Resource File	Materials Needed
animals	tiger	climbing	26	cassette/cassette player
butterfly	elephant	sitting		
caterpillar	crocodile	crawling		
crab	flying	swimming		
ant		jumping		
fish		walking		
monkey		bathing		

Step 1 Topic warm-up

a Tell pupils in their L1 that they are going to continue their English lessons by looking at animals. Introduce the word '**animals**' at this point.
b Ask pupils which words they think they might learn.
c Ask pupils what animals they have as pets. Can they name anything in English? Revise the pets they learnt in NEW STEPPING STONES 1.
d Discuss which animals they can touch and which they can't. Why? Why not?
e Ask pupils to think of animals that live in other countries but not their own. Why do they think they don't?

Step 2 Story warm-up

a Say '**Open your Coursebook at page 32. Look at the pictures.**' Demonstrate what you mean by holding up your CB and pointing to the pictures.
b Ask pupils in their L1 what they can see. Do they remember some of the animals from NEW STEPPING STONES 1?
c Ask pupils if they can see anything in the pictures they can name in English.

Step 3 Story listening

a Say '**Listen to the tape.**' Pupils look at the pictures and listen to the tape at the same time.
b Play the tape again.
c Ask questions in the pupils' L1 to check they have understood the story. Ask how many different colours they can see.

Tapescript:

Story One Blue Butterfly ...
One blue butterfly // flying in the air. //
Two red caterpillars // climbing up a chair. //
Three yellow crabs // sitting on the sand. //
Four black ants // crawling on my hand. //
Five pink and purple fish // swimming in the sea. //
Six brown monkeys // jumping in a tree. //
Seven orange tigers // walking through a wood. //
Eight grey elephants // bathing in the mud. //
Nine green crocodiles // sitting by a tree. //
How many different colours // can you see? //

Step 4 Listen and repeat

a Play the complete story again. Pupils listen and look at the pictures. Pupils can also mouth the words as they listen to the tape.
b Then play the story, pausing after each line for pupils to repeat.

Step 5 Story task

a Play the first part of the story and point to the butterfly.
b Play the complete story on tape again and demonstrate the task to pupils: point to each animal or group of animals in turn. Pupils listen to the tape and watch the demonstration.
c Then play the complete story again. Pupils listen, look at the pictures and point to the animals in turn.

Step 6 Story mime

a Divide the class into nine groups and allocate the roles of one type of animal to each group. Play the tape. Pupils stand up as their animal is mentioned.
b Play the tape again. This time pupils stand up and perform actions as appropriate, miming the movements of the animals, e.g. the butterfly flaps its wings. Pupils can also mouth the words as they listen to the tape.
c Finally, ask one group to volunteer to come to the front of the class and perform, listening to the tape.

Step 7 Story game

a Ask a volunteer to come to the front of the class and move like one of the animals in the story. The rest of the class guess which animal it is.
b The pupil that guesses correctly then takes a turn to mime an animal.

tep 2

tep 3

tep 4

tep 5

tep 6

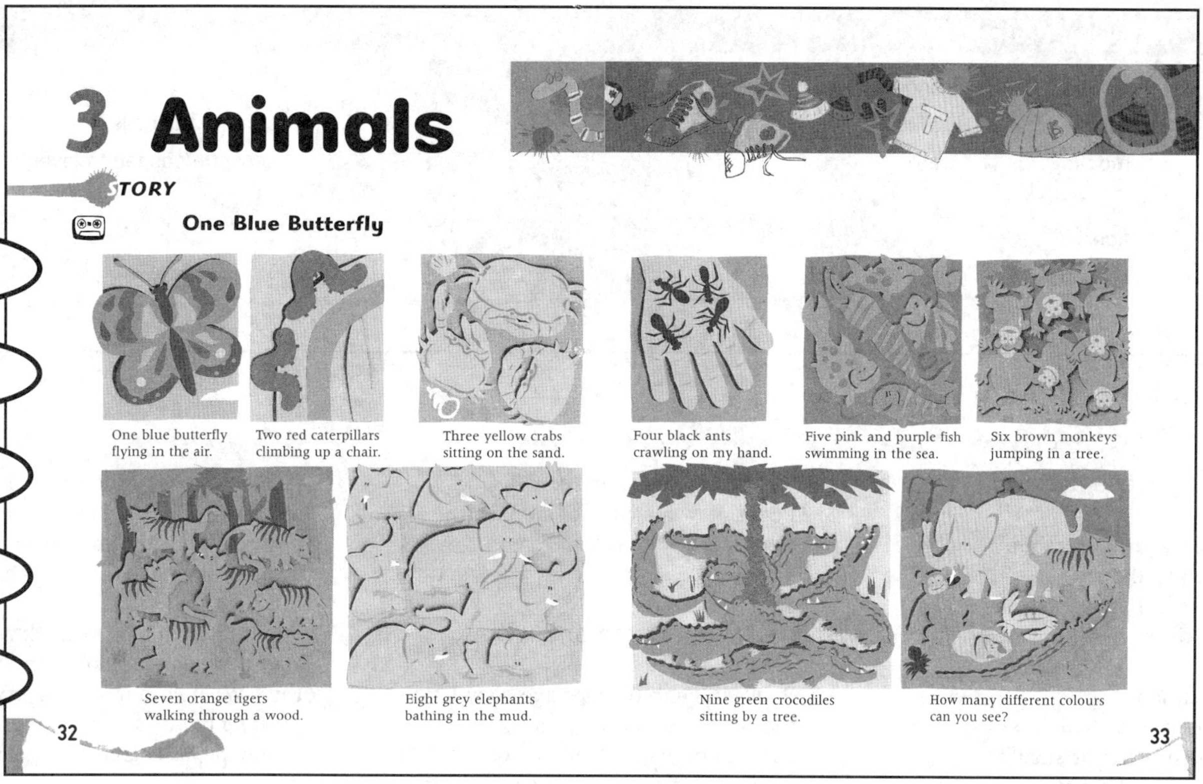

3 Animals

STORY

One Blue Butterfly

One blue butterfly flying in the air.

Two red caterpillars climbing up a chair.

Three yellow crabs sitting on the sand.

Four black ants crawling on my hand.

Five pink and purple fish swimming in the sea.

Six brown monkeys jumping in a tree.

Seven orange tigers walking through a wood.

Eight grey elephants bathing in the mud.

Nine green crocodiles sitting by a tree.

How many different colours can you see?

32

33

3A Lesson 1

Main Language Items			Resource File	Materials Needed
Do they eat ...? Are they ... or ...?	elephant panda monkey kangaroo tiger crocodile	penguin pelican trunk	10	coloured pencils cassette/cassette player

Step 1 Presentation

a Say '**Open your Coursebook at page 34. Listen to the tape.**'
b Play the tape. Pupils listen and read at the same time.
c Then ask questions to check comprehension:
What colour are elephants?
Are elephants big or small?
Do elephants like water?
How tall is a big elephant?
What do elephants eat?

Step 2 Pairwork

a Divide the class into pairs. Say '**Close your books.**'
b Play the tape. One pupil repeats the questions, the other answers.
c Then pupils ask and answer the questions without the help of the tape. The first pupil asks the questions using the words on page 35 as prompts and corrects their partner as appropriate.
d Change roles and repeat.

Step 3 Write. Then draw

a Pupils read the passage about the elephant on page 34 of the CB. When they are ready they close their CBs, turn to page 43 of the AB and complete the writing exercise at the top of the page.
b The pupils compare their answers with the correct version in the CB.
c Pupils draw a picture of an Asian elephant.

Step 4 Listen and write

a Pupils listen to the tape and complete the description of the animals in the chart on page 43. Pupils are only required to write one or two words for each animals.
b Play the tape three times, stopping after each description to allow pupils time to write the answers.

Tapescript:
Elephants are big and grey. // Monkeys are usually small and black or brown in colour. // There are two kinds of kangaroo. Both kinds are big, and they are either brown or grey. // Tigers are also big. They are mainly orange and black. // Crocodiles are big, long, green animals. // Penguins are small and are black and white. // Pandas are black and white too, but they are big animals.

c Go over the answers with the whole class by asking '**What colour are *penguins*? Are they big or small?**' etc.

Step 5 Pairwork

a Using the descriptions from Step 4, pupils work out which animal is which and write the names under each picture. Check the answers by holding up your book and asking '**What's this?**'
b Pupils work in pairs and ask and answer similar questions, e.g. '**What's this? What colour are *penguins*? Are *penguins* big or small?**'
c Finally pupils colour the animals.

tep 1

tep 3

Step 2

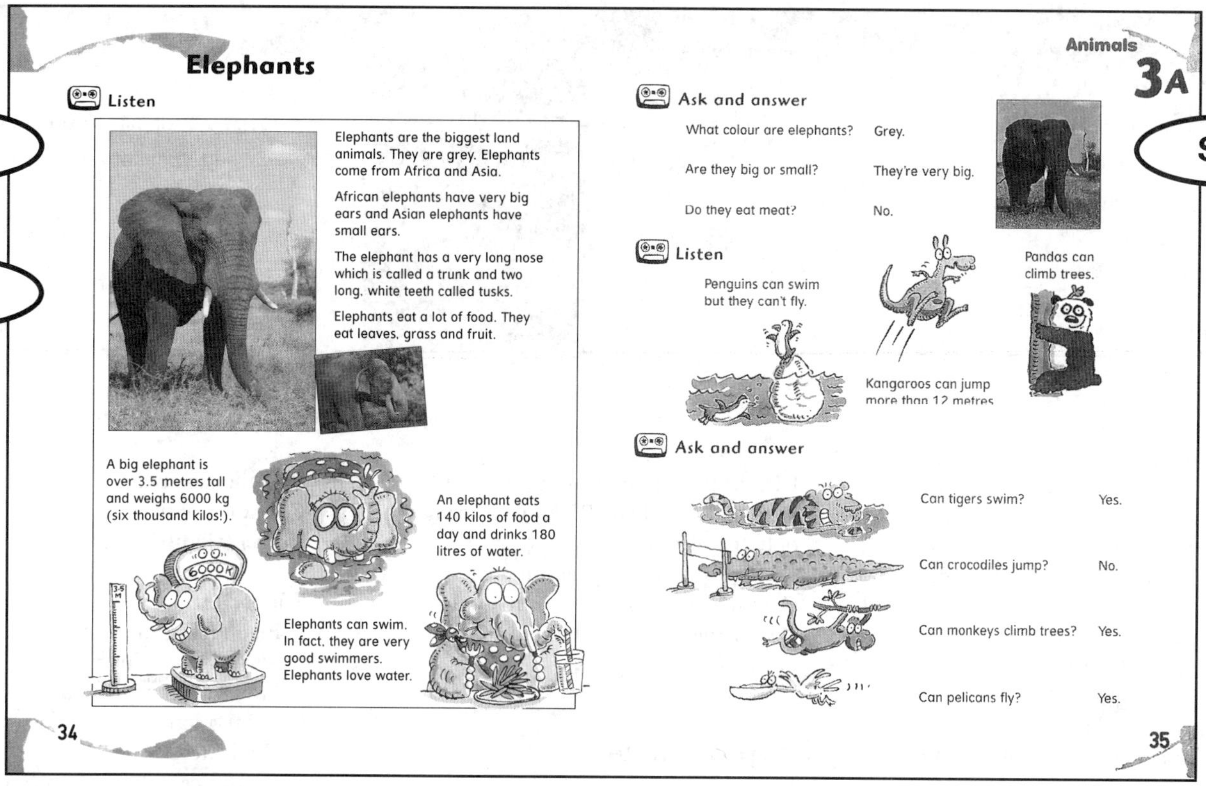

Elephants

Listen

Elephants are the biggest land animals. They are grey. Elephants come from Africa and Asia.

African elephants have very big ears and Asian elephants have small ears.

The elephant has a very long nose which is called a trunk and two long, white teeth called tusks.

Elephants eat a lot of food. They eat leaves, grass and fruit.

A big elephant is over 3.5 metres tall and weighs 6000 kg (six thousand kilos!).

An elephant eats 140 kilos of food a day and drinks 180 litres of water.

Elephants can swim. In fact, they are very good swimmers. Elephants love water.

6000K
3.5 M

34

Animals

3A

Ask and answer

What colour are elephants? Grey.

Are they big or small? They're very big.

Do they eat meat? No.

Listen

Penguins can swim but they can't fly.

Kangaroos can jump more than 12 metres.

Pandas can climb trees.

Ask and answer

Can tigers swim? Yes.

Can crocodiles jump? No.

Can monkeys climb trees? Yes.

Can pelicans fly? Yes.

35

Step 3

Step 4

Step 5

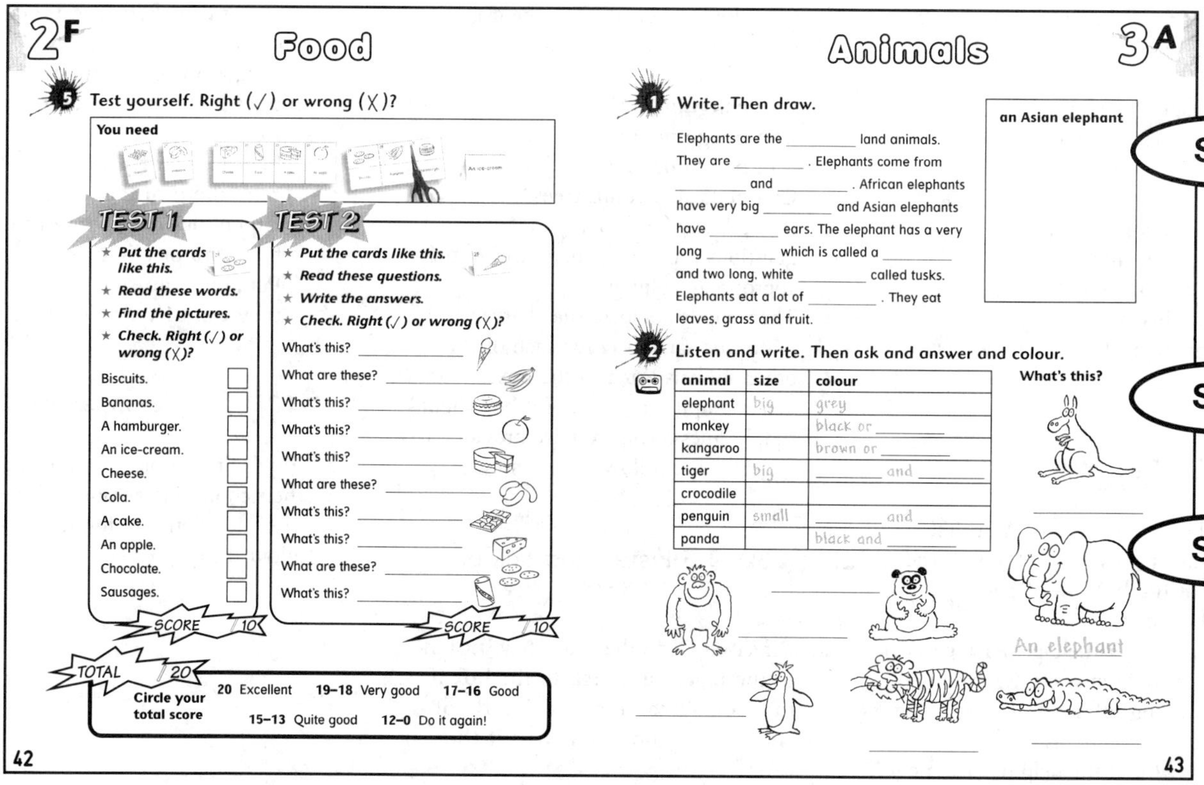

2F

Food

5 Test yourself. Right (✓) or wrong (✗)?

You need

TEST 1

- ★ Put the cards like this.
- ★ Read these words.
- ★ Find the pictures.
- ★ Check. Right (✓) or wrong (✗)?

Biscuits. ☐
Bananas. ☐
A hamburger. ☐
An ice-cream. ☐
Cheese. ☐
Cola. ☐
A cake. ☐
An apple. ☐
Chocolate. ☐
Sausages. ☐

SCORE /10

TEST 2

- ★ Put the cards like this.
- ★ Read these questions.
- ★ Write the answers.
- ★ Check. Right (✓) or wrong (✗)?

What's this? ________
What are these? ________
What's this? ________
What's this? ________
What's this? ________
What are these? ________
What's this? ________
What's this? ________
What are these? ________
What's this? ________

SCORE /10

TOTAL /20

Circle your total score

20 Excellent 19–18 Very good 17–16 Good
15–13 Quite good 12–0 Do it again!

42

Animals

3A

1 Write. Then draw.

Elephants are the ________ land animals. They are ________. Elephants come from ________ and ________. African elephants have very big ________ and Asian elephants have ________ ears. The elephant has a very long ________ which is called a ________ and two long, white ________ called tusks. Elephants eat a lot of ________. They eat leaves, grass and fruit.

an Asian elephant

2 Listen and write. Then ask and answer and colour.

animal	size	colour
elephant	big	grey
monkey		black or ________
kangaroo		brown or ________
tiger	big	________ and ________
crocodile		
penguin	small	________ and ________
panda		black and ________

What's this?

An elephant

43

3A Lesson 2

Main Language Items		Resource File	Materials Needed
can/can't Can ... swim/fly? (and, but, or)	pelican jump climb trees swim fly	1 9 10	paper for display (optional) cassette/cassette player

Step 1 Presentation

a Say **'Open your Coursebook at page 34.'** Briefly ask some questions about the passage, i.e.
Are elephants big or small?
Do elephants like water?
Have elephants got hair?
Can elephants swim?

b Play the tape. Pupils listen and read at the same time.

c Then hold your book up for the class. Point to each of the three animals in the centre of page 35 and ask **'What's this?'**

d Play the tape.

e Ask some questions about these pictures, i.e.
Can penguins fly?
Can pandas climb trees?
Can penguins climb trees?
Can kangaroos jump?
Can penguins swim?
Encourage pupils to answer **'Yes'** or **'No'**.

Step 2 Pairwork

a Divide the class into pairs. All pairs work simultaneously. Say **'Look at the pictures at the bottom of page 35. Cover the words.'**

b Pupils repeat after the tape. P1 repeats the questions, P2 answers. Repeat four times, changing roles.

c Then pupils ask and answer the questions without the help of the tape. P1 asks the questions using the words in the book to help, P2 answers using only the pictures.

d Change roles and repeat the procedure.

e Continue until the pupils can ask and answer the questions without the help of the words.

Step 3 Write

a Copy the grid on page 44 of the AB onto the blackboard. Ask the class questions about the first animal on the list:
Can penguins fly?
Can penguins swim?
Can penguins jump?
Can penguins climb trees?

b If pupils say **'yes'** to any of the questions then write **'penguin'** in the appropriate column.

c Then pupils compete the chart in the AB in the same way for each of the other animals listed in the box.

d Where pupils are uncertain they should simply guess. This exercise provides a focus for the following listening.

Step 4 Listen and tick or cross

a Direct pupils to the chart. Say **'Listen to the tape. Put a tick in the box if the animals can jump, swim, fly or climb trees, and put a cross if they can't.'**

b Play the tape two or three times.

c Check the answers by asking **'Can *elephants* jump?'** etc.

Tapescript:

Elephants can swim but they can't jump, fly or climb trees. // Monkeys can't fly but they can swim, jump and of course they can climb trees. // Pandas can climb trees but they can't fly, swim or jump. // Tigers can swim and jump but they can't fly or climb trees. // Kangaroos can't fly, swim or climb trees but they can jump very well. // Pelicans can fly and swim but they can't jump or climb trees. // Crocodiles can swim but they can't fly, jump or climb trees. // Penguins can swim and jump but they can't fly or climb trees. //

Step 5 Personal file

a Pupils draw a picture of an animal of their choice in the box and write a brief description using the sentence about the elephant as a model.

Step 1

Elephants

Listen

Elephants are the biggest land animals. They are grey. Elephants come from Africa and Asia.

African elephants have very big ears and Asian elephants have small ears.

The elephant has a very long nose which is called a trunk and two long, white teeth called tusks.

Elephants eat a lot of food. They eat leaves, grass and fruit.

A big elephant is over 3.5 metres tall and weighs 6000 kg (six thousand kilos!).

6000K
3.5 M

An elephant eats 140 kilos of food a day and drinks 180 litres of water.

Elephants can swim. In fact, they are very good swimmers. Elephants love water.

34

Animals

3A

Ask and answer

What colour are elephants? Grey.

Are they big or small? They're very big.

Do they eat meat? No.

Listen

Penguins can swim but they can't fly.

Kangaroos can jump more than 12 metres.

Pandas can climb trees.

Ask and answer

Step 2

Can tigers swim? Yes.

Can crocodiles jump? No.

Can monkeys climb trees? Yes.

Can pelicans fly? Yes.

35

3A

Animals

Step 3

3 Write.

Can penguins fly?

fly	swim	jump	climb trees
	penguin		

penguin
panda
kangaroo
crocodile
monkey
tiger
elephant
pelican

Step 4

4 Listen and tick (✓) or cross (✗).

fly								
swim								
jump								
climb trees								

Step 5

5 Draw and write.

Elephants can swim but they can't fly or climb trees!

Animals

44

Animals

3A

6 Ask and answer. Then tick (✓) or cross (✗).

Can you jump?

	me	friend 1	friend 2	friend 3
jump				
swim				
climb trees				

7 Match the pictures and the words.

1
2
3
4
5
6

This is a bird. It can swim but it can't fly or climb trees. 4

This animal has got four legs. It can't climb trees.

This is a white or brown bird.

This is a small, brown animal. It's got two arms and two legs.

This animal is black and white. It can climb trees.

This is a long, green animal.

45

3A Lesson 3

Main Language Items			Resource File	Materials Needed
Can you ...?	touch count stand draw pick up sing	write jump swim climb trees	4 8	Animal cards (see AB cut-outs section) cassette/cassette player

Step 1 Presentation (Action Game)

a Ask various pupils **'Can you swim?'** Then substitute **fly**, **jump** and **climb trees** for **swim**.

b Then revise vocabulary from NEW STEPPING STONES 1 using the same structure. Pupils should try to perform the actions before answering the questions. Try the following questions:
Can you touch your leg with your head?
Can you stand on one leg?
Can you pick up your chair?
Can you count in English?
Can you sing an English song?

c Also practise the question form **'Who can ... ?'** Ask pupils the following questions:
Who can jump?
Who can draw?
Who can write in English?

d Pupils answer using the structure **'I can ...'**

Step 2 Groupwork

a Copy the grid on page 45 of the AB onto the blackboard. Select one pupil. Ask **'Can you jump/swim/climb trees?'** and record the answers in the table with a tick or a cross.

b All pupils work simultaneously in groups of four, asking other group members similar questions and filling in the grid in their books.

c Finish off the exercise by asking pupils questions about other class members, e.g. **'Can *Maria* climb trees?'**

Step 3 Pictures and words

a Pupils read the sentences and match the animals to the descriptions by writing the appropriate numbers in the boxes.

Step 4 Card games (cut-outs)

Use the Animal cards from the cut-outs section. Both games are simple memory games. Pupils work in pairs. They require one pack of eight cards between them.

a Lay the cards face down. P1 points to any card and asks **'What's this?'** P2 guesses. If correct, he or she wins the card, and if not, the card is returned face down to the same position. Then P2 asks the question. The winner is the player to collect the most cards.

b Lay the cards face down. P1 asks **'Where's the elephant?'** P2 must guess where this particular card is. If correct, he or she wins the card, and if not, the card is returned face down to the same position. Then P2 asks a question using the same structure. The winner is the player to collect the most cards.

3A Animals

3 Write.

Can penguins fly?

fly	swim	jump	climb trees
	penguin		

penguin
panda
kangaroo
crocodile
monkey
tiger
elephant
pelican

4 Listen and tick (✓) or cross (X).

fly								
swim								
jump								
climb trees								

5 Draw and write.

Elephants can swim but they can't fly or climb trees!

Animals

44

Animals 3A

6 Ask and answer. Then tick (✓) or cross (X).

Can you jump?

	me	friend 1	friend 2	friend 3
jump				
swim				
climb trees				

Step 2

7 Match the pictures and the words.

1
2
3
4
5
6

- This is a bird. It can swim but it can't fly or climb trees. 4
- This animal has got four legs. It can't climb trees.
- This is a white or brown bird.
- This is a small, brown animal. It's got two arms and two legs.
- This animal is black and white. It can climb trees.
- This is a long, green animal.

Step 3

45

3B Lesson 1

Main Language Items			Resource File	Materials Needed
Can I have ...?	hippo	big	7	cassette/cassette player
What do you want?	crocodile	dangerous	7a	
What about ...?	fish	very		

Step 1 Presentation

a Say **'Open your Coursebook at page 36.'** Hold up your book for the class. Briefly ask some questions about the pictures. Use **'Who's this? Is this ...?'**

b Play the tape. Pupils look at the pictures and listen.

Step 2 Role play

a Divide the class into pairs. Give roles. One pupil in each pair plays Mr Kay and one pupil plays Gary.

b Play the dialogue. Pupils repeat after the tape twice.

c Then pupils act out the dialogue without the help of the tape. Insist upon actions and intonation to make the dialogue realistic, e.g. Mr Kay should look worried and put his hands up to his head.

d Volunteers can be invited to act out the dialogue for the class if they wish.

Step 3 Listen and number

a Look at the exercise at the top of page 46 in the AB.

b Pupils will hear seven animal noises and must decide which animal is making each noise. They should write the numbers 1–7 underneath each animal to indicate the order of the noises on the tape.

c Play the tape again. Stop after each noise and ask pupils **'What's that?'**.

Tapescript:

Shh! Listen! What's that? (Noise of all the animals) **I don't know ... Listen again ... 1** (Monkey), **2** (Crocodile), **3** (Pelican), **4** (Kangaroo), **5** (Penguin), **6** (Elephant), **7** (Tiger) **... Quick! Let's go.**

Step 4 Find the animals

a Pupils look at the picture on page 46 of the AB and try to find the hidden animals. Tell pupils to **'Circle all the animals you can find in the picture.'**

tep 1

tep 2

Crocodiles are Dangerous!

Listen

Dad, can I have a pet?
Yes, Gary. What do you want?
A hippo.
Hippos are very big.
OK. Er ... a crocodile.
But crocodiles are very dangerous!
What about a fish?
Yes. OK, a fish.

Tell your friend

Camels and zebras eat grass and leaves.
They don't eat meat or fish.

a camel

a zebra

36

Animals

3B

Ask and answer

What do lions eat?	Meat.
Do hippos eat meat?	No, they eat grass.
Do rhinos eat meat or grass?	Grass.
What do seals eat?	Fish.
Do giraffes eat fish?	No, they eat leaves.

BINGO

37

tep 3

tep 4

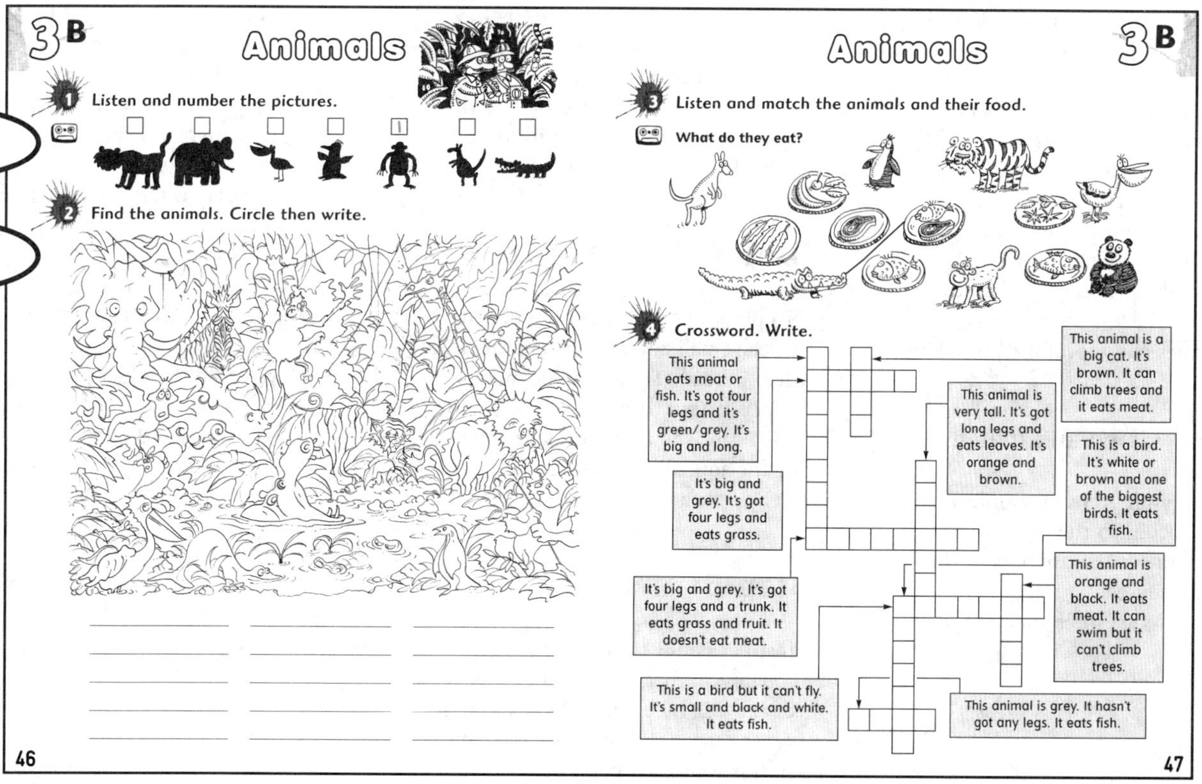

3B

Animals

1 Listen and number the pictures.

2 Find the animals. Circle then write.

46

Animals

3B

3 Listen and match the animals and their food.

What do they eat?

4 Crossword. Write.

This animal eats meat or fish. It's got four legs and it's green/grey. It's big and long.

This animal is a big cat. It's brown. It can climb trees and it eats meat.

This animal is very tall. It's got long legs and eats leaves. It's orange and brown.

This is a bird. It's white or brown and one of the biggest birds. It eats fish.

It's big and grey. It's got four legs and eats grass.

This animal is orange and black. It eats meat. It can swim but it can't climb trees.

It's big and grey. It's got four legs and a trunk. It eats grass and fruit. It doesn't eat meat.

This is a bird but it can't fly. It's small and black and white. It eats fish.

This animal is grey. It hasn't got any legs. It eats fish.

47

3B Lesson 2

Main Language Items			Resource File	Materials Needed
What do … eat?	seal	giraffe	23a	Bingo cover cards
Do … eat …?	hippo	rhino		cassette/cassette player
They eat …	lion	fish		
	leaves	grass		
	meat	fruit		

Step 1 Presentation

a Say '**Open your Coursebook at page 36. Look at the pictures at the bottom of the page.**'
b Play the tape. Pupils look at the pictures and listen.

Step 2 Pairwork

a Divide the class into pairs. All pairs work simultaneously. Say '**Look at the pictures on page 37. Cover the words.**'
b Pupils repeat after the tape. P1 repeats the questions, P2 answers. Repeat four times, changing roles.
c Then pupils ask and answer the questions without the help of the tape. P1 asks the questions, P2 answers using only the pictures. P1 should prompt and check P2's answers.
d Change roles and repeat the procedure.

Step 3 Listen and match

a Say '**Open your Activity Books on page 47. Listen to the tape. Draw lines to connect the animals to the food that they eat.**'
b Play each passage three times.

Tapescript:

1 **Crocodiles eat fish and meat // but they don't eat grass or leaves. //**
2 **Monkeys eat fruit and leaves // but they don't eat grass. //**
3 **Kangaroos eat grass and leaves. // They don't eat meat or fish. //**
4 **Penguins and pelicans eat fish // but they don't eat meat, grass, leaves or fruit. //**
5 **Tigers eat meat // but they don't eat fish, grass, leaves or fruit. //**
6 **Pandas eat leaves // but they don't eat grass, fruit, meat or fish.//**

Step 4 Make Bingo cards

a To play Bingo each pupil will need fifteen small cover cards (approximately 3cm x 3cm). These may be made from paper or thin card.
b Each card should have the name of one of the animals (on page 37 of the CB) clearly printed on it.

Step 5 Bingo

a Instruct pupils to cover any seven squares on their bingo card on page 37 of the CB, by placing the appropriate cover card face down over the picture. In this way, each pupil's card should now have eight different pictures showing.
b The Bingo Caller (teacher) will also need a set of word cards. Shuffle your cards. Lay them face down in front of you. Ask '**Are you ready?**' then select a card and read out the word.
c Pupils cover each animal that is called out, placing the cards with the words face up.
d Continue calling until one of the pupils has covered all the squares on his or her card. The first player to do so shouts '**Bingo!**' He or she must confirm that the Bingo card is correct by reading back the words that are face up. If correct, this pupil wins; if not, continue the game.
e Pupils play Bingo in small groups of 4–6 players.

Step 6 Crossword

a Pupils read the descriptions and then write the names of the animals in the crossword on AB page 47.

Step 1

Step 2

Step 5

Animals

3B

Crocodiles are Dangerous!

Listen

Dad, can I have a pet?
Yes, Gary. What do you want?
A hippo.
Hippos are very big.
OK. Er ... a crocodile.
But crocodiles are very dangerous!
What about a fish?
Yes. OK, a fish.

Tell your friend

Camels and zebras eat grass and leaves. They don't eat meat or fish.

a camel

a zebra

Ask and answer

What do lions eat?	Meat.
Do hippos eat meat?	No, they eat grass.
Do rhinos eat meat or grass?	Grass.
What do seals eat?	Fish.
Do giraffes eat fish?	No, they eat leaves.

BINGO

36

37

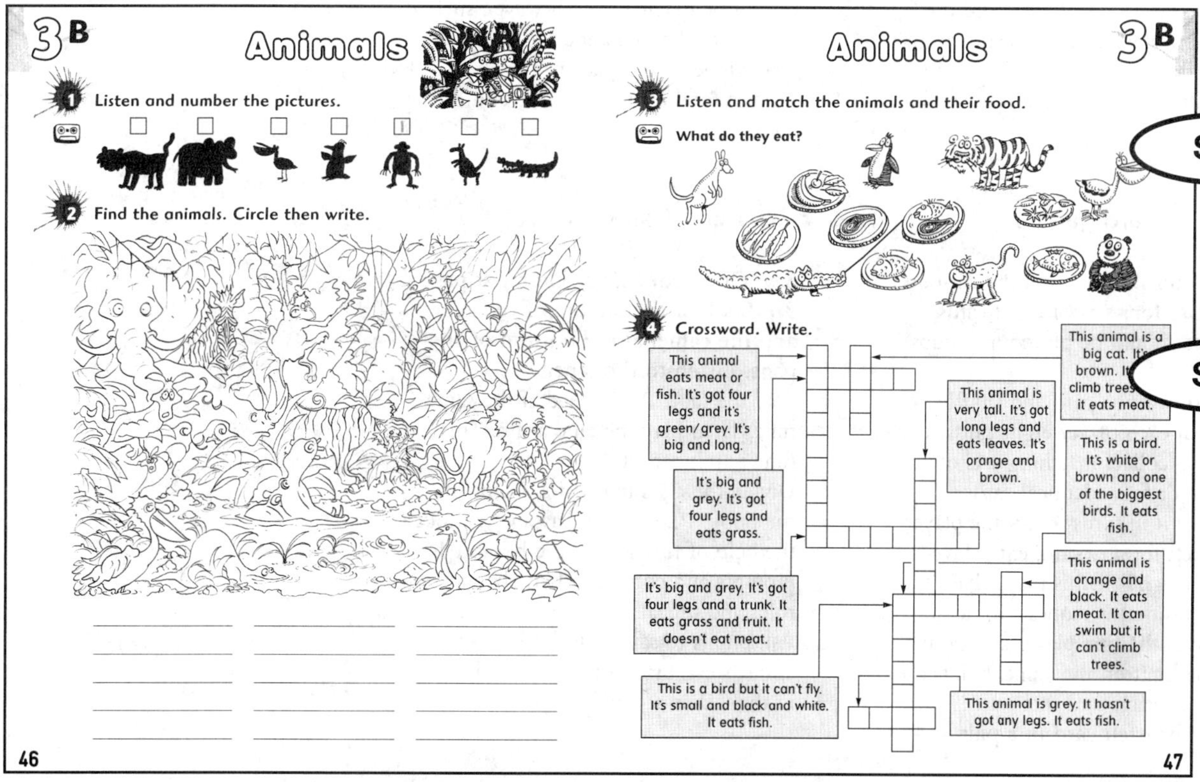

Step 3

Step 6

3B Animals

1 Listen and number the pictures.

2 Find the animals. Circle then write.

Animals 3B

3 Listen and match the animals and their food.

What do they eat?

4 Crossword. Write.

This animal eats meat or fish. It's got four legs and it's green/grey. It's big and long.

It's big and grey. It's got four legs and eats grass.

It's big and grey. It's got four legs and a trunk. It eats grass and fruit. It doesn't eat meat.

This is a bird but it can't fly. It's small and black and white. It eats fish.

This animal is very tall. It's got long legs and eats leaves. It's orange and brown.

This animal is a big cat. It's brown. It climb trees it eats meat.

This is a bird. It's white or brown and one of the biggest birds. It eats fish.

This animal is orange and black. It eats meat. It can swim but it can't climb trees.

This animal is grey. It hasn't got any legs. It eats fish.

46

47

3B Lesson 3

Main Language Items			Resource File	Materials Needed
Have you got ...?	camel	tigers	3	Materials to make word stones
They (don't) eat ...	zebra	penguins	10	Animal cards (see AB cut-outs section)
	elephants	crocodiles	55	cassette/cassette player
	kangaroos	pelicans		
	zebras	pandas		
	monkeys	meat		
	lions	fish		
	rhinos			

Step 1 Make word stones

a Pupils add twelve more word stones to their collection.
b Say **'Open your Activity Books at page 48.'** Point to the word stones. Check pupils are familiar with their meaning and point out that all the words are plurals.
c To make the word stones, each pupil requires twelve 'stones' (either real stones or stone-shaped pieces of card, as before). Pupils write one word on each stone in felt-tip pen, as shown in the pictures.
d Pupils then store their stones for future use.

Step 2 Card games

Use the Animal cards from the cut-outs section. Use four sets of eight cards. This game should be played in groups of four.
a Take all thirty-two card and shuffle them. Deal each player eight cards. The object is to collect matching sets of two, three or four identical cards.
b Pupils take it in turns to ask the player on their left for any card, e.g. **'Have you got a *tiger*?'** If this player hasn't got the card that is requested, then he or she gives the first player any card. Set a time limit on the game. Points are awarded for each card in a set:
2 points for each card in a pair = 4 points
3 points for each card in a three set = 9 points
4 points for each card in a four set = 16 points
Write the scoring system on the blackboard.
c Players must give any card that they are asked for, even if it is part of a set they are collecting. However, at any time in the game players may lay down a set in front of them. The value of this set is then awarded and the cards cannot be given away. However, such a set cannot then be added to.
d The winner is the player with the highest total of points at the end of the game.

Step 3 Pairwork

a Say **'Open your Coursebook at page 36. Look at the picture of the zebra and the camel at the bottom of the page. Listen to the tape.'**
b Play the tape. Pupils read at the same time. Then play the tape again. This time pupils repeat.
c Divide the class into pairs. P1 opens the book. P2 says the passage without the help of the tape or the book. P1 prompts and corrects. Then change roles and repeat.
d Ask pupils to say what food other animals eat, using the model sentence in the CB as a guide.

Step 4 Personal file

a Pupils draw a picture of an animal of their choice in the box, on page 48 of the AB, and write a brief description of what the animal eats, using the model on page 36 of the CB as a guide.

Step3

Crocodiles are Dangerous!
Listen
Dad, can I have a pet?
Yes, Gary. What do you want?
A hippo.
Hippos are very big.
OK. Er ... a crocodile.
But crocodiles are very dangerous!
What about a fish?
Yes. OK, a fish.
Tell your friend
Camels and zebras eat grass and leaves. They don't eat meat or fish.
a camel
a zebra
36
Animals
3B
Ask and answer
What do lions eat? Meat.
Do hippos eat meat? No, they eat grass.
Do rhinos eat meat or grass? Grass.
What do seals eat? Fish.
Do giraffes eat fish? No, they eat leaves.
BINGO
37

Step 1

Step 4

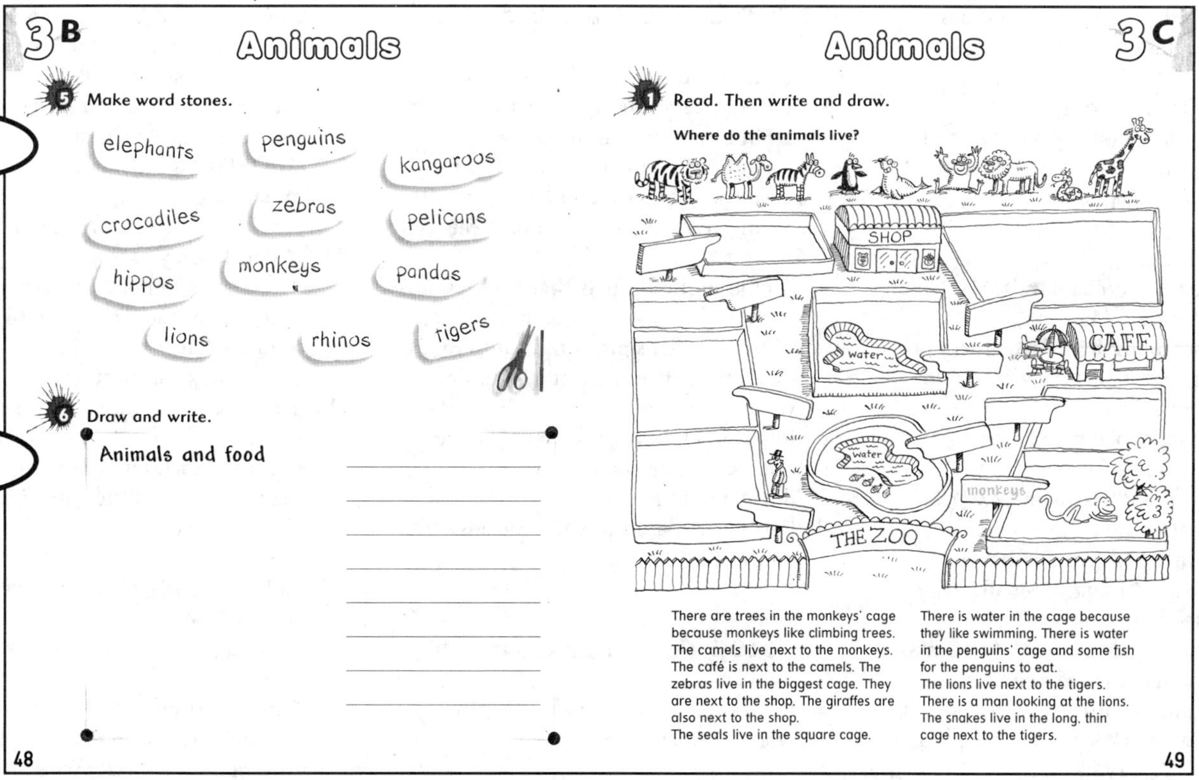
3B
Animals
5 Make word stones.
elephants
penguins
kangaroos
crocodiles
zebras
pelicans
hippos
monkeys
pandas
lions
rhinos
tigers
6 Draw and write.
Animals and food
48
Animals
3C
1 Read. Then write and draw.
Where do the animals live?
SHOP
CAFE
water
water
monkeys
THE ZOO
There are trees in the monkeys' cage because monkeys like climbing trees. The camels live next to the monkeys. The café is next to the camels. The zebras live in the biggest cage. They are next to the shop. The giraffes are also next to the shop. The seals live in the square cage.
There is water in the cage because they like swimming. There is water in the penguins' cage and some fish for the penguins to eat. The lions live next to the tigers. There is a man looking at the lions. The snakes live in the long, thin cage next to the tigers.
49

3c Lesson 1

Main Language Items		Resource File	Materials Needed
They are/can/eat ... Are they ...? Can they ...? What do they eat?	*Animal names (revision)*	19 26	cassette/cassette player

Step 1 Quiz

a All the questions in this quiz require factual answers.

b Divide the class into two teams. Play the first question on the tape. The first pupil to raise their hand gets a chance to answer, and if correct, wins two points for their team. If the answer is wrong, the opposing team may attempt the question for one point.

c Do all the questions in the same way pausing at the end of the questions before the answers.

Tapescript (with answers):

1 **Can penguins swim? // (Yes)**
2 **Which animal has got a trunk? // (An elephant)**
3 **What do giraffes eat? // (Leaves)**
4 **What is an elephant's nose called? // (A trunk)**
5 **How many legs have crocodiles got? // (Four)**
6 **What colour are tigers? // (Orange, black and white)**
7 **Do camels eat meat? // (No)**
8 **Can monkeys swim? // (Yes)**
9 **What is the biggest land animal? // (An elephant)**
10 **Is a giraffe big or small? // (Big)**
11 **What do rhinos eat? // (Grass)**
12 **What colour are pelicans? // (White or brown)**
13 **How many legs have penguins got? // (Two)**

Step 2 Pairwork

a Elicit questions from pupils that they can ask about the zoo picture on page 38 of the CB. Write the question forms on the blackboard.

b Divide the class into pairs. Using one book between each pair, pupils ask and answer as many questions as they can about the picture.

Step 3 Look and find

a Write the following on the blackboard.
1 **Find five animals that eat grass.**
2 **Find four grey animals.**
3 **Find nine animals that can swim.**
4 **Find the biggest animal.**
5 **Find ten animals that don't eat meat.**
6 **Find eight animals that can't climb trees.**

b The instructions direct the pupils to look carefully at the picture and find various animals.

c Pupils work in pairs to complete the tasks. Circulate and encourage discussion in English.

d Finally, get pupils to write the answers on the blackboard.

Step 4 Guess the animal

a Divide the class into pairs. All pairs work simultaneously.

b P1 thinks of an animal in the picture. P2 asks **'yes/no'** questions to determine which animal his or her partner has in mind. P2 cannot ask about animals by name: he or she cannot say **'Is it the penguin?'**

c Pupils should use the questions on page 38 as a guide.

Step 5 Game (Whole class)

a Ask the class to **'Name an animal'**. Ask questions about the animal and write the answers on the blackboard in the form of a description, e.g. if pupils suggest a **lion**, then ask:
Are lions big or small?
What colour are they?
Can they swim/jump/climb trees?
What do they eat?
The description on the blackboard might then read: **'They are big, brown animals. They can swim and climb trees. They eat meat.'**

b The description should not include the name of the animal.

c On paper each pupil then writes a description of a different animal. Leave the model description on the board as a guide.

d Collect pupils' descriptions when they have finished.

e Read out the descriptions one at a time.

f Pupils must guess the names of the animals from the description. The pupil who guesses correctly wins a point. (Give out the piece of paper to keep score.)

Step 2

Step 3

Step 4

The Zoo

Guess the animal

Is it big?
Is it black?
Can it swim?
Has it got four legs?
Does it eat grass?

Ask and answer

Where does the crocodile live?	Next to the rhino and the penguins.
Where do the zebras live?	Next to the giraffes.

38

Animals

3c

Sing

The Elephant

An elephant goes
Like this and that.
He's terribly big
And terribly fat.
He's got no fingers.
He's got no toes.
But goodness gracious.
What a NOSE!

Ask and answer

What is wrong with these animals?

39

3c Lesson 2

Main Language Items		Resource File	Materials Needed
do/does Where do(es) … live? Which …?	next to cage shop live (*v.*) biggest	51c	cassette/cassette player

Step 1 Presentation

a Say '**Open your Coursebooks at page 38. Look at the picture of the zoo.**' Ask pupils which cages the animals live in. Start with the simple question form '**Where's the *tiger*?**' and tell pupils to answer '**In cage number 7.**' Ask similar questions about other animals.

b When pupils are familiar with question and answer forms change the structure and ask '**Where does the *lion* live?**' or '**Where do the *penguins* live?**' Continue until pupils can answer freely about all the animals.

Step 2 Pairwork

a Divide the class into pairs. All pairs work simultaneously. Say '**Look at the picture of the zoo. Cover the words underneath.**'

b Pupils repeat after the tape. P1 repeats the questions, P2 answers. Repeat four times, changing roles.

c Then pupils ask and answer the questions without the help of the tape. P1 asks questions about all the animals using the words in the book to help; P2 answers, using only the pictures.

d Change roles and repeat the procedure.

Step 3 Read. Then draw

a Say '**Open your Activity Book at page 49. Look at the picture of the zoo. There are no animals in the cages. Read the description and write the names of the animals on the signs.**'

b Pupils can work individually or in pairs. During the exercise the teacher should circulate and help any pupils who are having difficulties. Try to focus pupils' attention on the key words in the text by asking questions, such as:
Which animals live next to the café?
Which animals have got the biggest cage?

c Go over the exercise with the whole class. Either sketch the zoo plan on the blackboard or hold up your book and ask:
Who lives in this cage?
Whose cage is this?
Which animals live here?

d Pupils can draw the animals in the zoo for homework.

Step 4 Write or draw

a Tell pupils to '**Look at the plan of the zoo on page 50 of the Activity Book. Put animals in the cages.**'

b Pupils may put any animals they want in their zoo. They can write the names in the cages or draw the animals if they wish.

c Pupils then complete the written description of their zoo in the space provided.

Step 5 Pairwork

a Ask one of the pupils '**Have you got a *camel* in your zoo?**' If the answer is 'yes', ask '**Which cage is it in?**' then ask '**What's next to the *camel*?**' Repeat with other pupils.

b Divide the class into pairs. Pupils ask and answer similar questions to find out what is in their partner's zoo.

Step 1

Step 2

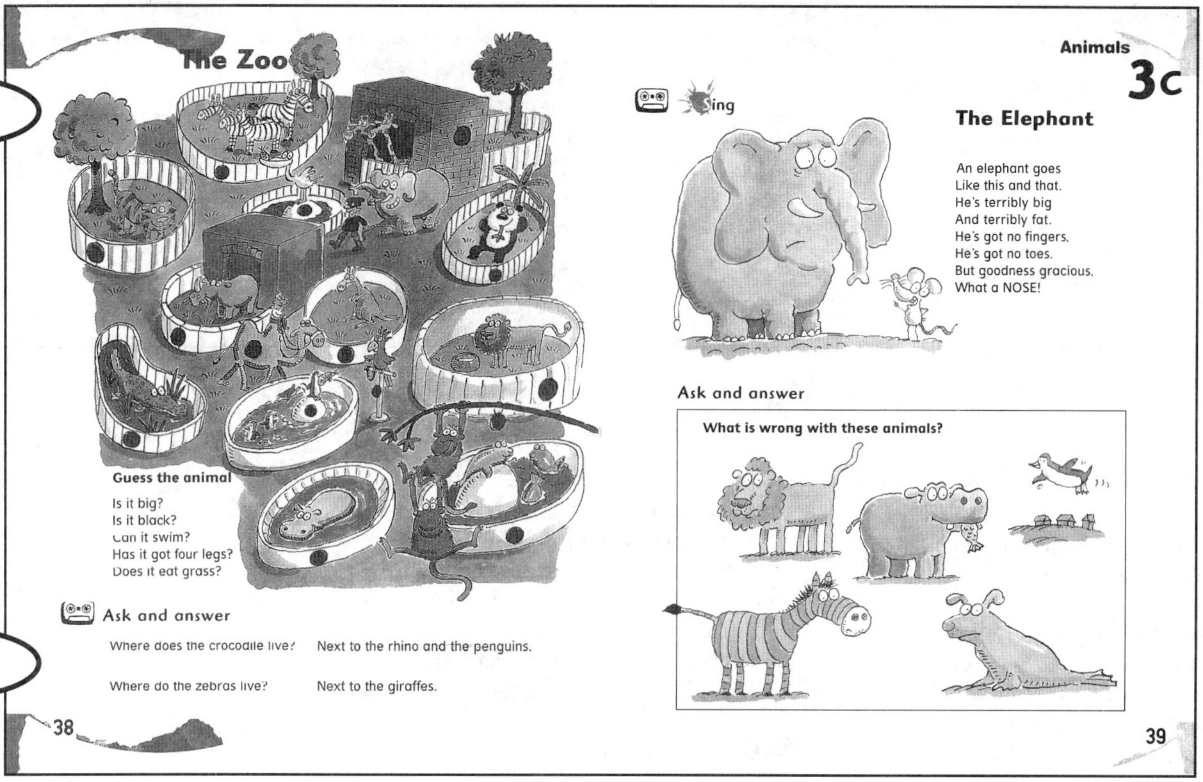

The Zoo

Guess the animal

Is it big?
Is it black?
Can it swim?
Has it got four legs?
Does it eat grass?

Ask and answer

Where does the crocodile live? Next to the rhino and the penguins.

Where do the zebras live? Next to the giraffes.

38

Animals

3c

Sing

The Elephant

An elephant goes
Like this and that.
He's terribly big
And terribly fat.
He's got no fingers,
He's got no toes,
But goodness gracious,
What a NOSE!

Ask and answer

What is wrong with these animals?

39

Step 3

Step 4

Step 5

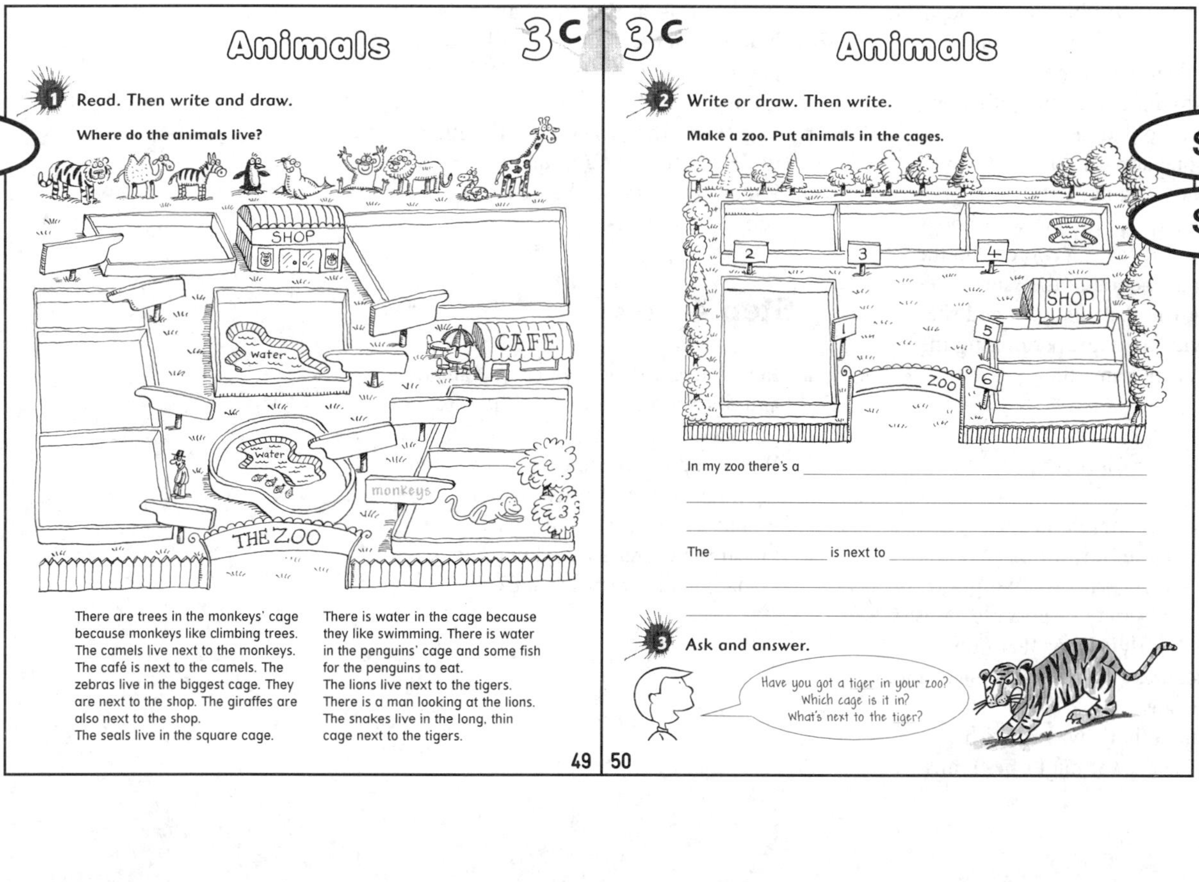

Animals 3c

1 Read. Then write and draw.

Where do the animals live?

SHOP
CAFE
water
water
monkeys
THE ZOO

There are trees in the monkeys' cage because monkeys like climbing trees. The camels live next to the monkeys. The café is next to the camels. The zebras live in the biggest cage. They are next to the shop. The giraffes are also next to the shop.
The seals live in the square cage.

There is water in the cage because they like swimming. There is water in the penguins' cage and some fish for the penguins to eat.
The lions live next to the tigers.
There is a man looking at the lions.
The snakes live in the long, thin cage next to the tigers.

49

3c Animals

2 Write or draw. Then write.

Make a zoo. Put animals in the cages.

1
2
3
4
5
6
SHOP
ZOO

In my zoo there's a ______

The ______ is next to ______

3 Ask and answer.

Have you got a tiger in your zoo?
Which cage is it in?
What's next to the tiger?

50

3c Lesson 3

Main Language Items		Resource File	Materials Needed
goodness gracious!	terribly	1	coloured pencils
What's wrong with ... ?	big	47	cassette/cassette player
Negatives:	fat		
haven't got			
can't			

Step 1 Song

a Say **'Look at the song and picture at the top of page 39. Listen to the tape.'**
b Pupils listen to the song, reading at the same time.
c Check comprehension of the words, directing pupils through an action sequence to go with each of the four lines:
  1 Move from one foot to the other and back, swaying like an elephant.
  2 Put your hands above your head and then out to the sides.
  3 Hold your hands out with your fingers folded in.
  4 Put one arm out in front of your nose as a trunk. Repeat.
d Listen again line by line with books closed and repeat the words. Do the appropriate action at the same time.
e Play the whole song again and sing along with the tape, performing the actions at the same time.

Step 2 Pairwork

a Say **'Look at the pictures of the animals at the bottom of page 39. What's wrong with the penguin?'** There are a variety of possible answers such as **'It's flying.'** or **'Penguins can't fly.'** Encourage pupils to produce more than one answer.
b Then ask **'What's wrong with the lion?'** The answer might be **'Lions haven't got five legs'** or **'Lions have got four legs'.**
c Divide the class into pairs. Pupils ask and answer similar questions about the other animals.
d Finish the exercise by asking the whole class questions about all the animals.

Step 3 Write

a Say **'Turn to page 51 in your Activity Book. Look at the crazy animals. Number one is a monkey's head on a penguin's body.'** Then ask **'What's number two?'**
b Say **'Write the answers on the lines under each crazy animal.'**
c Pupils can work on their own or cooperate in pairs.

Step 4 Draw

a Pupils invent their own crazy animal and draw a picture of it in the box provided.
b When pupils have finished they should try to guess the identity of their friends' pictures.
c Finish the exercise by asking pupils **'What's your crazy animal?'**

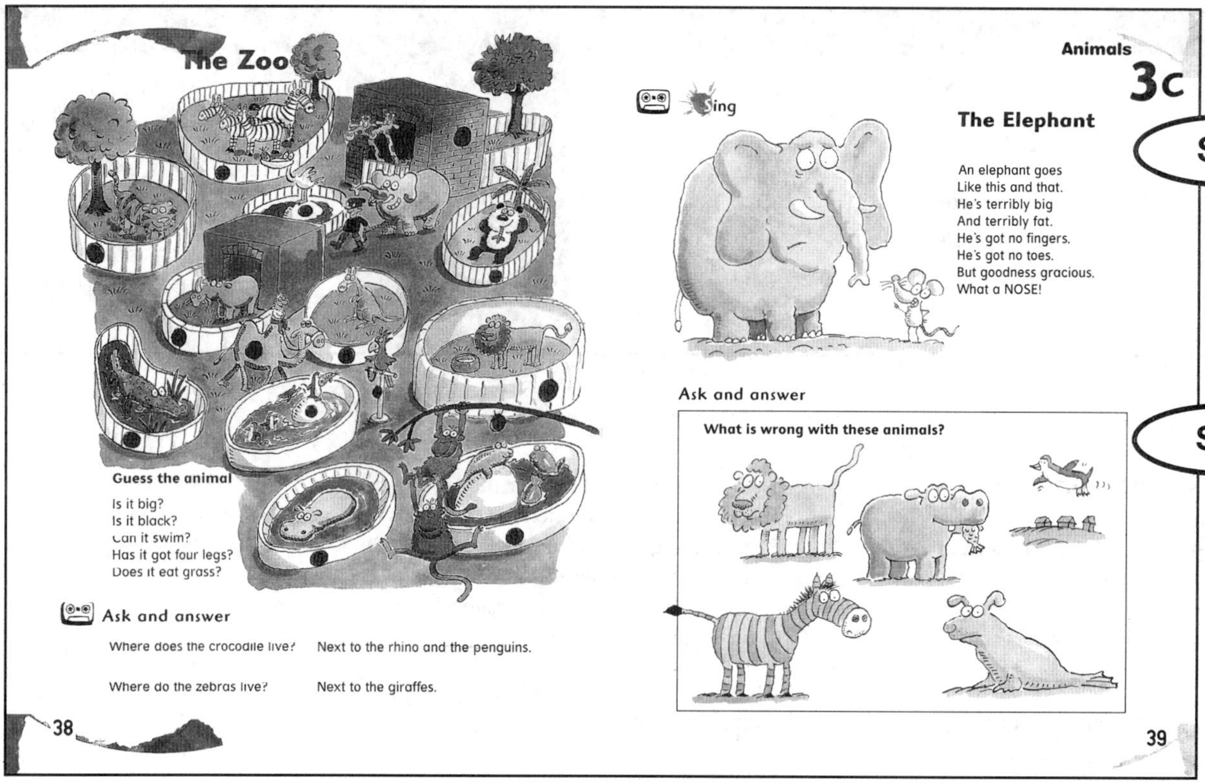

The Zoo

Guess the animal

Is it big?
Is it black?
Can it swim?
Has it got four legs?
Does it eat grass?

Ask and answer

Where does the crocodile live?	Next to the rhino and the penguins.
Where do the zebras live?	Next to the giraffes.

38

Animals

3c

Sing

The Elephant

An elephant goes
Like this and that.
He's terribly big
And terribly fat.
He's got no fingers,
He's got no toes,
But goodness gracious,
What a NOSE!

Ask and answer

What is wrong with these animals?

39

Step 1

Step 2

3c

Animals

2 Write or draw. Then write.

Make a zoo. Put animals in the cages.

1
2
3
4
5
6
SHOP
ZOO

In my zoo there's a ______________________

The __________ is next to ______________

3 Ask and answer.

Have you got a tiger in your zoo?
Which cage is it in?
What's next to the tiger?

50

Animals

3c

4 Write. Then draw and ask and answer.

Crazy animals! Whose head, body, legs and tail?

1 A monkey's head / A penguin's body

2

3

4

5

6

7

My crazy animal

51

Step 3

Step 4

3D Lesson 1

Main Language Items		Resource File	Materials Needed
Where do … live? What colour are …?	Africa Asia spots stripes tallest biggest	7	cassette /cassette player

Step 1 Presentation

a Say **'Open your Coursebook at page 40. Listen to the tape.'**
b Play the tape. Pupils listen and read at the same time.

Tapescript:
The Giraffe. The giraffe has got brown spots on a yellow body. It eats leaves. It's the tallest animal in the world. It's got long legs, a long neck and a long tail. Giraffes live in Africa.
The Tiger. The tiger has got black stripes on an orange and white body. It eats meat and fish. The tiger is one of the cat family. It's the biggest cat. It's got a long body, a long tail and big teeth. Tigers live in Asia.

c Then ask some questions to check comprehension.
What colour are tigers?
What's the tallest animal in the world?
Do tigers have spots?
Where do giraffes live?
Do tigers eat grass?
What do giraffes eat?
What colour are giraffes?

Step 2 Pairwork

a Divide the class into pairs. Say **'Close your books.'**
b Play the tape. P1 repeats the questions, P2 answers.
c Then pupils ask and answer the questions without the help of the tape. P1 asks the questions, using the words on page 40 as prompts, and corrects his or her partner as appropriate.
d Change roles and repeat.

Step 3 Match the animals

a Say **'Open your Activity Book at page 52.'**
b Pupils read the descriptions of the animals that the zoo keeper has dropped. Pupils must decide which description matches which animal and then write the appropriate number alongside the descriptions.

Step 4 Write

a Using the descriptions in the AB and the CB as models, pupils write the description of an elephant.
b Faster pupils can then choose an animal of their choice and draw a picture and write a similar description in their exercise books.

Step 5 Write

a Pupils look at the close-up pictures at the top of page 53 in their ABs and try to identity the animals.
b Pupils then write the names of the animals in the spaces provided.
Answers: 1 zebra, **2** giraffe, **3** crocodile, **4** seal, **5** elephant, **6** tiger.

Step 1

Step 2

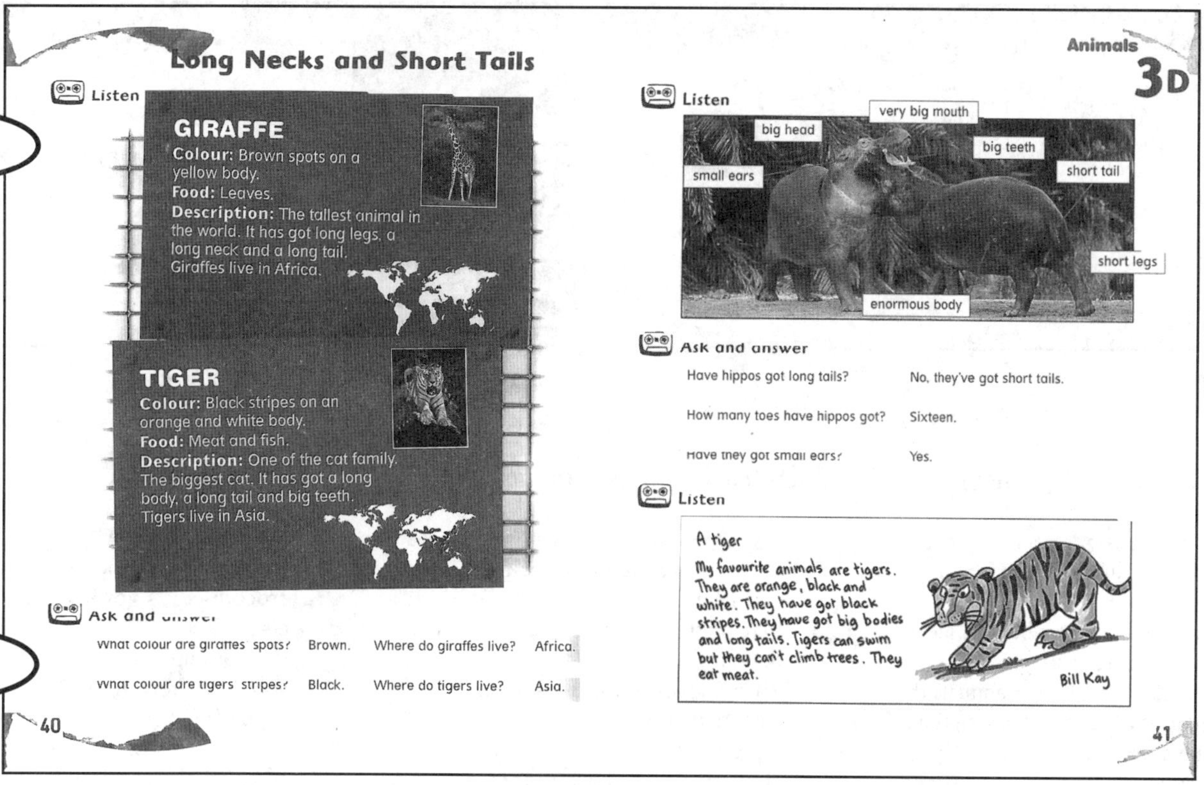

Long Necks and Short Tails

Listen

GIRAFFE
Colour: Brown spots on a yellow body.
Food: Leaves.
Description: The tallest animal in the world. It has got long legs, a long neck and a long tail. Giraffes live in Africa.

TIGER
Colour: Black stripes on an orange and white body.
Food: Meat and fish.
Description: One of the cat family. The biggest cat. It has got a long body, a long tail and big teeth. Tigers live in Asia.

Ask and answer

What colour are giraffes spots? Brown. Where do giraffes live? Africa.

What colour are tigers stripes? Black. Where do tigers live? Asia.

40

Animals 3D

Listen

very big mouth
big head
big teeth
small ears
short tail
short legs
enormous body

Ask and answer

Have hippos got long tails? No, they've got short tails.

How many toes have hippos got? Sixteen.

Have they got small ears? Yes.

Listen

A tiger

My favourite animals are tigers. They are orange, black and white. They have got black stripes. They have got big bodies and long tails. Tigers can swim but they can't climb trees. They eat meat.

Bill Kay

41

Step 3

Step 4

Step 5

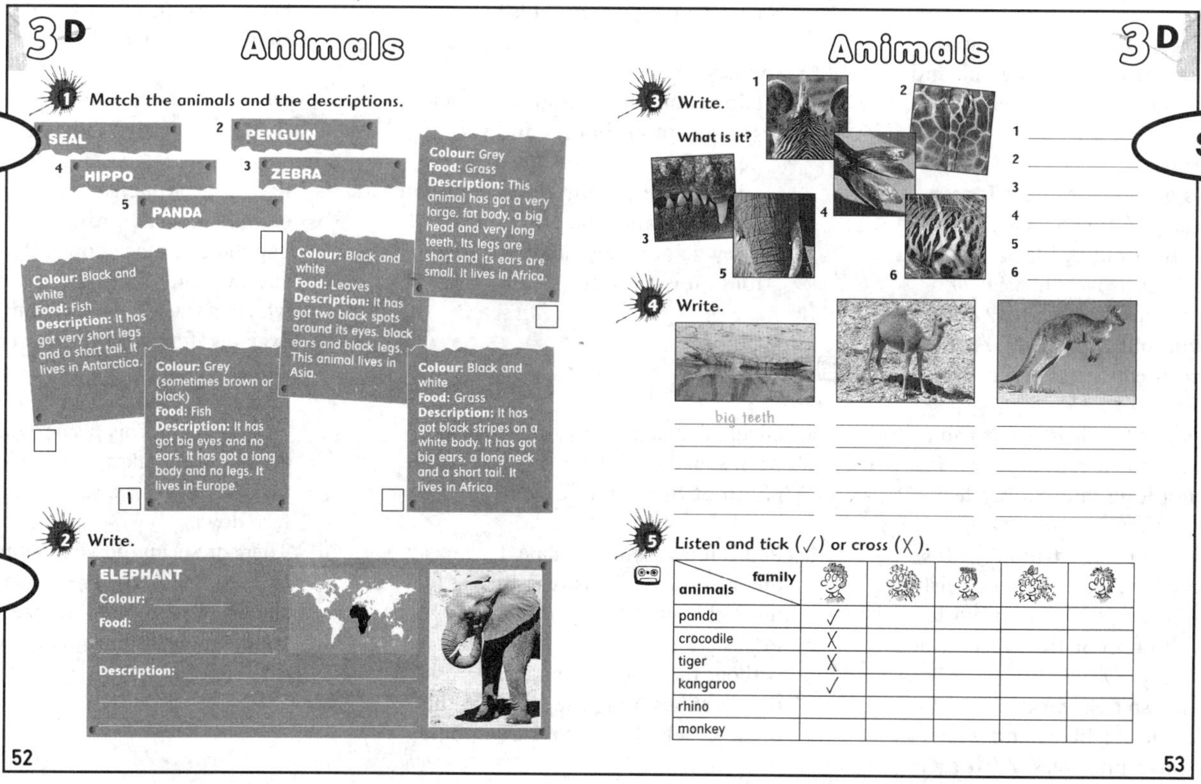

3D Animals

1 Match the animals and the descriptions.

SEAL
2 PENGUIN
4 HIPPO
3 ZEBRA
5 PANDA

Colour: Grey
Food: Grass
Description: This animal has got a very large, fat body, a big head and very long teeth. Its legs are short and its ears are small. It lives in Africa.

Colour: Black and white
Food: Leaves
Description: It has got two black spots around its eyes, black ears and black legs. This animal lives in Asia.

Colour: Black and white
Food: Fish
Description: It has got very short legs and a short tail. It lives in Antarctica.

1 **Colour:** Grey (sometimes brown or black)
Food: Fish
Description: It has got big eyes and no ears. It has got a long body and no legs. It lives in Europe.

Colour: Black and white
Food: Grass
Description: It has got black stripes on a white body. It has got big ears, a long neck and a short tail. It lives in Africa.

2 Write.

ELEPHANT
Colour: ______
Food: ______
Description: ______

52

Animals 3D

3 Write.

What is it?

1 ______
2 ______
3 ______
4 ______
5 ______
6 ______

4 Write.

big teeth

5 Listen and tick (✓) or cross (X).

family / animals					
panda	✓				
crocodile	X				
tiger	X				
kangaroo	✓				
rhino					
monkey					

53

3D Lesson 2

Main Language Items		Resource File	Materials Needed
Have they got ...?	funny	7	Animal cards (see AB cut-outs section)
How many ... have they got?	tail	7a	cassette/cassette player
They've got ...	enormous		
Adjectives (Revision)	very		

Step 1 Listening (Task)

a Each pupil needs one pack of eight Animal cards. Lay the cards face up on the table.

b An animal will be described on the tape. As each part of the description is given, pupils eliminate the animals that do not correspond to the description, e.g. if the animal has got 'long legs', pupils can eliminate the crocodile and the penguin by turning those cards face down.

c By a process of elimination, pupils should eventually have only one card remaining face up.

Tapescript:

1 **It's got four legs. // It eats meat. // It can swim very well. // It's orange, black and white // and it lives in Asia. //**

2 **It's black and white. // It can swim but it can't fly. // It's big and it eats grass. // It lives in Africa. //**

3 **It's got two legs. // It can't swim but it can jump. // It's got a long tail and big feet. // It's brown or grey. //**

4 **It hasn't got a trunk. // It's got short legs. // It eats fish or meat. // It can swim but it can't jump or fly. // It's green or grey. //**

5 **It doesn't eat meat. // It's big // and it's black and white. // It can climb trees. // It eats leaves. // It lives in Asia.**

Step 2 Presentation

a Say **'Open your Coursebook at page 41. Look at the photo of the hippo and listen to the tape.'**

b Play the tape. Pupils listen and read at the same time.

c Then ask some questions to check comprehension:
Have hippos got big bodies?
How many legs have hippos got?
Are they small animals?
Have hippos got long tails?

Tapescript:

Hippos are funny animals. They've got enormous bodies and very big heads. Their mouths are very big and they've got big, long teeth but their eyes and ears are quite small. They've got short legs and four toes on each foot.

Step 3 Pairwork

a Divide the class into pairs. All pairs work simultaneously. Say **'Look at the photo of the hippo. Cover the words.'**

b Pupils repeat after the tape. P1 repeats the questions, P2 answers. Repeat four times changing roles.

c Pupils ask and answer the questions without the help of the tape. P1 asks the questions using the words in the book to help, P2 answers using only the picture.

d Change roles and repeat the procedure.

Step 4 Write

a Say **'Turn to page 53 in your Activity Book. Look at the photo of the crocodile. It's got big teeth. What else?'**
Prompt pupils with other questions about the crocodile's features, e.g. **'Has it got *long legs*?'**

b Then pupils work in pairs and complete the physical descriptions of the three animals.

c Finally, list the characteristics of each animal on the blackboard.

Step 5 Card games

Each pair of pupils requires one pack of eight Animal cards.

a Lay the cards face down. P1 turns over any two cards and says one sentence which is true about both animals. For example if a player turns over a **zebra** and an **elephant**, then the sentence **'They eat grass'** would be true for both animals. This player wins the cards and P2 takes a turn. If P1 cannot say a sentence, the cards are returned face down.

b There are many possible sentences for each pair of cards. The sentences should relate to **colour, size, features, food**, and what the animals **'can/can't do'**, etc.

Long Necks and Short Tails

Listen

GIRAFFE

Colour: Brown spots on a yellow body.
Food: Leaves.
Description: The tallest animal in the world. It has got long legs, a long neck and a long tail. Giraffes live in Africa.

TIGER

Colour: Black stripes on an orange and white body.
Food: Meat and fish.
Description: One of the cat family. The biggest cat. It has got a long body, a long tail and big teeth. Tigers live in Asia.

Ask and answer

What colour are giraffes spots?	Brown.	Where do giraffes live?	Africa.
What colour are tigers stripes?	Black.	Where do tigers live?	Asia.

40

Animals **3D**

Listen

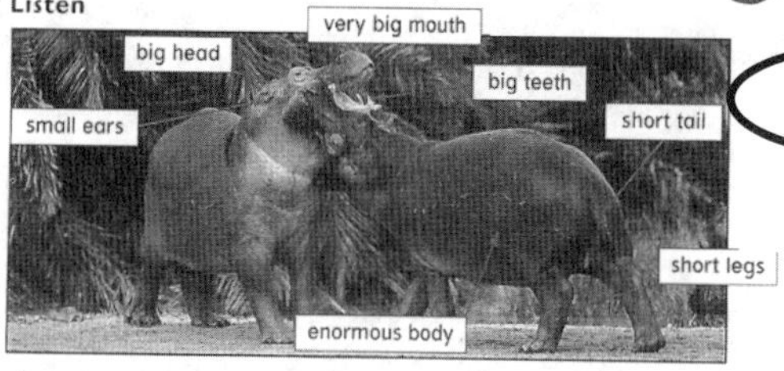

very big mouth
big head
big teeth
small ears
short tail
short legs
enormous body

Step 2

Ask and answer

Have hippos got long tails?	No, they've got short tails.
How many toes have hippos got?	Sixteen.
Have they got small ears?	Yes.

Step 3

Listen

A tiger

My favourite animals are tigers. They are orange, black and white. They have got black stripes. They have got big bodies and long tails. Tigers can swim but they can't climb trees. They eat meat.

Bill Kay

41

3D Animals

1 Match the animals and the descriptions.

1 SEAL
2 PENGUIN
3 ZEBRA
4 HIPPO
5 PANDA

Colour: Grey
Food: Grass
Description: This animal has got a very large, fat body, a big head and very long teeth. Its legs are short and its ears are small. It lives in Africa. ☐

Colour: Black and white
Food: Fish
Description: It has got very short legs and a short tail. It lives in Antarctica. ☐

Colour: Black and white
Food: Leaves
Description: It has got two black spots around its eyes, black ears and black legs. This animal lives in Asia. ☐

Colour: Grey (sometimes brown or black)
Food: Fish
Description: It has got big eyes and no ears. It has got a long body and no legs. It lives in Europe. 1

Colour: Black and white
Food: Grass
Description: It has got black stripes on a white body. It has got big ears, a long neck and a short tail. It lives in Africa. ☐

2 Write.

ELEPHANT
Colour: ____________
Food: ____________
Description: ____________

52

Animals **3D**

3 Write.

What is it?

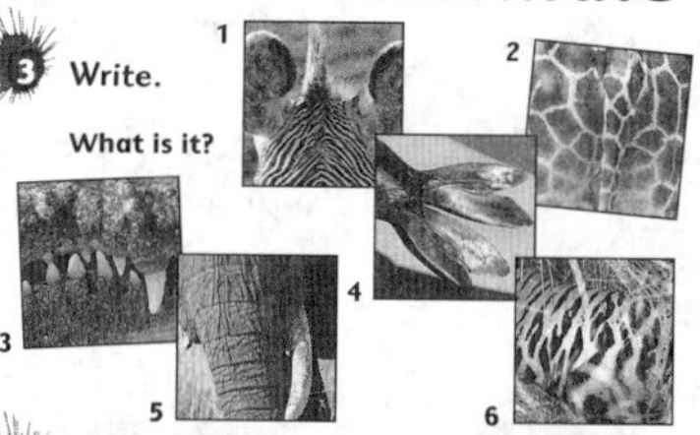

1 ____________
2 ____________
3 ____________
4 ____________
5 ____________
6 ____________

4 Write.

big teeth

Step 4

5 Listen and tick (✓) or cross (✗).

animals \ family	1	2	3	4	5
panda	✓				
crocodile	✗				
tiger	✗				
kangaroo	✓				
rhino					
monkey					

53

3D Lesson 3

Main Language Items	Resource File	Materials Needed
Do you like …? What's your favourite …?	1 4 8 9	paper for display (optional) coloured pencils cassette/cassette player

Step 1 Listen and tick or cross

a Tell pupils to look at the chart on page 53 of their ABs. Pupils place a tick in the grid to indicate the animals that the characters like and a cross for those they dislike.
b Play the tape two or three times.
c Check the answers by asking, **'What animals does *Mr Kay* like?'** or **'Does *Mr Kay* like *monkeys*?'** etc.

Tapescript:

Mr Kay's favourite animals are pandas. He also likes kangaroos but he doesn't like crocodiles and tigers. //
Mrs Kay also likes pandas and she likes tigers too. She doesn't like rhinos much. //
Bill's favourite animals are tigers. He likes the colour. He also likes crocodiles and rhinos but he doesn't really like kangaroos. //
Suzy likes all animals. She loves cats. Her favourite animals are lions and tigers. She also likes pandas and monkeys. //
Gary likes monkeys, kangaroos and pandas and his favourite animals are crocodiles. //

Step 2 Groupwork

a Ask various pupils in the class **'Do you like *snakes*?'** Ask about other animals.
b Copy the chart on page 54 of the AB onto the blackboard. Select one pupil to draw any animal in the left-hand column of the grid and then write the names of four pupils along the top. If he or she draws a monkey, they should ask other pupils **'Do you like monkeys?'** and record their answers in the chart, using ticks and crosses. Also ask pupils **'What's your favourite animal?'** and write the answer in the chart.
c Then all pupils work simultaneously in groups of four asking other group members similar questions and filling in their charts on page 54.
d Each pupils chooses the animals that they want to ask about, so their charts will be different.
e Finish by asking pupils questions about other class members, e.g. **'Does Alex like *monkeys*? What animals does *Maria* like?'**

Step 3 Listen/Presentation

a Say **'Look at Bill's drawing on page 41 of your Coursebook.'** Pupils listen and read at the same time. Then cover the words, look at the picture and listen again.

Step 4 Personal file

a Pupils draw a picture of their favourite animal in the space provided on AB page 54 and write a description alongside. Encourage pupils to compare their description with Bill's on page 41 of the CB and use any other information given in the topic. Provide extra vocabulary if required.
b Expect differences in terms of accuracy and length, according to individual ability. Pupils need not limit their descriptions as in the CB and should be encouraged to write as much as they want.

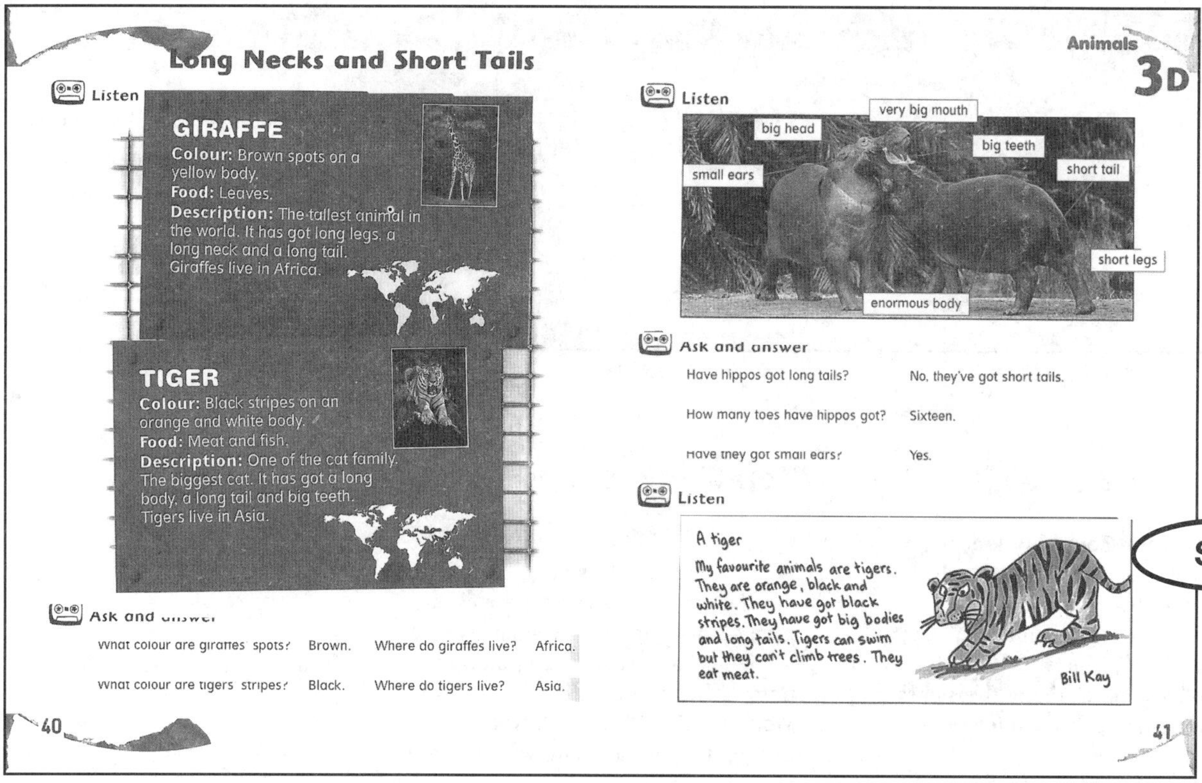

Long Necks and Short Tails

Listen

GIRAFFE
Colour: Brown spots on a yellow body.
Food: Leaves.
Description: The tallest animal in the world. It has got long legs, a long neck and a long tail. Giraffes live in Africa.

TIGER
Colour: Black stripes on an orange and white body.
Food: Meat and fish.
Description: One of the cat family. The biggest cat. It has got a long body, a long tail and big teeth. Tigers live in Asia.

Ask and answer

What colour are giraffes spots? Brown. Where do giraffes live? Africa.

What colour are tigers stripes? Black. Where do tigers live? Asia.

40

Animals **3D**

Listen

very big mouth
big head
big teeth
small ears
short tail
short legs
enormous body

Ask and answer

Have hippos got long tails? No, they've got short tails.

How many toes have hippos got? Sixteen.

Have they got small ears? Yes.

Listen

A tiger
My favourite animals are tigers. They are orange, black and white. They have got black stripes. They have got big bodies and long tails. Tigers can swim but they can't climb trees. They eat meat.
Bill Kay

41

Step 3

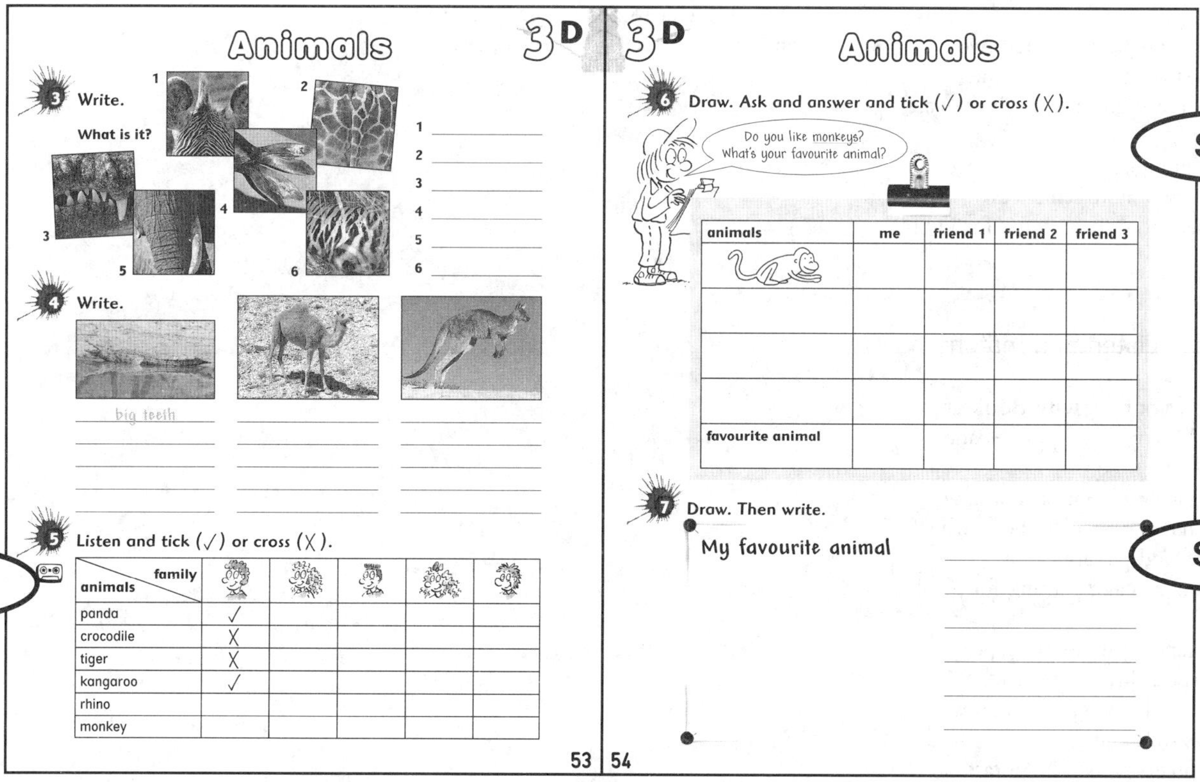

Animals **3D**

3 Write.

What is it?

1 ______
2 ______
3 ______
4 ______
5 ______
6 ______

4 Write.

big teeth

5 Listen and tick (✓) or cross (✗).

family / animals					
panda	✓				
crocodile	✗				
tiger	✗				
kangaroo	✓				
rhino					
monkey					

53

Step 1

54

3D Animals

6 Draw. Ask and answer and tick (✓) or cross (✗).

Do you like monkeys?
What's your favourite animal?

animals	me	friend 1	friend 2	friend 3
favourite animal				

Step 2

7 Draw. Then write.

My favourite animal

Step 4

3E Lesson 1

Main Language Items	Resource File	Materials Needed
can/can't *(Revision)*	18 25	materials to make word stones word stone collections cassette/cassette player

Step 1 Word stones

a Say **'Open your Coursebook at page 42.'** To make the word stones, each pupil requires five 'stones'. Pupils write one word on each stone in felt-tip pen, as shown in the pictures.
b Each pupil also needs the twelve stones shown from their collection (**elephants**, **hippos**, etc.).
c Pupils play the game shown, putting appropriate stones together, **'elephants can't fly'**, etc.
d When pupils have completed two sentences, they can compare their stones with a friend's to see if they are the same.
e Pupils then repeat the above procedure and make two more sentences
f Pupils then store their stones for future use.

Step 2 Listen and match

a Say **'Open your Activity Book at page 55.'** Point to the phrases and pictures.
b Play the tape, one phrase at a time. Pupils listen and draw a line to match the phrase and picture.
c Play the tape again, pausing for pupils to repeat.
d Play the tape again. Pupils repeat the phrases as quickly as they can.
e Pupils practise saying the phrases as quickly as they can.
f Ask volunteers to say the phrases as fast as they can in front of the class.

Step 3 The Stepping Stones Game

a Pupils make sentences going from left to right across the stepping stones on page 42 of their CBs. They must begin in the first column and take one word from each column.
b Work in pairs. Give the class ten minutes to make as many sentences as possible from the words on the stones.
c Check the answers with the whole class. The pair to get the most correct and true sentences are the winners.

Step 1

Step 3

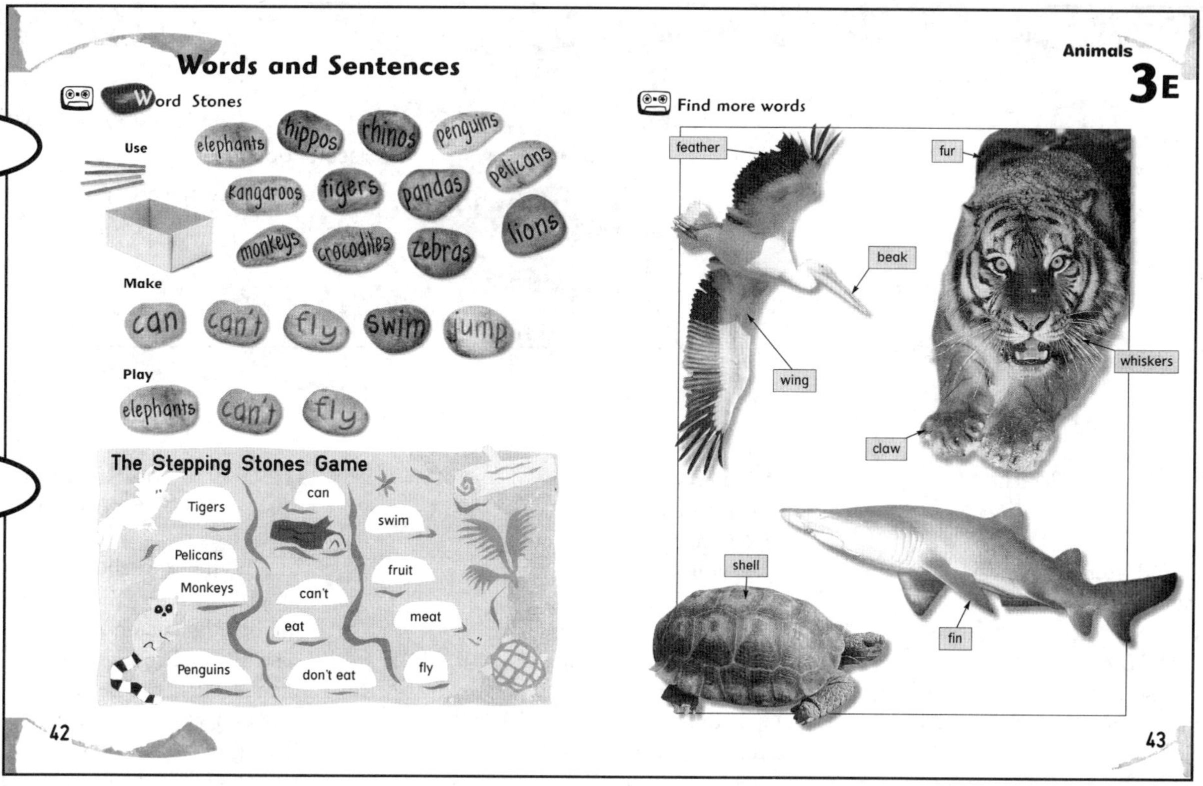

Words and Sentences

Word Stones

Use

elephants hippos rhinos penguins kangaroos tigers pandas pelicans monkeys crocodiles zebras lions

Make

can can't fly swim jump

Play

elephants can't fly

The Stepping Stones Game

Tigers
can
swim
Pelicans
fruit
Monkeys
can't
meat
eat
Penguins
don't eat
fly

42

Animals

3E

Find more words

feather
fur
beak
whiskers
wing
claw
shell
fin

43

Step 2

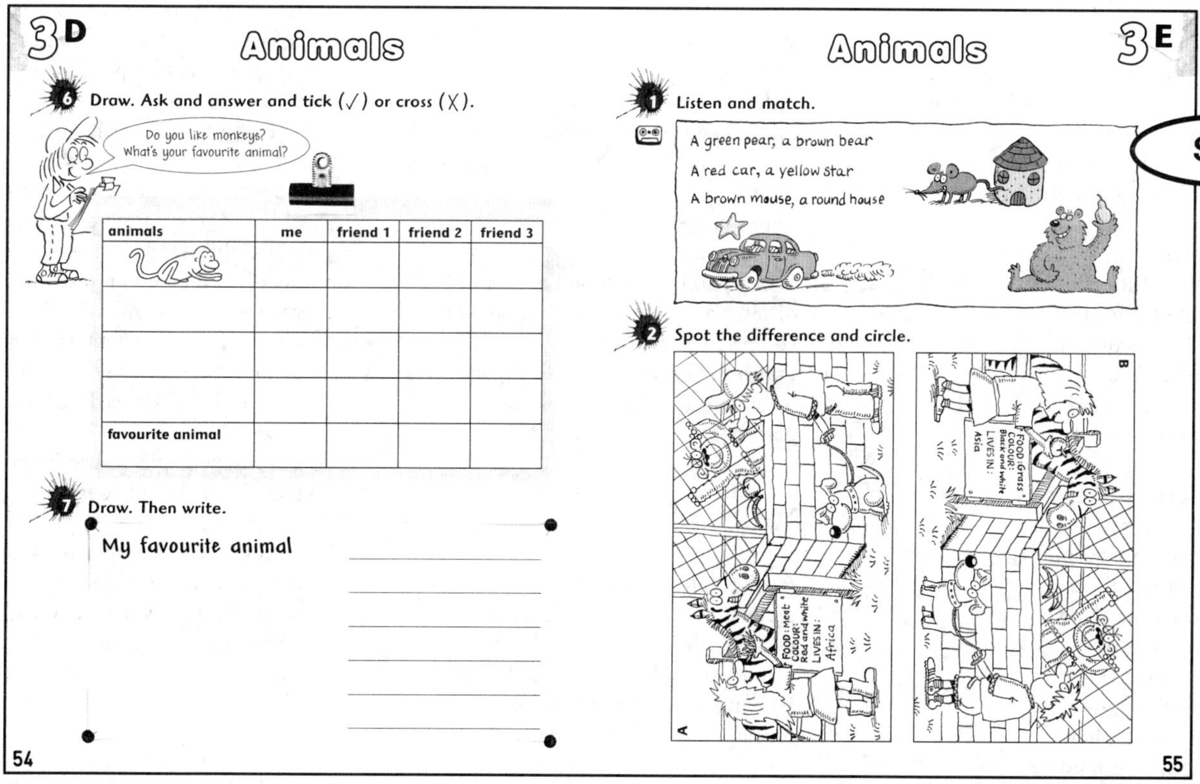

3D

Animals

6 Draw. Ask and answer and tick (✓) or cross (✗).

Do you like monkeys?
What's your favourite animal?

animals	me	friend 1	friend 2	friend 3
favourite animal				

7 Draw. Then write.

My favourite animal

54

Animals

3E

1 Listen and match.

A green pear, a brown bear

A red car, a yellow star

A brown mouse, a round house

2 Spot the difference and circle.

A
FOOD: Meat
COLOUR: Red and white
LIVES IN: Africa
B
FOOD: Grass
COLOUR: Black and white
LIVES IN: Asia

55

3E Lesson 2

Main Language Items	Resource File	Materials Needed
Animals (*Revision*)	26	Story strips 3 (see AB cut-outs section) scissors (optional) cassette/cassette player dice/counters

Step 1 Jigsaw Reading/ Listening

a Play the introductory story again. Pupils listen.
b The cut-outs 'Story strips 3' in the centre of the AB form the text to the introductory story on pages 32–33 of the CB. Pupils should cut them out and jumble them up.
c Pupils then try to put their story strips in the correct order, without looking at their CBs.
d When pupils have finished the jigsaw reading task, they should look at the pictures on pages 32–33 of their CBs to check the order.
e Finally, play the complete story again on tape to confirm the correct order.

Tapescript:

One Blue Butterfly ...
One blue butterfly
flying in the air.
Two red caterpillars
climbing up a chair.
Three yellow crabs
sitting on the sand.
Four black ants
crawling on my hand.
Five pink and purple fish
swimming in the sea.
Six brown monkeys
jumping in a tree.
Seven orange tigers
walking through a wood.
Eight grey elephants
bathing in the mud.
Nine green crocodiles
sitting by a tree.
How many different colours
can you see?

Step 2 Pairwork

a Divide the class into pairs. P1 looks at picture A on page 55 of the AB and P2 looks at picture B. The pictures of the zoo scene are similar but not identical.
b Without looking at each other's pictures, pupils must find the differences between the two pictures.
c Pupils can use any structures they want to describe the pictures and complete the task.
d Pupils circle the differences they find in their pictures.
e When pupils have found as many differences as they can, they should compare their pictures.
f Finish the exercise by asking volunteers to write the differences on the blackboard.

Optional

Each pupil colours in one of the two pictures used in Step 2. Then P1 describes his or her picture while P2 colours the other picture, following P1's instructions. Change roles and repeat.

Step 3 The Stepping Stones Spelling Game 3

a Ideally the game should be played in groups. Each group needs one copy of the board game on AB page 56 and a dice. (If no dice is available, the numbers 1–6 can be written on each side of a six-sided pencil.)
Each group nominates a referee. The referee's job is to check the answers and adjudicate. The rest of the group are the players. Each player needs a coloured counter (or small coloured piece of paper), a pencil and a sheet of paper.
b The object of the game is to make your way from the start to the finish.
c Players take it in turns to throw the dice and move around the board. When they land on a letter they must say a word beginning with that letter, write the word and say each letter as they write. When they land on a picture they must say the word, write the word and say each letter as they write.
d Encourage pupils to use English as they play. They should count in English and use phrases such as **'Your/My turn'**.
E In addition, ask pupils questions about the game as you monitor their progress, e.g. **'Is it your turn?'**, **'What's your colour?'**

Step 1

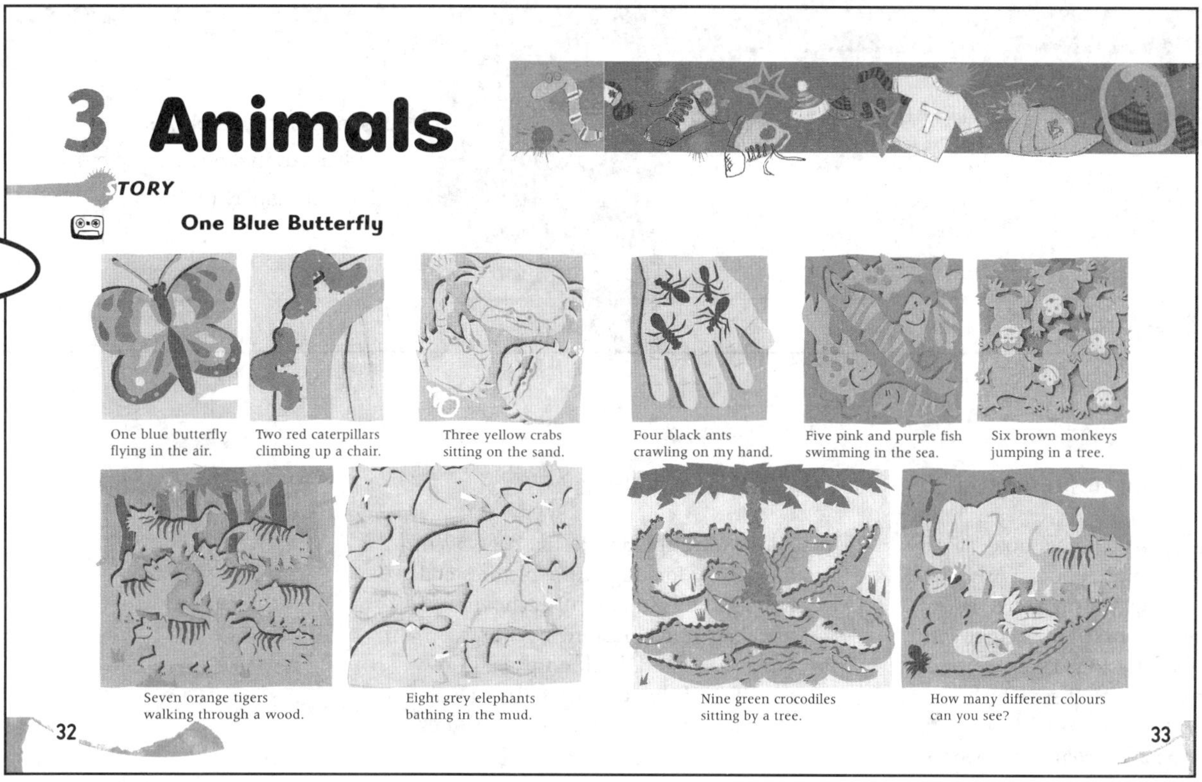

3 Animals

STORY

One Blue Butterfly

One blue butterfly flying in the air.

Two red caterpillars climbing up a chair.

Three yellow crabs sitting on the sand.

Four black ants crawling on my hand.

Five pink and purple fish swimming in the sea.

Six brown monkeys jumping in a tree.

Seven orange tigers walking through a wood.

Eight grey elephants bathing in the mud.

Nine green crocodiles sitting by a tree.

How many different colours can you see?

32 33

Step 2

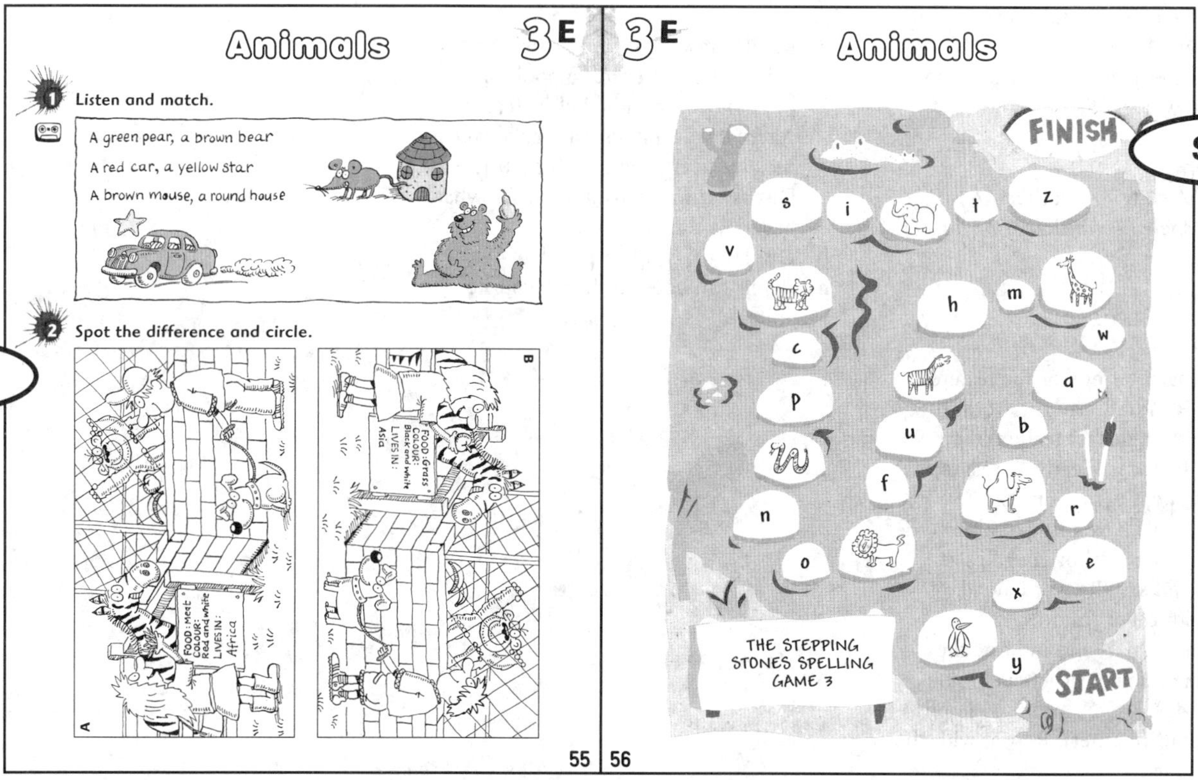

Animals 3E

1 Listen and match.

A green pear, a brown bear
A red car, a yellow star
A brown mouse, a round house

2 Spot the difference and circle.

A
FOOD: Meat
COLOUR: Red and white
LIVES IN: Africa
B
FOOD: Grass
COLOUR: Black and white
LIVES IN: Asia

55

3E Animals

FINISH
s i t z
v
h m
w
c
a
p
u b
f
r
n
o
e
x
y
START
THE STEPPING STONES SPELLING GAME 3

56

Step 3

3E Lesson 3

Main Language Items		Resource File	Materials Needed
beak	whiskers	37	cassette/cassette player
claw	wing	39	materials to make collage pictures (optional)
feather			paper for display (optional)
fin			
fur			
shell			

Step 1 Find more words

a Say **'Open your Coursebooks at page 43'** and look at the photos. Ask pupils in their L1 if any of them can see an animal they have seen in their country. Ask if any of the animals has features similar to their pets. If so, which animals, features and pets?

b Play the tape and listen to the words while looking at the pictures.

c Play the tape again. This time pupils point to the appropriate feature as they hear the word.

d Play the tape again. Pupils listen and repeat the words.

Tapescript:
beak // claw // feather // fin // fur // shell // whiskers // wing //

Step 2 Games

a Spell the name of one of the features, e.g. 'F-U-R'. Pupils say the word **'fur'**. Repeat with the other features.

b Stand at the front, clearly visible to the class, and silently 'say' one of the features. Pupils have to guess the word using the movement of your lips as their cue and say the word aloud. Repeat with other features.

c Ask **'What's this?'** and indicate the appropriate number of letters on the blackboard, e.g. _ _ _ _ _ _ _. Pupils say the word **(feather)**. Repeat with the other features.

Step 3 Write

a Pupils solve the puzzles on page 57 of the AB, by looking at the pictures and writing the first letter of each word to reveal an animal feature, e.g. **fur.**

b Pupils can check back on page 43 of the CB and the rest of the Animals topic if they are unsure of the features.

Step 4 Draw and label

a Pupils draw a picture of their favourite animal in their exercise book or on a piece of paper and label its features. Alternatively, pupils, can make collage pictures using feathers, fur fabric, etc. Discuss with pupils in their L1 what materials they could use.

b Display the work if possible.

c Pupils can vote on their favourite animal.

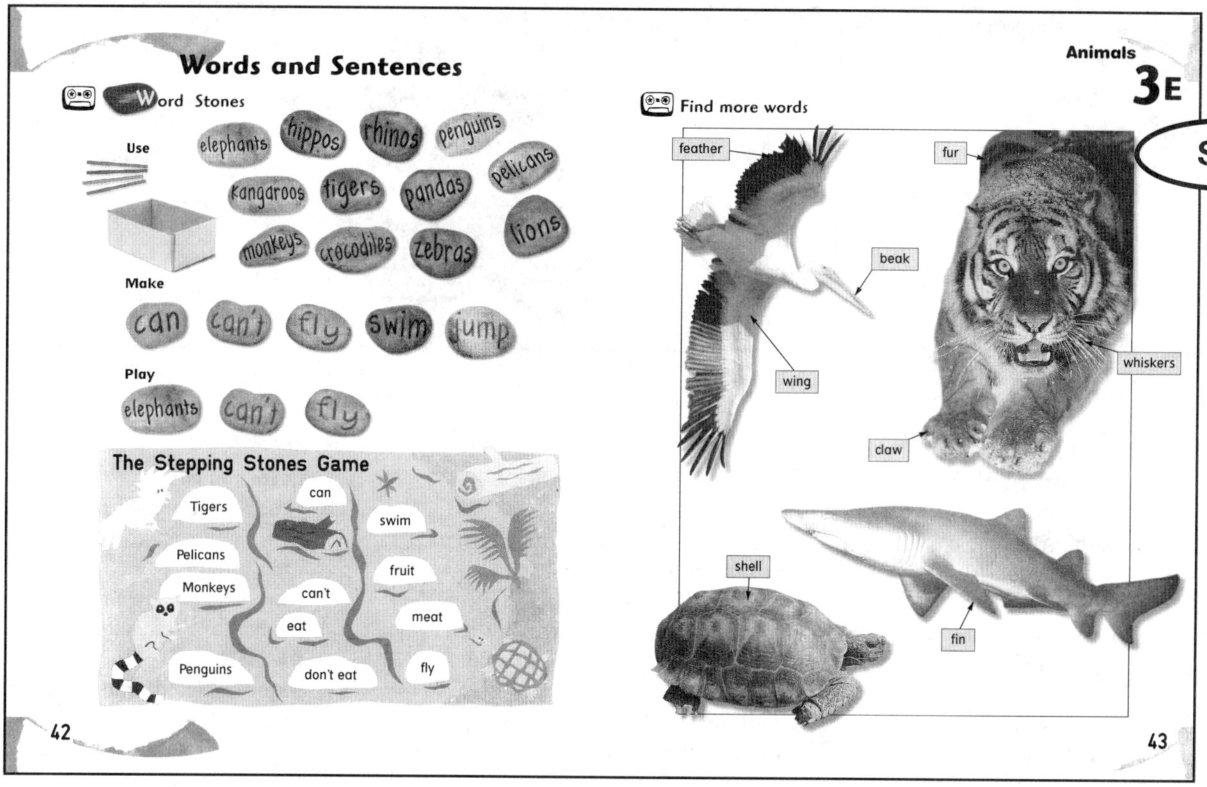
Words and Sentences
Word Stones
Use
elephants hippos rhinos penguins
kangaroos tigers pandas pelicans
monkeys crocodiles zebras lions
Make
can can't fly swim jump
Play
elephants can't fly
The Stepping Stones Game
Tigers
Pelicans
Monkeys
Penguins
can
can't
eat
don't eat
swim
fruit
meat
fly
42
Animals
3E
Find more words
feather
beak
wing
fur
whiskers
claw
shell
fin
43

Step 1

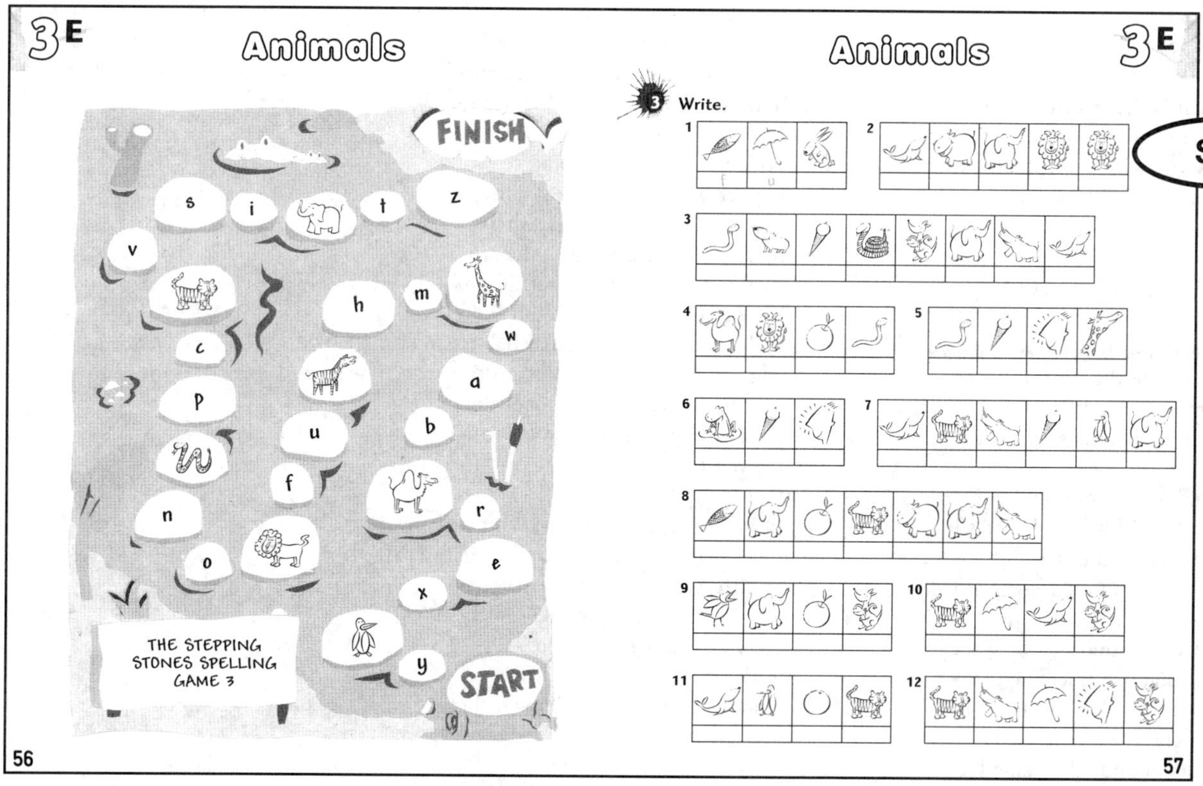
3E
Animals
FINISH
s i t z
v
h m
w
c
a
p
b
u
f
r
n
o
e
x
y
START
THE STEPPING STONES SPELLING GAME 3
56
Animals
3E
3 Write.
1
2
3
4
5
6
7
8
9
10
11
12
57

Step 3

3F Lesson 1 – Project

Main Language Items	Resource File	Materials Needed
Am I ... ? Have I got ... ?	10 47	cassette/cassette player project materials

Step 1 Listen and number

a Tell pupils to open the ABs on page 58. Play the three descriptions of animals, pausing after each one.
b Pupils listen to the tape and write the appropriate number in the box next to the picture.
c Play the tape three times. Allow pupils to compare their answers before replaying the tape.

Tapescript:

1 **It's got four legs and a hard shell. It can't fly.**
2 **It can't fly. It's brown and it's got fur and claws.**
3 **It's got wings and feathers and a beak. It's black and white.**

Step 2 Play the game

a In groups, pupils use labels or pieces of paper and write the names of an animal on each label.
b Each group then mixes up all the labels.
c Each member of the group then selects a label and sticks it on a friend's back. (The friend can either be in the same group or can be in a different group.)
d The friend with the label should then ask questions to find out what they are, e.g. **'Am I black?'**. Encourage other pupils to answer **'Yes'** or **'No'** appropriately.
e Pupils can continue the game in groups or with the rest of the class.

Step 3 Start a project

NOTE A week or two before you start this project, prepare a collection box in class and ask pupils to bring objects and materials such as corks, buttons, feathers, bits of string, wire, walnut shells, etc.

a Say **'Look at the pictures on page 44 of the Coursebook'**. In their L1, ask pupils what they can see and have a class discussion about animals and models. Ask some questions to help pupils focus their attention on the subject: **'Have you ever made models? Of what? What materials did you use? Was it difficult?'**
b Explain that they are going to work together in small groups in order to make models of animals in their different habitats. Suggest the following list: jungle/desert/farm/town/sea/North Pole/South Pole. Ask pupils to suggest additional habitats, and stick the completed list on the wall. Pupils write their names down next to the project they want to be involved in, and groups are formed accordingly.
c Before they start, sit down with each group in turn and help pupils organise the different tasks and materials so that everyone is fully involved. Tell them that the project consists in
• making models of the different animals that live in the habitat they have selected.
• providing a suitably detailed background of painted cardboard for those animals.
• marking the habitats on a world map (hand out a photocopy of this map to each group).
• preparing a short description of each animal for presentation to the rest of the class.
The completed projects are then displayed around the room. Make sure that pupils have the necessary English vocabulary.
d Encourage pupils to continue their project work outside their English class and find out as much as they can about their chosen group of animals.

tep 3

START A PROJECT

SUPERSNAKE
HOMEWORK
Write about snakes
That's easy!
So, Willy asks Supersnake.
Supersnake, can you swim? Can you fly? Can you ...
Yes, yes.
Later, Willy finishes his homework.
SNAKES
Snaiks can fli.
Snaiks can swim.
Snaiks wear blak coats.
Snaiks are GREAT!
Next day, in the classroom.
Willy! Snakes can't fly. They can't jump and they don't wear clothes!
Snakes can't fly
Oh yes they can!
Teachers don't know everything!

Animals

tep 1

1 Listen and number.

tep 2

2 Play the game.

You need

1 Write the name of an animal on the label.

giraffe

2 Mix up all the labels.

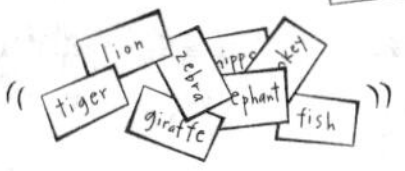
lion
zebra
hippo
monkey
tiger
elephant
giraffe
fish

3 Pin a label on a friend.

giraffe

4 Ask questions to guess what you are. Answer 'yes' or 'no'.

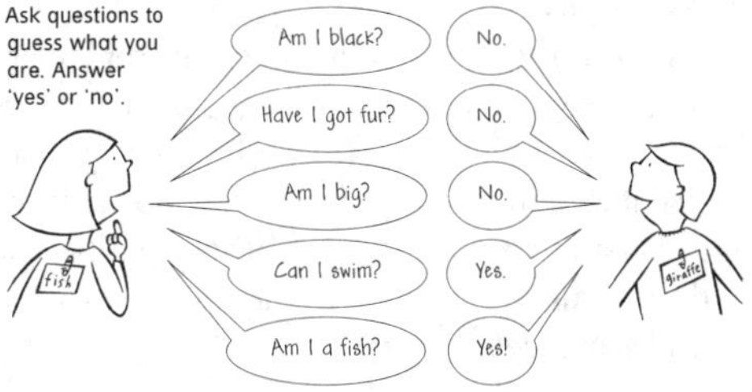
Am I black?
No.
Have I got fur?
No.
Am I big?
No.
Can I swim?
Yes.
Am I a fish?
Yes!
fish
giraffe

3 Listen and number the picture.

1

4 Write.

A

1 Can penguins fly? ______
2 What colour are zebras? ______
3 How many legs have hippos got? ______
4 What do lions eat? ______
5 What colour are giraffes? ______

B

Elephants are big, grey animals. They have got ______ legs and a big body. They ______ swim but they ______ climb trees. They ______ grass. They have got a very long ______. It is called a trunk.

3F Lesson 2 - Evaluation

Main Language Items		Resource File	Materials Needed
Can you ...?	swim fly wear		test cards 3F (see photocopy master on TG p.175) scissors (optional) Supersnake puppets cassette/cassette player

Step 1 Listen and number

a Look at the pictures at the top of page 59 in the AB. There is a short dialogue or sentence on the tape referring to each of the pictures. Pupils must decide which dialogue or sentence refers to which picture and write the appropriate numbers in the boxes.

b Number 1 is given as an example. Play each one three times.

Tapescript:

1 **Gosh! Isn't it tall! ~ Yes, it's the tallest animal in the world. //**
2 **How many animals are there in that cage? ~ Three, I think. //**
3 **This animal is a big cat. It's got black stripes. //**
4 **Look at this hippo's teeth. They're enormous. //**
5 **It's big and it's got black and white stripes. //**
6 **Can it fly? ~ Yes, of course it can. It's a pelican. //**
7 **What's that animal in the tree? Is it a monkey or a panda? ~ It's a monkey. //**
8 **This animal has got a long tail and big feet. It can't walk but it jumps. //**
9 **What's that in the grass? ~ It looks like a crocodile. //**
10 **These are birds but they can't fly. //**

Step 2 Write (Test)

a Pupils work individually. In Part A they read the questions and write the answers. In Part B they read the passage and write the missing words.

b The tests are designed to test communication as much as accuracy. Credit should be given for answers which show that pupils have understood the meaning of the questions, and where answers are comprehensible and appropriate to the question.

Step 3 Test yourself

a Photocopy one set of test cards 3F for each pupil (see photocopy master on TG page 175).

b Say '**Open your Activity Books at page 60 and look at the pictures.**' Hand out the test card sheets and ask pupils to cut out the cards. Alternatively, give each pupil a set of cards already cut out. Pupils then fold the eight cards along the dotted line.

c To do the first self-test, pupils place all their cards in front of them with the pictures showing, following the visual instructions. Demonstrate.

d Pupils then read the first sentence in the left-hand list, '**Penguins can't fly**'. Pupils must find the card with the picture which illustrates the sentence, pick it up and read the sentence on the card. They then put a tick or cross in the box in their ABs if they were right or wrong. Repeat for the other cards.

e To do the second self-test, pupils first cover the words in the left-hand list and then place all their cards in front of them again with the pictures showing, following the visual instructions. Demonstrate.

f Pupils then look at the first picture in the right-hand list. Pupils must write the appropriate sentence in the space provided ('**Seals eat fish.**') they then find the card with the appropriate picture, pick it up and look at the words to check. They put a tick or a cross in the box accordingly. Repeat for the other pictures.

g Pupils add up their scores out of eight for each test and total them. Finally, they circle the comment.

h Pupils can create other cards to test themselves or their friends using other animal vocabulary they have met in the topic and project work. The photocopy master includes some blank cards.

Step 4 Supersnake

a Look at the Supersnake cartoon on page 45 of the CB. Listen to the story and read at the same time.

b Follow up with role play with or without puppets, as with previous Supersnake stories.

START A PROJECT

44

Animals

3F

SUPERSNAKE
HOMEWORK
Write about snakes.
That's easy!
So, Willy asks Supersnake.
Supersnake, can you swim? Can you fly? Can you....
Yes, yes...
Later, Willy finishes his homework.
SNAKS
Snaiks can fli.
Snaiks can swim.
Snaiks wear blak coats.
Snaiks are GREAT!
Next day, in the classroom.
Willy! Snakes can't fly. They can't jump and they don't wear clothes!
Snakes can't fly
Oh yes they can!
Teachers don't know everything!

45

Step 4

Animals

3F

3 Listen and number the picture.

Step 1

4 Write.

A

1 Can penguins fly? ________
2 What colour are zebras? ____________________
3 How many legs have hippos got? ________
4 What do lions eat? ______________
5 What colour are giraffes? ____________________

B

Elephants are big, grey animals. They have got ________ legs and a big body. They ________ swim but they ________ climb trees. They ________ grass. They have got a very long ________. It is called a trunk.

59

3F

Animals

5 Test yourself. Right (✓) or wrong (X)?

Step 3

You need

TEST 1

* *Put the cards like this.*
* *Read these words.*
* *Find the pictures.*
* *Check. Right (✓) or wrong (X)?*

Penguins can't fly. ☐
Tigers eat meat. ☐
Kangaroos can jump. ☐
Seals eat fish. ☐
Monkeys can climb. ☐
Zebras eat grass. ☐
Elephants can't fly. ☐
Giraffes eat leaves. ☐

SCORE /8

TEST 2

* *Put the cards like this.*
* *Read these questions.*
* *Write the descriptions.*
* *Check. Right (✓) or wrong (X)?*

SCORE /8

TOTAL /16

Circle your total score

16 Excellent **15–14** Very good **13–12** Good
11–10 Quite good **9–0** Do it again!

60

4 Story lesson

Main Language Items			Resource File	Materials Needed
There's a ...	dark cupboard shelf box wood house	in on	11	cassette/cassette player

Step 1 Topic warm-up

a Tell pupils in their L1 that they are going to continue their English lessons by looking at homes. Introduce the word '**homes**' at this point

b Then ask pupils what words they think they might learn.

c Ask pupils about their homes. Can they name anything in English?

d Discuss what different homes they can think of and who or what lives in which type of home.

e Ask pupils if they think homes in other countries are the same as their own. Why do they think they are/aren't?

Step 2 Story warm-up

a Say '**Open your Coursebooks at page 46. Look at the pictures.**' Demonstrate what you mean by holding up your CB and pointing to the pictures.

b Ask pupils in their L1 what they can see. Where do they think it is?

c Ask pupils if they can see anything in the pictures they can name in English.

Step 3 Story listening

a Say '**Listen to the tape.**' Pupils look at the pictures and listen to the tape at the same time.

b Play the tape again.

c Ask questions in the pupils' L1 to check they have understood the story.

Tapescript:

In a Dark, Dark Wood ...
In a dark, dark wood // there's
A dark, dark house. //
In the dark, dark house // there's
A dark, dark cupboard. //
In the dark, dark cupboard //
there's a dark, dark shelf. //
On the dark, dark shelf // there's
A dark, dark box. //
And in the dark, dark box //
there's a ... //

Step 4 Listen and repeat

a Play the complete story again. Pupils listen and look at the pictures. Pupils can also mouth the words as they listen to the tape.

b Then play the story pausing after each line for pupils to repeat.

Step 5 Story task

a Pupils close their CBs. Then write **wood**, **house**, **cupboard**, **shelf** and **box** on the blackboard, in a random order.

b Say each word for pupils to repeat two or three times.

c Pupils then say in what order they appear in the story.

d Listen to the tape again to confirm the correct order.

e Finally, listen to the tape again, or say the story, leaving gaps for the nouns (**wood**, **house**, etc.). Pupils try to join in and say the story.

f Finally, you may like to ask pupils to say, or alternatively to draw, what they think is in the box.

Step 6 Story learn and say

a Play the tape again, pausing after each line for pupils to repeat.

b Finally, pupils say as much of the story as they can without the tape.

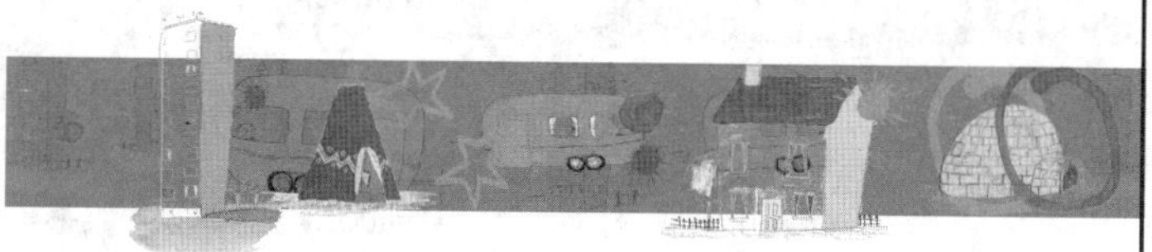

4 Homes

STORY

In a Dark, Dark Wood

Step 2

Step 3

Step 4

In a dark, dark wood there's a dark, dark house.
In the dark, dark house there's a dark, dark cupboard.
In the dark, dark cupboard there's a dark, dark shelf. On the dark, dark shelf there's a dark, dark box.
And in the dark, dark box there's a ...

46 47

4A Lesson 1

Main Language Items			Resource File	Materials Needed
Do/Does ... live ...?	house kitchen garden living room	flat bathroom balcony	1 2 8	paper for display (optional) coloured pencils cassette/cassette player

Step 1 Presentation

a Say **'Open your Coursebooks at page 48. Listen to the tape.'**
b Play the tape. Pupils listen and read at the same time.
c Then ask some questions to check comprehension:
Does Kev live in a house or a flat?
How many rooms are there in Julie's house?
What's the biggest room in Julie's house?
Is Julie's bedroom the biggest or the smallest? etc.

Step 2 Pairwork

a Hold up your book for the class. Say **'Look at the small pictures of the rooms. These are four of the rooms in Kev and Kate's flat.'** Point to the first room and ask **'Is this the kitchen?'**
b Point to the second room and ask **'Which room is this?'**
c Ask similar questions about all four rooms.
d Divide the class into pairs. Pupils ask and answer similar questions about the four rooms.

Step 3 Pairwork

a Say **'Close your books.'** Pupils remain in pairs.
b Play the tape. P1 repeats the question, P2 answers.
c Then pupils ask and answer the questions without the help of the tape. P1 asks the questions using the words at the bottom of page 48 to help, and corrects his or her partner as appropriate.
d Change roles and repeat.

Step 4 Listen and number

a Say **'Look at the four houses at the top of page 61 in your Activity Book. Read the description of each house.'**
b Pupils must decide in which house each family lives.
c Pupils listen to the tape and write the number of each description on the door of the appropriate house.
d Play the tape two or three times.
e Go over the answers with the whole class asking:
How many rooms in ***Mr and Mrs Black's*** **house?**
Has ***Mr and Mrs Green's*** **house got a garden?**
How many bedrooms in ***Mr and Mrs Grey's*** **house?** etc.

Tapescript:

1 **Mr and Mrs Green have a small house with a garden. // It's got two small bedrooms, // a living room, a kitchen and a bathroom. //**
2 **Mr and Mrs Black's house is quite big. // There are four bedrooms: two big and two small. // They've got a big garden and a balcony at the front of the house. // There are two bathrooms upstairs and a kitchen and a large living room downstairs. //**
3 **Mr and Mrs Grey haven't got a garden. Their house is quite small. // They've got a small kitchen, a living room and two small bedrooms. // Their bathroom is very small and the house has no balconies. //**
4 **Mr and Mrs White live in a big house. // They've got a large garden at the back of the house. // There are three bedrooms and a bathroom upstairs. // Downstairs there is a living room, a dining room and a large kitchen. //**

Step 5 Personal file

a Tell pupils to open their ABs at page 61. Pupils draw a picture of their house/flat from the outside and write a brief description alongside. Use the models on page 48 of the CB to help.
b Descriptions may range from a list of rooms to a few sentences as in the CB, according to individual abilities.
c Then pupils answer the questions about their own home.
d Faster pupils can ask questions about their friends' homes.

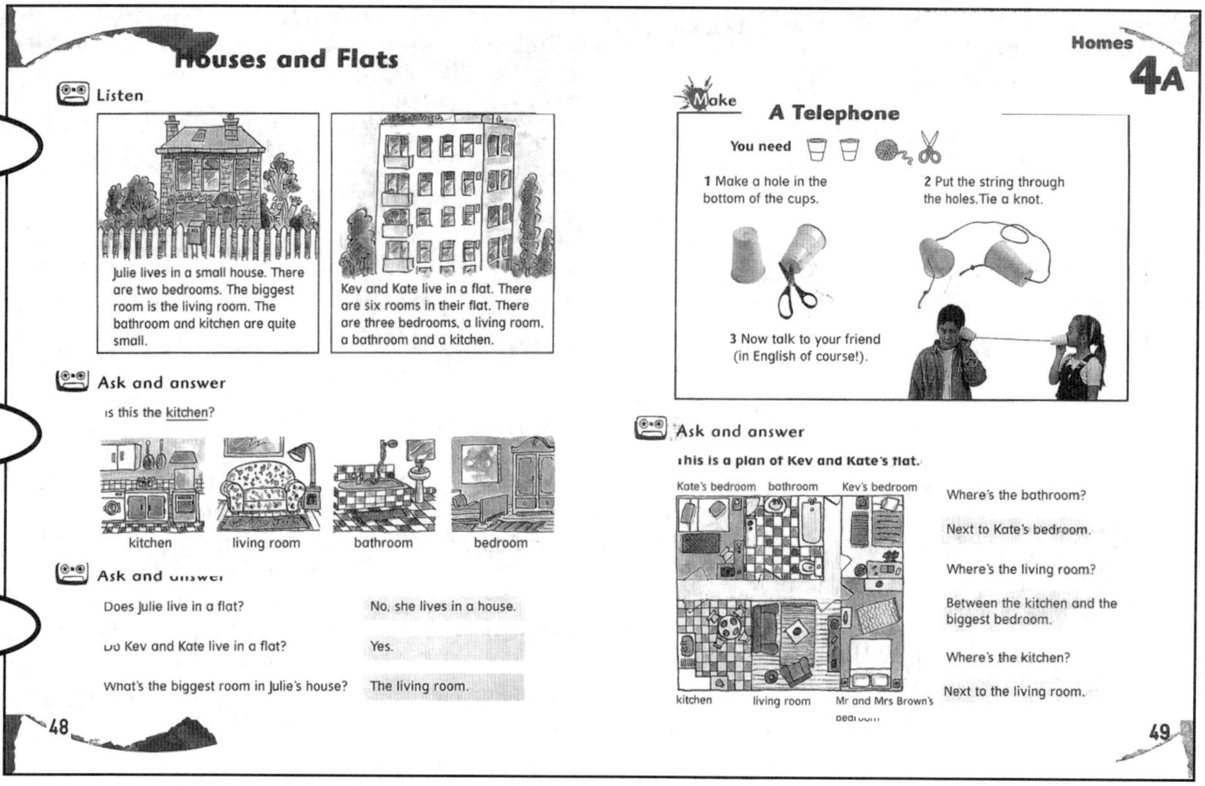

Step 1

Step 2

Step 3

Houses and Flats

Homes **4A**

Listen

Julie lives in a small house. There are two bedrooms. The biggest room is the living room. The bathroom and kitchen are quite small.

Kev and Kate live in a flat. There are six rooms in their flat. There are three bedrooms, a living room, a bathroom and a kitchen.

Ask and answer

Is this the kitchen?

kitchen · living room · bathroom · bedroom

Ask and answer

Does Julie live in a flat?	No, she lives in a house.
Do Kev and Kate live in a flat?	Yes.
What's the biggest room in Julie's house?	The living room.

Make

A Telephone

You need

1 Make a hole in the bottom of the cups.

2 Put the string through the holes. Tie a knot.

3 Now talk to your friend (in English of course!).

Ask and answer

This is a plan of Kev and Kate's flat.

Kate's bedroom · bathroom · Kev's bedroom · kitchen · living room · Mr and Mrs Brown's bedroom

Where's the bathroom?	Next to Kate's bedroom.
Where's the living room?	Between the kitchen and the biggest bedroom.
Where's the kitchen?	Next to the living room.

48 · 49

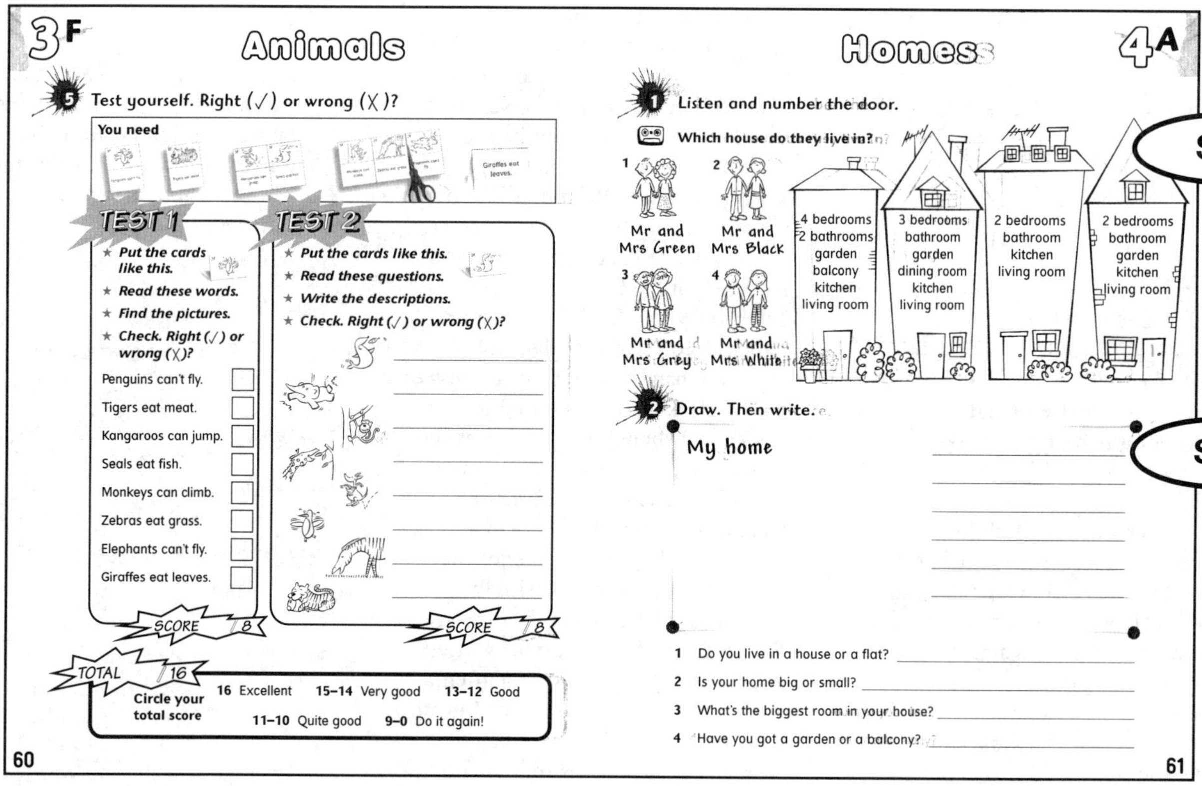

Step 4

Step 5

3F Animals

Homes **4A**

5 Test yourself. Right (✓) or wrong (✗)?

You need

TEST 1

- Put the cards like this.
- Read these words.
- Find the pictures.
- Check. Right (✓) or wrong (✗)?

Penguins can't fly.
Tigers eat meat.
Kangaroos can jump.
Seals eat fish.
Monkeys can climb.
Zebras eat grass.
Elephants can't fly.
Giraffes eat leaves.

SCORE /8

TEST 2

- Put the cards like this.
- Read these questions.
- Write the descriptions.
- Check. Right (✓) or wrong (✗)?

SCORE /8

TOTAL /16

Circle your total score: 16 Excellent · 15–14 Very good · 13–12 Good · 11–10 Quite good · 9–0 Do it again!

1 Listen and number the door.

Which house do they live in?

1 Mr and Mrs Green · 2 Mr and Mrs Black · 3 Mr and Mrs Grey · 4 Mr and Mrs White

4 bedrooms 2 bathrooms garden balcony kitchen living room	3 bedrooms bathroom garden dining room kitchen living room	2 bedrooms bathroom kitchen living room	2 bedrooms bathroom garden kitchen living room

2 Draw. Then write.

My home

1 Do you live in a house or a flat?
2 Is your home big or small?
3 What's the biggest room in your house?
4 Have you got a garden or a balcony?

60 · 61

4A Lesson 2

Main Language Items		Resource File	Materials Needed
What's your telephone number? Do you live in ...? How many ...? Have you got ...?	Numbers 0-9	4 12	materials to make a telephone cassette/cassette player

Step 1 Make a telephone

a Using the words and pictures on page 49 of the CB as a guide, pupils each make their own telephone out of plastic cups and string.

b If insufficient materials are available, one or two telephones can be made as a whole class activity and used for role plays, etc.

c Encourage pupils to talk to one another in English down their completed telephones. (The telephones only work effectively when the string is pulled taut.)

d Pupils ask each other **'What's your telephone number?'** Explain that the number '0' is said like the letter 'O' in a telephone number, not 'zero' or 'nought'.

Step 2 Groupwork

a Ask pupils the following questions:
Do you live in a house or flat?
Have you got a garden/balcony?
How many rooms are there in your home?

b When pupils are familiar with the question forms, direct them to the grid on page 62 of their ABs. Copy the grid onto the blackboard. Select one pupil. Ask the above questions again. Write the answers in the grid.

c Then pupils ask each other similar questions using their telephones and fill in the grid in their ABs.

d Round up the exercise by asking pupils questions about other class members, e.g. **'Does *Maria* live in a house?'**

Step 3 Classwork (Survey)

a The aim of this survey is to find out how many pupils live in houses; how many pupils live in flats; how many homes have gardens and balconies; and how big pupils' homes are in terms of the number of bedrooms.

b Copy the three graphs on page 62 of the AB onto the blackboard. Ask for volunteers to record the answers on the board and others to count hands.

c Then ask the first question. Say **'Who lives in a house? Put up your hands if you live in a house.'** Pupils count the number of hands and the answer is recorded on the blackboard. Then ask **'Who lives in a flat? Put up your hands if you live in a flat.'** Again, count the hands and record the answer on the blackboard. (The total on the blackboard should be the same as the number of pupils in the class. If not, someone has either not raised their hand or has more than one home!)

d Repeat the above procedure for the other parts of the survey. Use the following questions and instructions:
Whose home has a garden? Put up your hand if you've got a garden.
Whose home has a balcony? Put up your hand if you've got a balcony.
How many bedrooms in your home? Put up your hand if there are *two* bedrooms.

e Encourage pupils to do all the arithmetic in English.

f When all the figures have been recorded on the blackboard direct pupils to the graphs on page 62 of the AB. Pupils transfer the figures into their books.

Homework

Pupils measure the rooms in their homes and record the answers in the AB on page 63 (measurements should be made in centimetres). One bedroom (preferably their own), plus the kitchen, bathroom and main living room will be sufficient.

Step 1

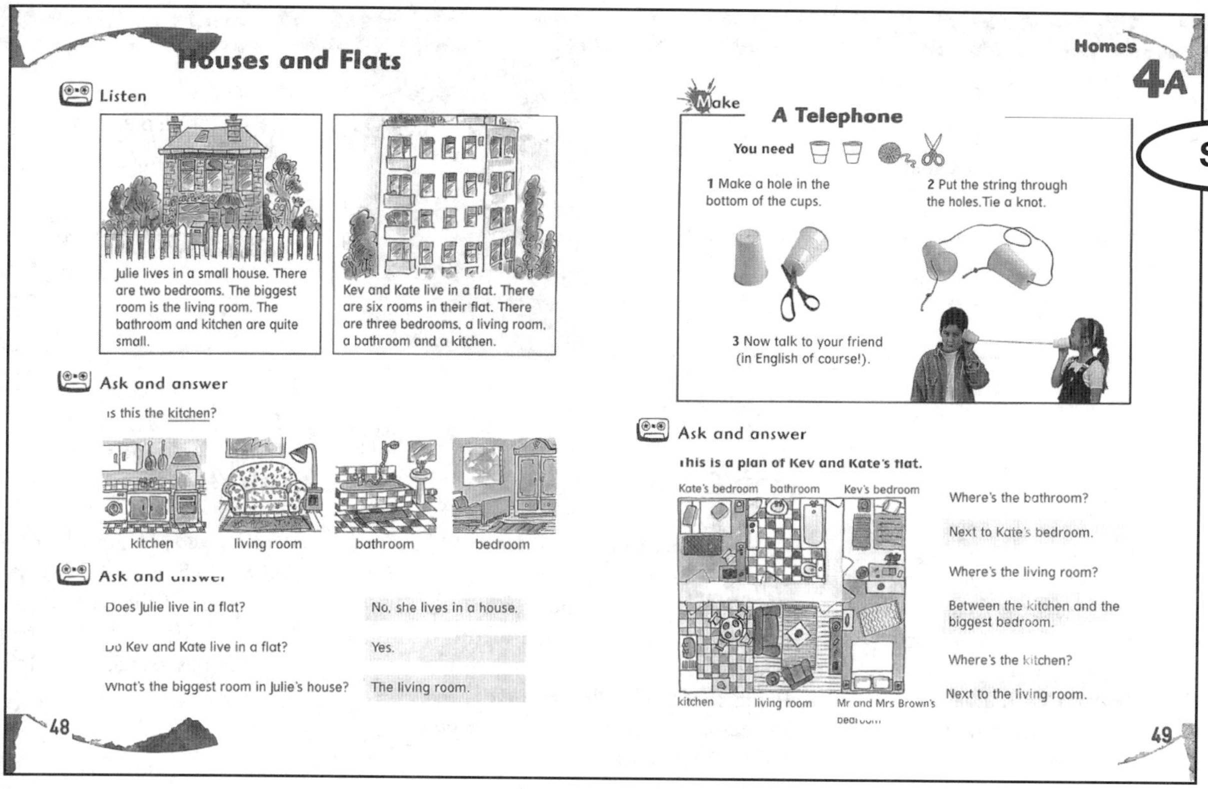

Houses and Flats

Homes 4A

Listen

Julie lives in a small house. There are two bedrooms. The biggest room is the living room. The bathroom and kitchen are quite small.

Kev and Kate live in a flat. There are six rooms in their flat. There are three bedrooms, a living room, a bathroom and a kitchen.

Ask and answer

Is this the kitchen?

kitchen | living room | bathroom | bedroom

Ask and answer

Does Julie live in a flat?	No, she lives in a house.
Do Kev and Kate live in a flat?	Yes.
What's the biggest room in Julie's house?	The living room.

Make

A Telephone

You need

1 Make a hole in the bottom of the cups.

2 Put the string through the holes. Tie a knot.

3 Now talk to your friend (in English of course!).

Ask and answer

This is a plan of Kev and Kate's flat.

Kate's bedroom | bathroom | Kev's bedroom | kitchen | living room | Mr and Mrs Brown's bedroom

Where's the bathroom?

Next to Kate's bedroom.

Where's the living room?

Between the kitchen and the biggest bedroom.

Where's the kitchen?

Next to the living room.

48 49

Step 2

Step 3

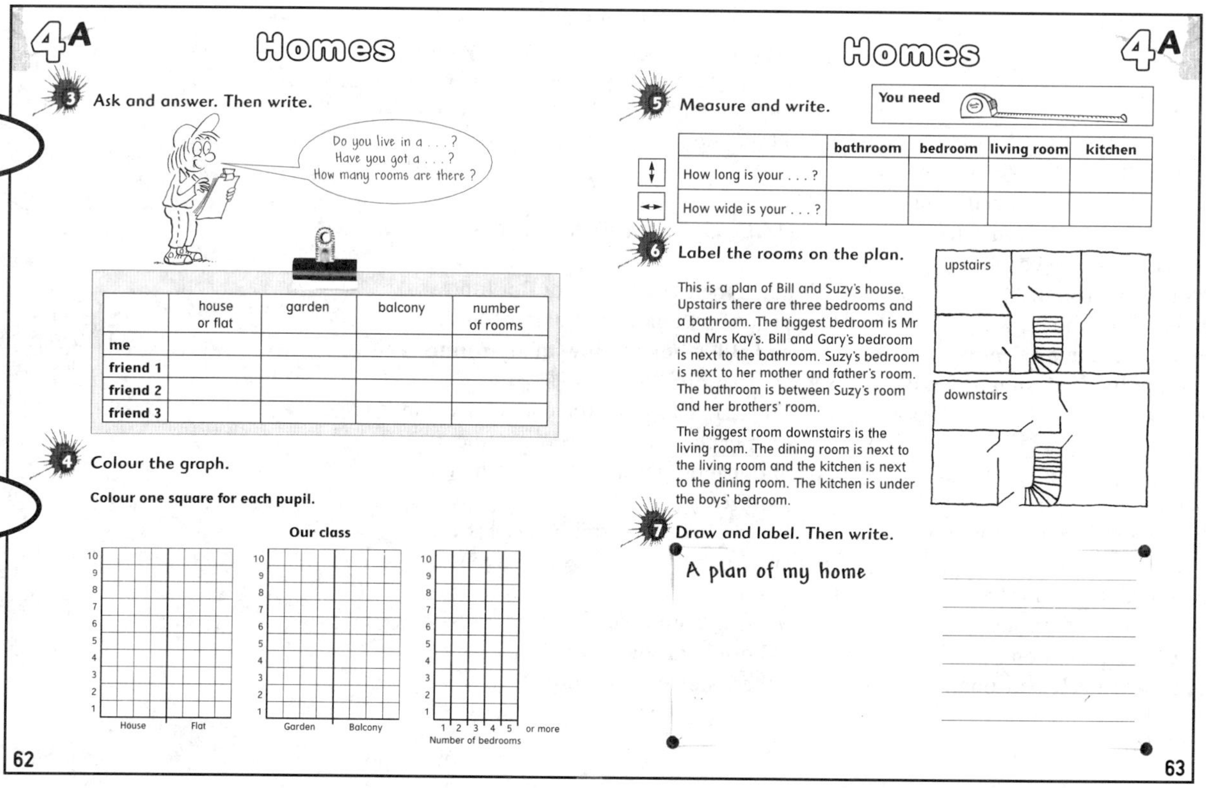

4A **Homes**

3 Ask and answer. Then write.

Do you live in a . . . ?
Have you got a . . . ?
How many rooms are there ?

	house or flat	garden	balcony	number of rooms
me				
friend 1				
friend 2				
friend 3				

4 Colour the graph.

Colour one square for each pupil.

Our class

House | Flat | Garden | Balcony | 1 2 3 4 5 or more Number of bedrooms

Homes 4A

5 Measure and write. You need

	bathroom	bedroom	living room	kitchen
How long is your . . . ?				
How wide is your . . . ?				

6 Label the rooms on the plan.

This is a plan of Bill and Suzy's house. Upstairs there are three bedrooms and a bathroom. The biggest bedroom is Mr and Mrs Kay's. Bill and Gary's bedroom is next to the bathroom. Suzy's bedroom is next to her mother and father's room. The bathroom is between Suzy's room and her brothers' room.

The biggest room downstairs is the living room. The dining room is next to the living room and the kitchen is next to the dining room. The kitchen is under the boys' bedroom.

upstairs | downstairs

7 Draw and label. Then write.

A plan of my home

62 63

4A Lesson 3

Main Language Items		Resource File	Materials Needed
Where's ...? Which is ...?	plan next to between	12 12a	paper for display (optional) coloured pencils cassette/cassette player

Step 1 Presentation

a Ask pupils about their homework, e.g. '*Maria*, **how long/wide is your bedroom?**'

b Then say '**Open your Coursebook at page 49. Look at the picture. This is a plan of Kev and Kate's flat.**' Reinforce the meaning of the word '**plan**'. (Draw a house and a plan on the blackboard. Ask pupils '**Which picture is a plan?**')

c Play the tape. Pupils look at the plan and listen.

Tapescript:

Kev and Kate live in a three-bedroomed flat with their mother and father. The smallest bedroom is Kev's. It's next to his mother and father's. Kate's bedroom is next to the bathroom. Mr and Mrs Brown have got the biggest bedroom. The living room is between the big bedroom and the kitchen.

d Then ask some questions to check comprehension.
How many rooms are there in Kev and Kate's flat?
How many bedrooms are there?
Which is the smallest room?
Which is the biggest room?
Who's got the biggest bedroom?

Step 2 Pairwork

a Divide the class into pairs, with only one book between each pair open at page 49. Say '**Cover the words on page 49. Look at the plan of the flat.**'

b Pupils repeat after the tape. P1 repeats the question, P2 answers. Repeat twice then change roles.

c Then pupils ask and answer the questions without the help of the tape. P1 uses the questions and answers on page 49 as prompts, P2 uses only the plan to help. Change roles and repeat.

d Pupils then ask similar questions about all the rooms in the flat.

Step 3 Label the rooms

a Say '**Open your Activity Book at page 63. Look at the plan of Suzy and Bill's house. How many rooms are there in the house?**'

b The task is to write the correct name in each of the rooms based upon the information given in the written passage.

c When pupils have finished check the answers by asking questions about the house:
Which room is this?
Whose bedroom is this?
Where's Suzy's bedroom? etc.

Step 4 Personal file

a Pupils draw a plan of their house/flat and label all the rooms. Write a brief description of the location and size of the rooms alongside. Use the model in the previous exercise to help.

Houses and Flats

Homes

4A

Listen

Julie lives in a small house. There are two bedrooms. The biggest room is the living room. The bathroom and kitchen are quite small.

Kev and Kate live in a flat. There are six rooms in their flat. There are three bedrooms, a living room, a bathroom and a kitchen.

Ask and answer

Is this the kitchen?

kitchen | living room | bathroom | bedroom

Ask and answer

Does Julie live in a flat?	No, she lives in a house.
Do Kev and Kate live in a flat?	Yes.
What's the biggest room in Julie's house?	The living room.

Make

A Telephone

You need

1 Make a hole in the bottom of the cups.

2 Put the string through the holes. Tie a knot.

3 Now talk to your friend (in English of course!).

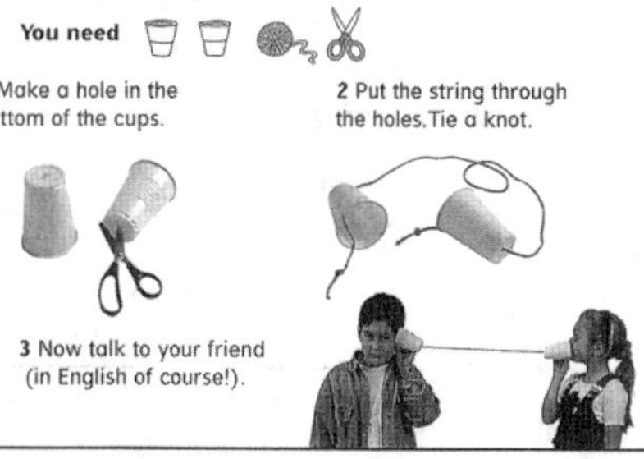

Ask and answer

This is a plan of Kev and Kate's flat.

Kate's bedroom
bathroom
Kev's bedroom
kitchen
living room
Mr and Mrs Brown's bedroom

Where's the bathroom?

Next to Kate's bedroom.

Where's the living room?

Between the kitchen and the biggest bedroom.

Where's the kitchen?

Next to the living room.

48 49

Step 1

Step 2

4A

Homes

3 Ask and answer. Then write.

Do you live in a . . . ?
Have you got a . . . ?
How many rooms are there ?

	house or flat	garden	balcony	number of rooms
me				
friend 1				
friend 2				
friend 3				

4 Colour the graph.

Colour one square for each pupil.

Our class

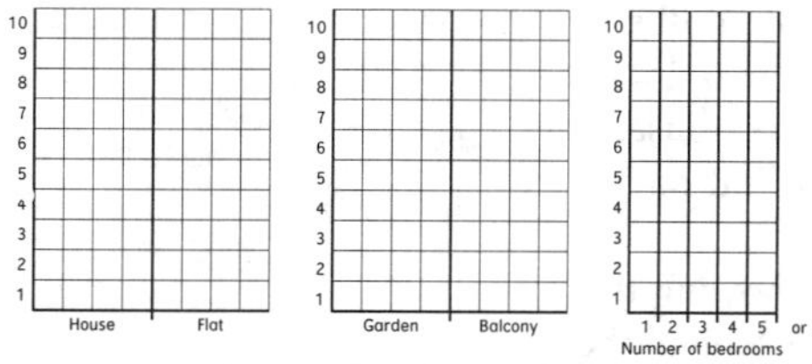

House
Flat
Garden
Balcony
or more
Number of bedrooms

62

Homes

4A

5 Measure and write.

You need

	bathroom	bedroom	living room	kitchen
How long is your . . . ?				
How wide is your . . . ?				

6 Label the rooms on the plan.

This is a plan of Bill and Suzy's house. Upstairs there are three bedrooms and a bathroom. The biggest bedroom is Mr and Mrs Kay's. Bill and Gary's bedroom is next to the bathroom. Suzy's bedroom is next to her mother and father's room. The bathroom is between Suzy's room and her brothers' room.

The biggest room downstairs is the living room. The dining room is next to the living room and the kitchen is next to the dining room. The kitchen is under the boys' bedroom.

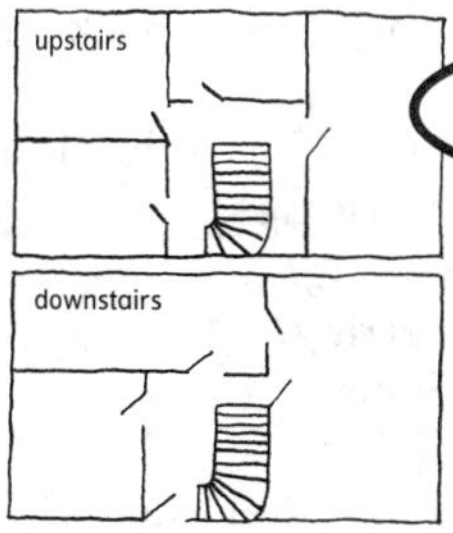

upstairs
downstairs

Step 3

7 Draw and label. Then write.

A plan of my home

Step 4

63

4B Lesson 1

Main Language Items		Resource File	Materials Needed
Prepositions: next to between under	upstairs downstairs sofa armchair cooker sink	17 26	cassette/cassette player

Step 1 Presentation

a Say **'Open your Coursebook at page 50 and look at the pictures.'** Ask a few questions to set the scene before pupils listen to the story: **'Who can you see in the pictures? Where are they?'** etc.
b Play the tape. Pupils listen and read at the same time.
c Then pupils listen again.
d Ask some questions to check comprehension:
Who's in the doll's house?
Which rooms does Wow go in?

Step 2 Pairwork

a Say **'Look at the pictures at the top of page 50.'** Hold up your book for the class.
b Ask pupils questions about the pictures:
What's this? What are these?
What's *Kev* wearing?
What's *Kate* wearing?
What's *Kate* doing?
What's *Wow* doing?
What colour is the doll's house?
c Divide the class into pairs. Pupils ask and answer as many questions as they can about the picture using a variety of question forms.
d Encourage pupils to help and prompt each other.

Step 3 Pairwork

a Pupils remain in pairs. Say **'Look at the pictures of Wow in the doll's house at the bottom of page 50. Cover the words.'**
b Pupils repeat after the tape. P1 repeats the questions, P2 answers. Repeat four times, changing roles.
c Then pupils ask and answer the questions without the help of the tape. P1 asks the questions using the words in the book to help, P2 answers using only the pictures. (Ensure pupils point at the appropriate picture when they ask the questions.)
d Change roles and repeat the procedure.
e Continue until pupils can ask and answer the questions without the help of the words.

Step 4 Write

a Pupils write answers to the questions on page 64 of the AB.

Step 5 Draw a line

a Say **'Look at the plan of the doll's house at the bottom of page 64. Wow is running around the house. Read the description and find out where he runs.'**
b The task is to draw a line showing the route Wow takes as he runs around the house.
c Go over the exercise with the whole class. Sketch the plan on the blackboard. Pupils take turns to say where Wow runs and draw one part of his route on the blackboard.

Step 1

Step 2

Step 3

Step 4

Step 5

Upstairs and Downstairs

Listen

Kate, Where's Wow?
He's in my doll's house.
I can't see him!
Look! He's upstairs, under the bed.
Quick! Get him!
Come here!
Too late. Now he's downstairs in the kitchen.

Ask and answer

Where's Wow?	Where's Wow?	Where's Wow?	Where's Wow?
Under the TV.	On the sofa.	Next to the armchair.	Between the sink and the cooker.

Listen to your friend

Which room is it?

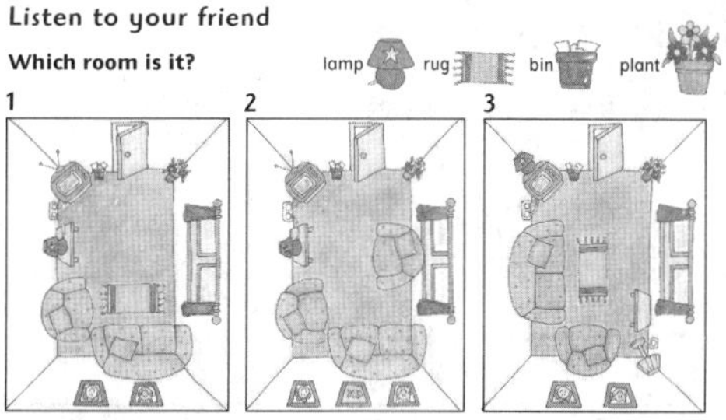
lamp
rug
bin
plant
1
2
3

BINGO

1 Write.

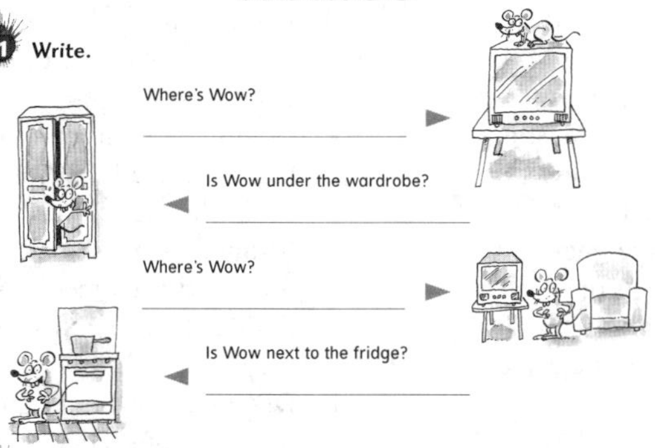

Where's Wow?

____

Is Wow under the wardrobe?

____

Where's Wow?

____

Is Wow next to the fridge?

____

2 Draw a line.

Where does Wow go?

Wow is sitting on the sofa in the living room. He stands up and runs to the television. He jumps onto the square table and then he runs to the armchair. He doesn't sit down.

Next he opens the door and goes into the kitchen. He runs to the big table and jumps onto it. Then he jumps onto the chair next to the sink and sits down.

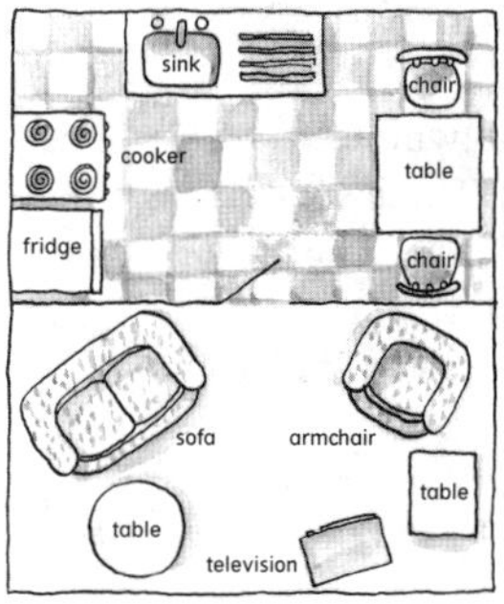
sink
chair
cooker
table
fridge
chair
sofa
armchair
table
table
television

3 Listen and colour.

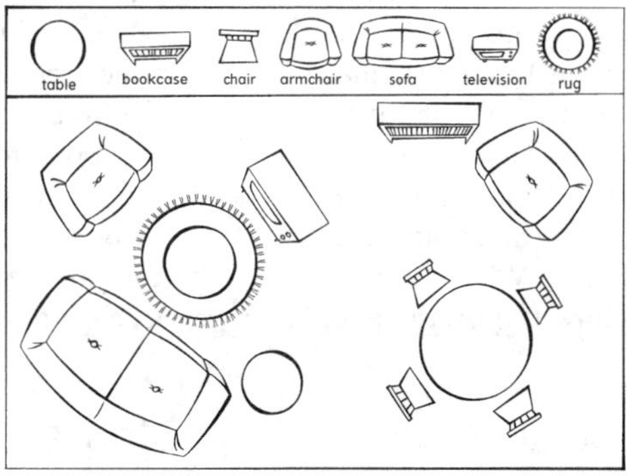
table
bookcase
chair
armchair
sofa
television
rug

4 Read to your friend.

Which room is it? Look at the plans on page 51 in your Coursebook.

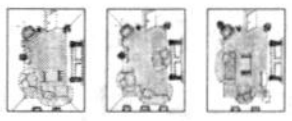

A

There's a sofa next to the wall and an armchair next to the sofa. Next to the armchair there's a small table. There's a lamp on the table. There's a rug on the floor next to the sofa and there are two pictures on the wall. There's a bin between the television and the door and a plant in the corner next to the door.

B

In this room there's a sofa, a table, an armchair, a rug and a television. There's a plant next to the door and two pictures on the wall. There's a small bin next to the television and a big rug between the table and the sofa. The table is next to the window and there's a big lamp on the floor next to the table.

4B Lesson 2

Main Language Items		Resource File	Materials Needed
Is the sofa by the door? There is/are ...	rug bin bookcase lamp plant	2 12	coloured pencils cassette/cassette player Bingo cover cards

Step 1 Listen and colour

a Say '**Open your Activity Book at page 65. Look at the plan of the living room.**' Point to one of the shapes in the picture. Ask pupils '**What's this?**'

b Then play the tape. Pupils colour the furniture in the plan.

Tapescript:

In the living room, there's a sofa and two armchairs. The sofa is red // and the armchair next to the sofa is blue. // The other armchair is red. // There are two tables. One is big and one is small. The small table is black // and the big table is brown. // The four chairs next to the table are green. // There's also a bookcase and a TV in the room. The bookcase is pink // and the TV is grey. // There is a yellow rug on the floor.

Step 2 Reading (Task)

a Divide the class into pairs. Say '**One pupil in each pair open your Coursebook at page 51. Look at the plans of the living rooms ... Now one pupil open your Activity Book at page 65. Do not show your partner your book.**'

b Ensure each pair have their books open at the correct pages before continuing.

c Then the pupil with the AB reads description A to their partner. The task is to determine which picture in the CB is being described.

d Change roles and repeat the procedure using description B.

Step 3 Listen to your friend

a This is a continuation of the Reading (Task) exercise in Step 2.

b Pupils remain in their pairs. Both pupils look at the three living room plans on page 51 of their CBs.

c P1 chooses one of the rooms and without telling his or her partner which room, describes the location of the furniture. P2 tries to guess which room is being described.

d P2 may ask yes/no type questions before coming to a decision, e.g. '**Is the sofa next to the door?**'

e Change roles and repeat the exercise.

Step 4 Make Bingo cards

a To play Bingo each pupil will need twelve small cover cards. These should be approximately 3cm x 3cm. They may be made from paper or thin card.

b Each card should have the word for the items of furniture (CB page 51) clearly printed on it.

Step 5 Bingo

a Instruct pupils to cover any six squares on their bingo card on page 51 of their CB by placing the appropriate cover card face down over the picture. Each pupil's card should now have six different pictures showing.

b The Bingo Caller (teacher) will also need a set of word cards. Shuffle your cards. Lay them face down in front of you. Ask '**Are you ready?**' Encourage pupil's to answer '**Yes**' or '**No**'.

c Select a card. Read the word.

d Pupils cover each furniture item that is called out with the cards face up (i.e. words showing).

e Continue calling until one of the pupils has covered all the squares on their card. The first player to do so shouts '**Bingo!**' He or she must confirm that their card is correct by reading back the words that are face up. If correct, they win.

f Divide the class into groups of 4–6 players. Pupils continue the game simultaneously in groups.

Upstairs and Downstairs

Listen

Kate, Where's Wow?
He's in my doll's house.
I can't see him!
Look! He's upstairs, under the bed.
Quick! Get him!
Come here!
Too late. Now he's downstairs in the kitchen.

Ask and answer

Where's Wow?	Where's Wow?	Where's Wow?	Where's Wow?
Under the TV.	On the sofa.	Next to the armchair.	Between the sink and the cooker.

Listen to your friend

Which room is it? lamp rug bin plant

Step 2

Step 3

1 2 3

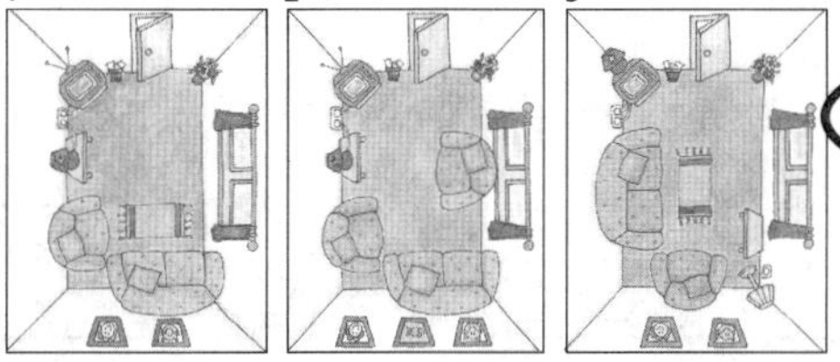

Step 5

BINGO

Homes

1 Write.

Where's Wow? ____________

Is Wow under the wardrobe? ____________

Where's Wow? ____________

Is Wow next to the fridge? ____________

2 Draw a line.

Where does Wow go?

Wow is sitting on the sofa in the living room. He stands up and runs to the television. He jumps onto the square table and then he runs to the armchair. He doesn't sit down.

Next he opens the door and goes into the kitchen. He runs to the big table and jumps onto it. Then he jumps onto the chair next to the sink and sits down.

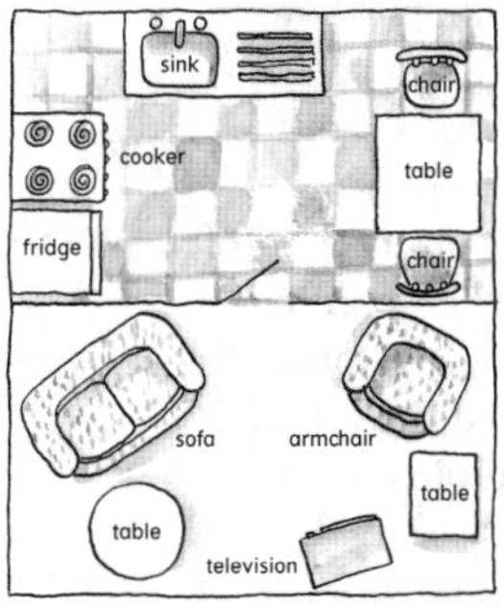

sink
chair
cooker
table
fridge
chair
sofa
armchair
table
table
television

Homes

3 Listen and colour.

Step 1

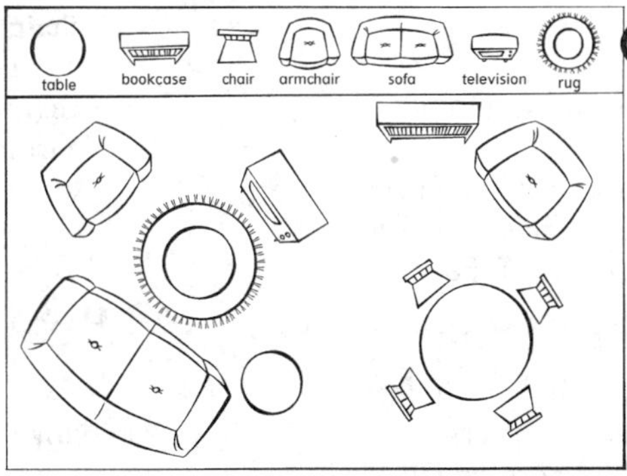

table
bookcase
chair
armchair
sofa
television
rug

4 Read to your friend.

Which room is it? Look at the plans on page 51 in your Coursebook.

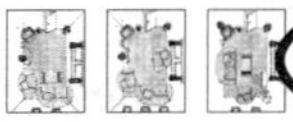

Step 2

A

There's a sofa next to the wall and an armchair next to the sofa. Next to the armchair there's a small table. There's a lamp on the table. There's a rug on the floor next to the sofa and there are two pictures on the wall. There's a bin between the television and the door and a plant in the corner next to the door.

B

In this room there's a sofa, a table, an armchair, a rug and a television. There's a plant next to the door and two pictures on the wall. There's a small bin next to the television and a big rug between the table and the sofa. The table is next to the window and there's a big lamp on the floor next to the table.

4B Lesson 3

Main Language Items		Resource File	Materials Needed
What's next to ...?	*Furniture items* (revision)	49 50 55	materials to make word stones furniture pieces (see AB cut-outs section) cassette/cassette player

Step 1 Make word stones

a Pupils add eight more word stones to their collection.

b Say **'Open your Activity Books at page 66.'** Point to the word stones. Check pupils are familiar with their meaning.

c To make the word stones, each pupil requires eight 'stones' (either real stones or stone-shaped pieces of card, as before). Pupils write one word on each stone in felt-tip pen as shown in the pictures.

d Pupils then store their stones for future use.

Step 2 Listening (Task)

Each pupil needs the 24 Furniture pieces from the cut-outs section and the baseboard picture of the room on page 63 of the CB.

a Pupils listen to the description and place the items of furniture in the appropriate place on the baseboard. After each complete description, pupils should compare their answers with their partners'.

b Ask pupils a few questions to check their finished picture. Use the structure **'Where's the ...?'**

Tapescript:

1 **The sofa is under the window // and the purple armchair is next to the sofa. // There's a picture on the wall by the door // and a rug on the floor. // The TV is on the rug.**

2 **– Let's put the sofa next to the door.**
– No, no. Let's put the TV next to the door.
– OK. We'll put the TV next to the door. // What about the table?
– Let's put that under the window. // And put the two chairs next to the table. //
– Fine. So the sofa goes there next to the big wall. And the purple armchair between the sofa and the table. Great!

Step 3 Read and put the furniture in the room

Pupils use the 24 Furniture pieces from the cut-outs section and the baseboard picture of the room on page 63 of the CB.

a Pupils read instruction A on page 66 of the AB and place the furniture in the appropriate place on their baseboard.

b When pupils have finished they should compare their completed picture with their partners'.

c Repeat the above procedure with instruction B.

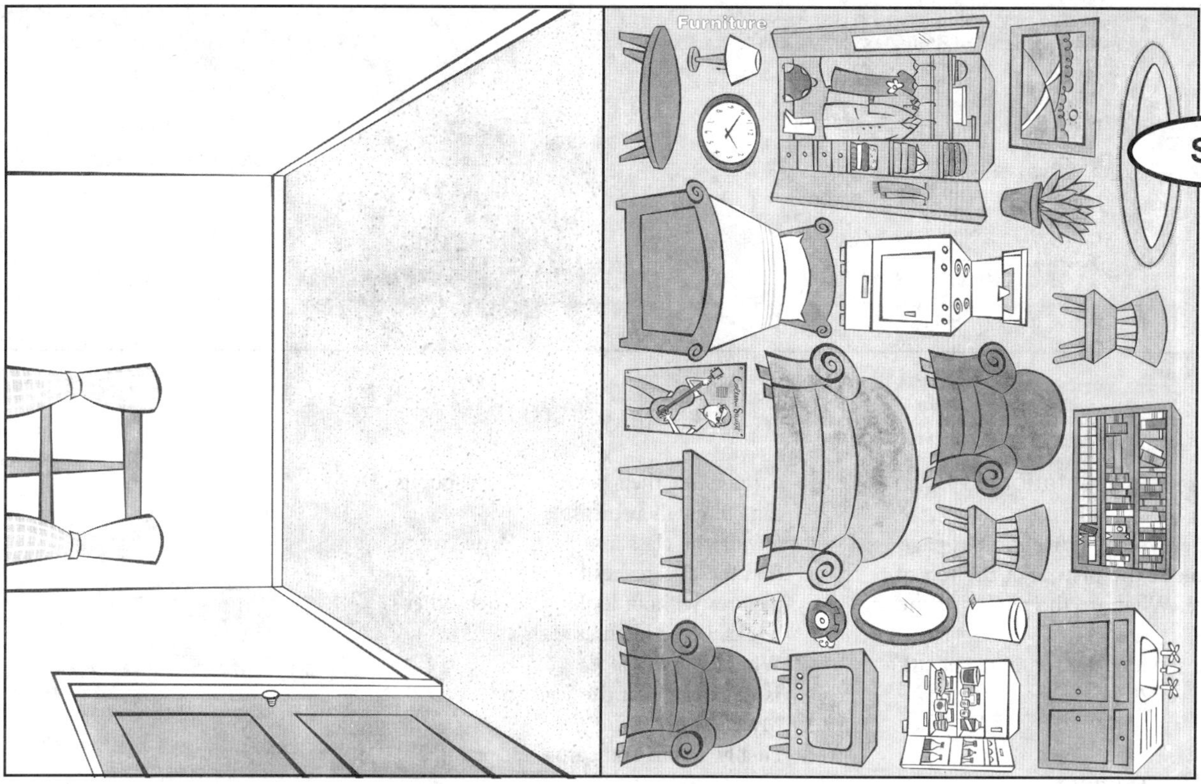
Furniture

Step 2

Step 1

Step 3

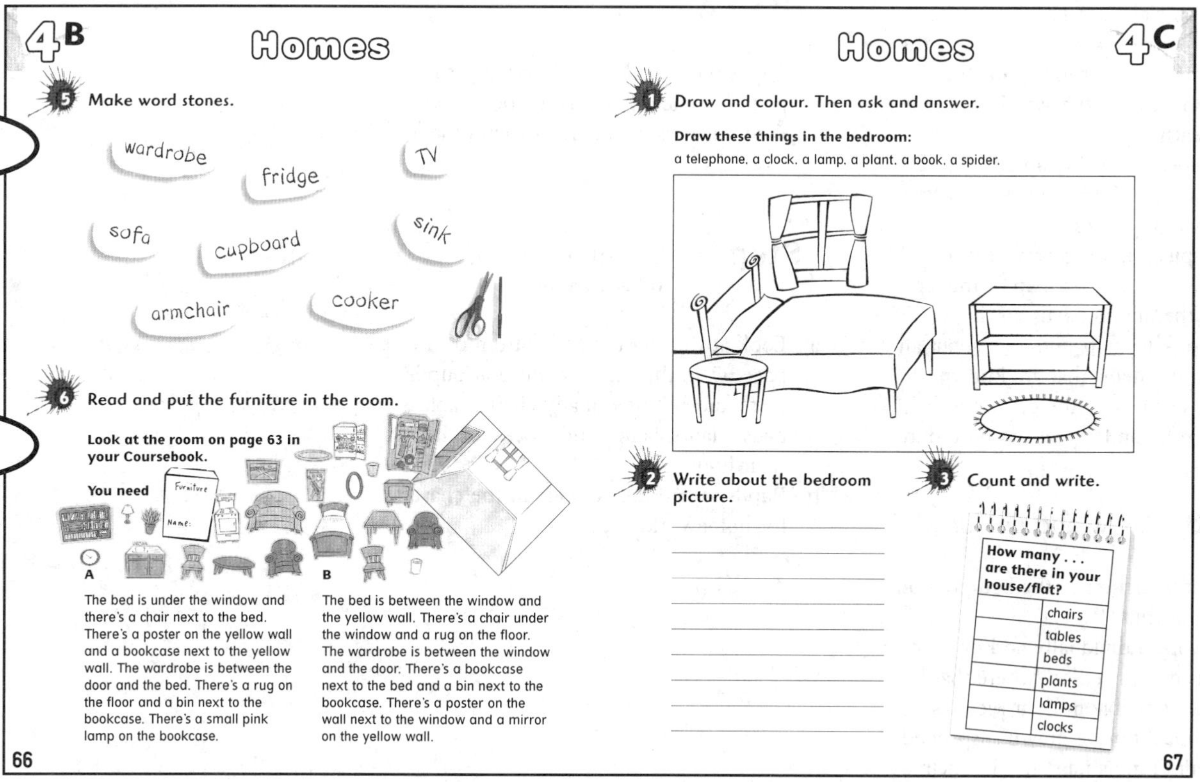

4B **Homes**

5 Make word stones.

wardrobe
fridge
TV
sofa
cupboard
sink
armchair
cooker

6 Read and put the furniture in the room.

Look at the room on page 63 in your Coursebook.

You need

Furniture
Name:

A

The bed is under the window and there's a chair next to the bed. There's a poster on the yellow wall and a bookcase next to the yellow wall. The wardrobe is between the door and the bed. There's a rug on the floor and a bin next to the bookcase. There's a small pink lamp on the bookcase.

B

The bed is between the window and the yellow wall. There's a chair under the window and a rug on the floor. The wardrobe is between the window and the door. There's a bookcase next to the bed and a bin next to the bookcase. There's a poster on the wall next to the window and a mirror on the yellow wall.

66

Homes **4C**

1 Draw and colour. Then ask and answer.

Draw these things in the bedroom:

a telephone, a clock, a lamp, a plant, a book, a spider.

2 Write about the bedroom picture.

3 Count and write.

How many ... are there in your house/flat?	
	chairs
	tables
	beds
	plants
	lamps
	clocks

67

4c Lesson 1

Main Language Items			Resource File	Materials Needed
upstairs my clock is on ...	clock toilet boat telephone bath	lamp plant book spider	3 3b	coloured pencils cassette/cassette player

Step 1 Presentation

a Say '**Open your Coursebook at page 52. Look at the picture at the top of the page. What are the names of the rooms?**'
b Point to some of the furniture and ask '**What's this?**'

Step 2 Pairwork

a Divide the class into pairs. All pairs work simultaneously. Say '**Look at the picture of the bedroom and the bathroom. Cover the words underneath.**'
b Pupils repeat after the tape. P1 repeats the questions, P2 answers. Repeat four times changing roles.
c Then pupils ask and answer the questions without the help of the tape. P1 asks the questions, using the words in the book to help, and asks about all the furniture items that are known. P2 answers, using only the picture to help.
d Change roles and repeat the procedure.

Step 3 Draw and colour

a Look at the picture of the bedroom on page 67 of the AB.
b Pupils work individually and draw the six items mentioned anywhere that is physically possible in their pictures, (objects must not be drawn suspended in mid-air.) Pupils must not let their partners see their pictures. Faster pupils can colour their pictures.
c Divide the class into pairs. Pupils try to find the differences between their pictures without looking at each other's books. Use structures such as:
Where's your *clock*?
Is your *clock* on the *bookcase*?
My *clock* is on the *floor*.
d Finally, pupils compare their pictures.

Step 4 Write

a Pupils write sentences describing their pictures. They then change books with their partners' and correct each other's work.

Step 5 Count and write (Homework)

a Look at the chart at the bottom of page 67 in the AB. Explain that pupils must find out how many chairs, tables, beds, plants, lamps and clocks are in their house/flat.
b Pupils record the answers in the chart for homework.

Step 1

Step 2

Rooms and Furniture

Ask and answer

This is the upstairs of a house.

What's on the table in the bedroom?

A telephone.

What's on the bookcase?

A clock.

What's next to the sink in the bathroom?

The toilet.

What's in the bath?

A boat.

Look and find

1. Find twelve things that you know. Write the words.
2. Find three things that you can't name in English. Draw pictures.
3. Find four 3-letter words. Write the words.
4. Find four things that you can wear. Draw them.

52

Homes

4C

Play

the House Game
bedroom
bathroom
start here
living room
kitchen

53

4B Homes

5 Make word stones.

wardrobe
fridge
TV
sofa
cupboard
sink
armchair
cooker

6 Read and put the furniture in the room.

Look at the room on page 63 in your Coursebook.

You need

Furniture
Name:

A

The bed is under the window and there's a chair next to the bed. There's a poster on the yellow wall and a bookcase next to the yellow wall. The wardrobe is between the door and the bed. There's a rug on the floor and a bin next to the bookcase. There's a small pink lamp on the bookcase.

B

The bed is between the window and the yellow wall. There's a chair under the window and a rug on the floor. The wardrobe is between the window and the door. There's a bookcase next to the bed and a bin next to the bookcase. There's a poster on the wall next to the window and a mirror on the yellow wall.

66

Homes **4C**

1 Draw and colour. Then ask and answer.

Draw these things in the bedroom:

a telephone, a clock, a lamp, a plant, a book, a spider.

Step 3

Step 4

2 Write about the bedroom picture.

3 Count and write.

Step 5

How many . . . are there in your house/flat?

	chairs
	tables
	beds
	plants
	lamps
	clocks

67

4c Lesson 2

Main Language Items		Resource File	Materials Needed
How many ...? Which room is it in? I've got ... I can't remember	*Furniture items (Revision)*	38 48 50	dice/counters

Step 1 Presentation

a Ask pupils questions about their homework, e.g. '*Maria*, **how many** ***chairs*** **are there in your home?**'

b Then play a game. Using the information gathered for homework, set up a chain-sentence around the class. One pupil begins and produces a sentence about any of the furniture in their list such as '**I've got ten *chairs*.**' The next pupil must add another phrase using the same structure and remembering the first pupil's phrase, e.g. '**I've got three *tables* and he/she's got *ten chairs*.**'

c Pupils continue building up the chain-sentence in this way until someone is unable to remember part of the sentence or makes a mistake. The game then begins again with the next pupil in sequence providing the opening sentence. Continue around the class.

d It may be useful to teach the phrase '**I can't remember.**'

Step 2 Look and find

a Direct pupils to the instructions under the picture of the bedroom and the bathroom on page 52 of the CB. The instructions direct pupils to look carefully at the picture and find specific things.

b Pupils work in pairs and complete the tasks in their exercise books.

c Finish the activity by checking if pairs have completed each task. Tell pupils the names of the objects that they do not know. The most likely words are **cup**, **pillow**, **poster**, **towel**, **toothbrush**, **shelf**, **shower** and **tap**. If any of the pupils know these words in English, they can tell their classmates.

Step 3 Write

a Say '**Look at the photos on page 68 of your Activity Book.**'

b Pupils work in pairs and try to determine the identity of the household objects in the six photos.

c Finish the exercise with the whole class. Ask pupils: '**What is it? Which room is it in?**' etc.
Answers: 1 A telephone, **2** A cooker, **3** Taps, **4** A clock, **5** Pillows, **6** An armchair

Step 4 Crossword

a Using the pictures as clues, pupils complete the crossword.

Step 5 The House Game

a This is a dice game to be played in groups of four, using counters, a dice and one CB open at page 53 for each group.

b Quickly revise the names of all the items in the game on page 53 of the CB. Say '**Point to a *sofa*. Point to a *clock*. Point to a *cooker*.**' etc. Pupils must point to the appropriate picture on the board. Then ask some questions regarding which rooms the objects are usually found in, e.g. '**Do you find *sofas* in the *bathroom*?**'

c Each player chooses one of the four rooms (**bathroom**, **bedroom**, **kitchen** or **living room**). All players place their counters on the centre square.

d Players take turns to throw the dice and move around the board the appropriate number of squares. Players may move in any direction. The aim is to collect items of furniture that can be found in their room. Each time pupils land on a square, the group must decide if this object/item of furniture is ever located in their room. If 'yes' then they write the name of the object in their exercise books. Each item may only be written once.

e When a player has collected six different items they must return to their room on the board. They must enter through the door. The first player to do so is the winner.

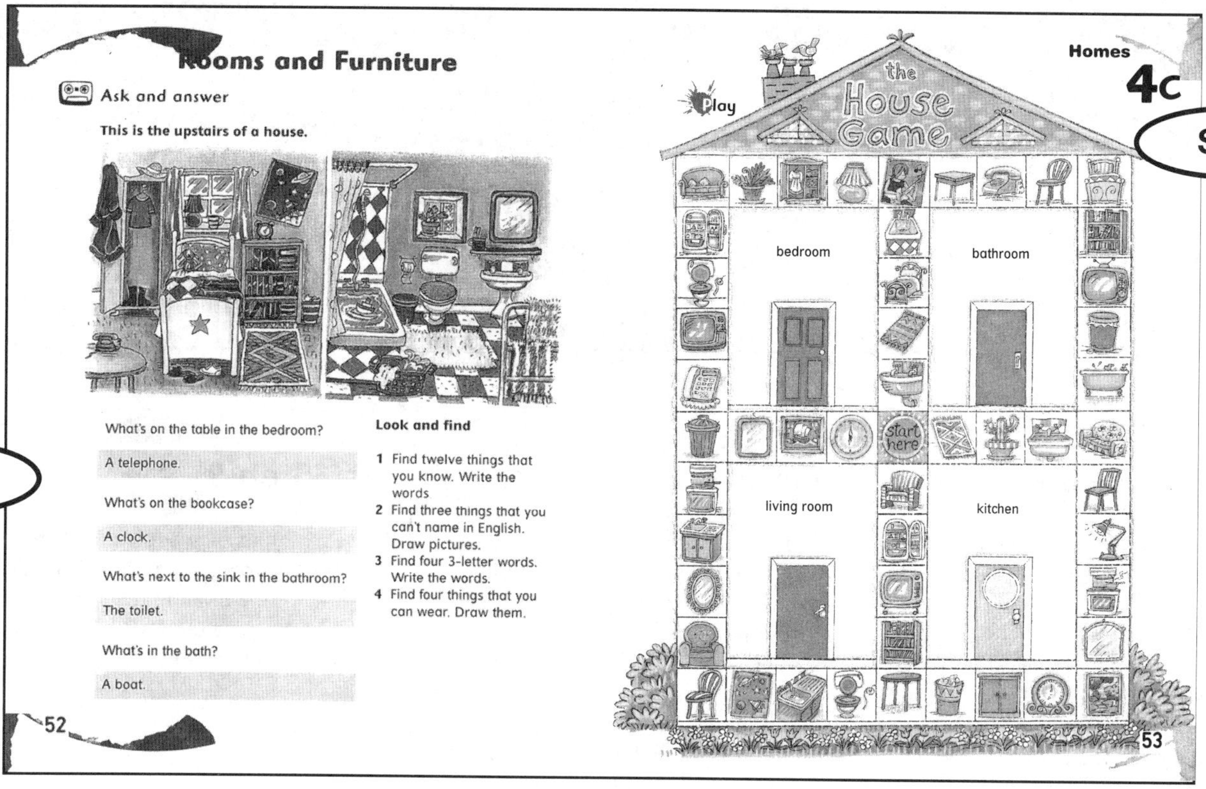

Rooms and Furniture

Ask and answer

This is the upstairs of a house.

What's on the table in the bedroom?

A telephone.

What's on the bookcase?

A clock.

What's next to the sink in the bathroom?

The toilet.

What's in the bath?

A boat.

Look and find

1 Find twelve things that you know. Write the words
2 Find three things that you can't name in English. Draw pictures.
3 Find four 3-letter words. Write the words.
4 Find four things that you can wear. Draw them.

52

Homes

4C

Play

the House Game
bedroom
bathroom
start here
living room
kitchen

53

Step 5

Step 2

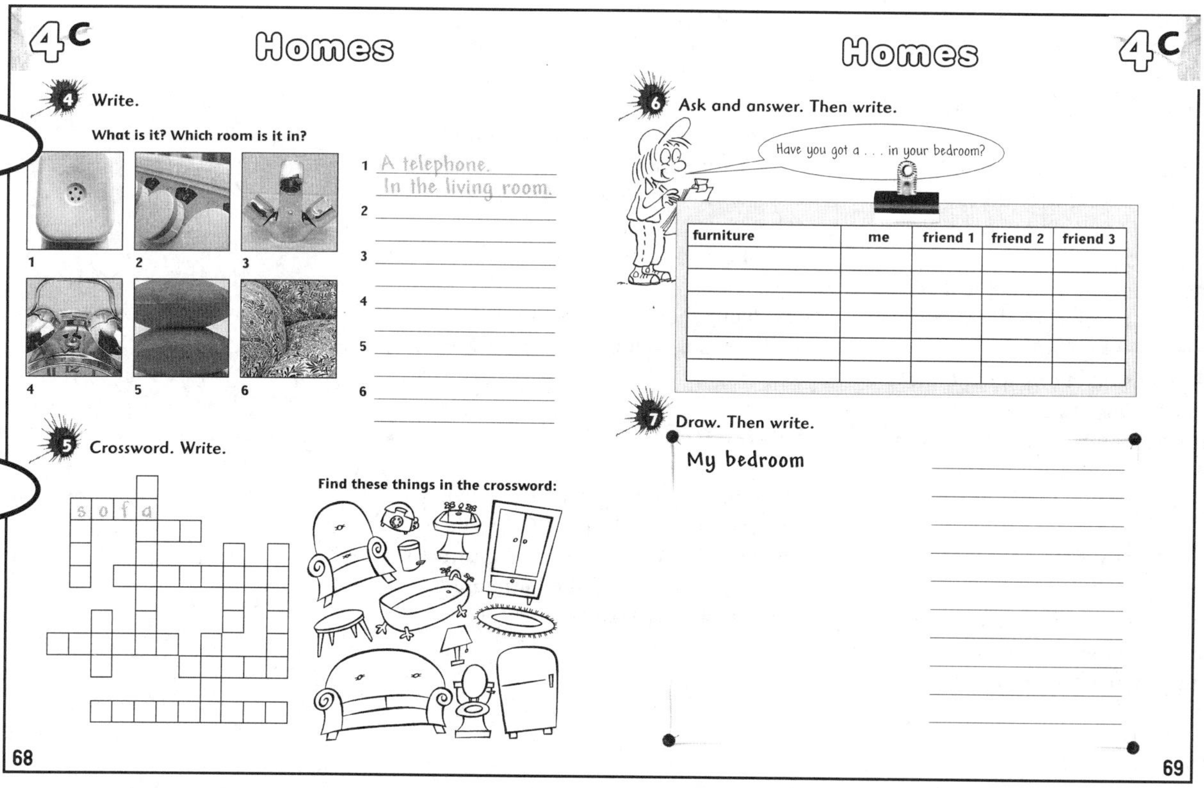

4C

Homes

4 Write.

What is it? Which room is it in?

1 A telephone. In the living room.
2
3
4
5
6

5 Crossword. Write.

Find these things in the crossword:

sofa

68

Homes

4C

6 Ask and answer. Then write.

Have you got a . . . in your bedroom?

furniture	me	friend 1	friend 2	friend 3

7 Draw. Then write.

My bedroom

69

Step 3

Step 4

4c Lesson 3

Main Language Items		Resource File	Materials Needed
Have you got ...? What's in your bedroom?	on under next to between	2 8 17	Furniture pieces (see AB cut-outs section) coloured pencils paper for display (optional)

Step 1 Groupwork

a Ask various pupils about the furniture in their bedrooms. Use the following question form: **'Have you got a ... in your bedroom?'**

b Then copy the chart on page 69 of the AB onto the blackboard. Select one pupil to write the name of any furniture item in the left-hand column of the grid and the names of four pupils along the top. If he or she chooses the word **'table'**, then ask the other pupils **'Have you got a table in your bedroom?'** and record the answers in the grid using ticks and crosses.

c Then all pupils work simultaneously in groups of four asking each other similar questions and filling in the charts.

d Each pupil chooses the furniture items that they want to ask about, so each pupil's chart will be different.

e Then ask pupils questions about other class members, e.g. **'Has *Alex* got a *sofa* in his bedroom? What has *Maria* got in her bedroom?'**

Step 2 Pairwork

Each pupil needs the Furniture pieces from the cut-outs section and the baseboard picture of the room on page 63 of the CB.

a Quickly revise the names of the furniture, instructing pupils to **'Pick up the *sofa*.'** etc.

b One pupil places various furniture pieces on his or her baseboard. Then using the structures:
There is a ... on/under/next to/between the ... or **The ... is on/under/next to/between the ...**, he or she describes the picture. The other pupil must try to reconstruct an identical picture following the instructions.

c The second pupil may ask questions in English to help if necessary, e.g.
Where's your *armchair*?
Where's the *sofa* in your picture?
What's *next to* the *bed*?
After each complete description pupils should compare their pictures.

d Then change roles and repeat the exercise.

NOTE Pupils should only use the furniture items they can name at this stage.

Optional

One pupil describes one of the living rooms on page 51 of the CB to their partner. The other tries to reconstruct a similar picture using the Furniture pieces and baseboard picture of the room.

Step 3 Personal file

a Pupils draw a picture of their own bedroom and write a brief description of the room in the space provided on AB page 69. Use the models on page 66 of the AB to help.

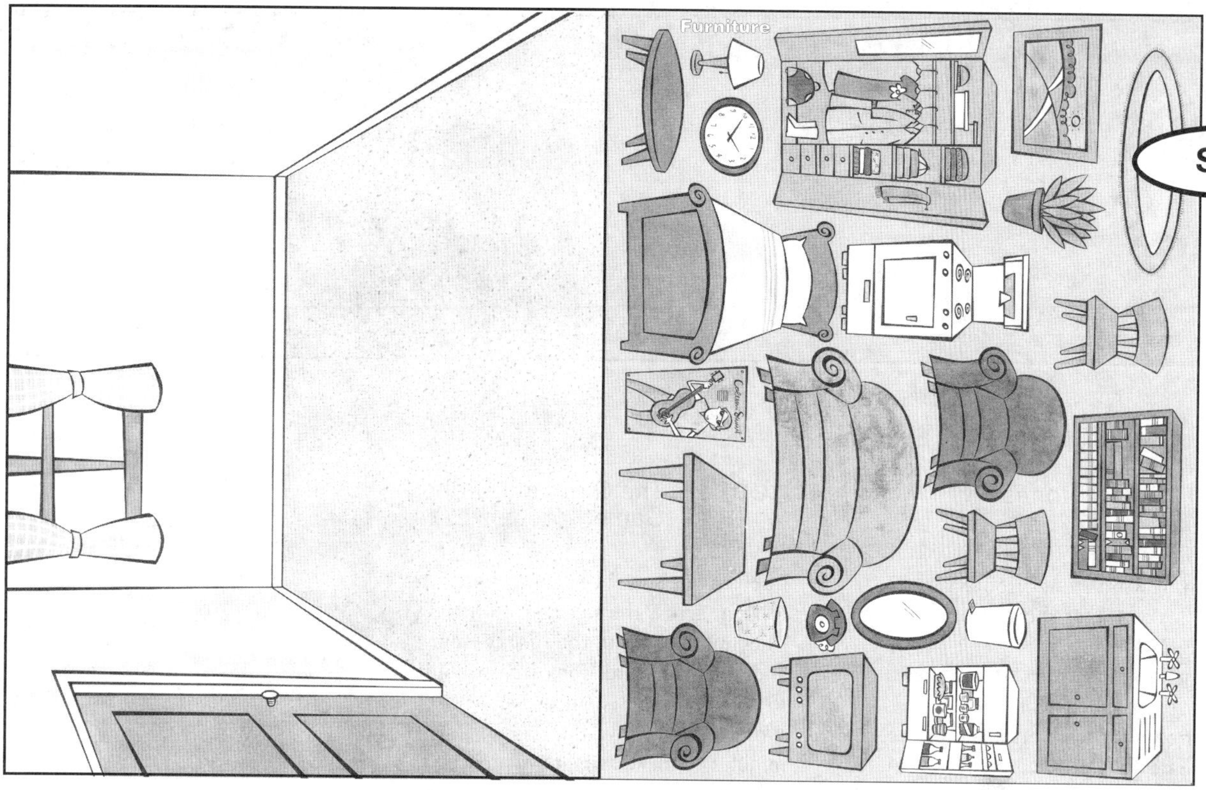
Furniture

Step 2

4C Homes

4 Write.

What is it? Which room is it in?

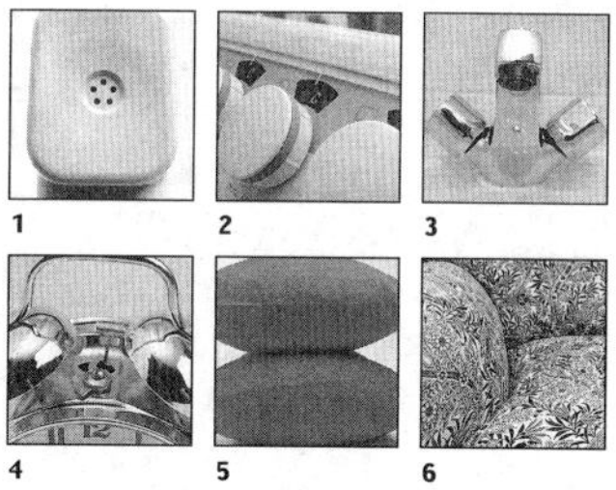
1
2
3
4
5
6

1 A telephone.
In the living room.

2

3

4

5

6

5 Crossword. Write.

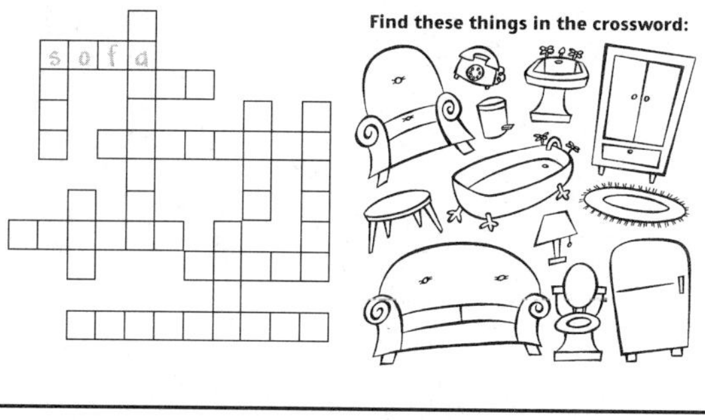
s o f a
Find these things in the crossword:

Homes 4C

6 Ask and answer. Then write.

Step 1

Have you got a . . . in your bedroom?

furniture	me	friend 1	friend 2	friend 3

7 Draw. Then write.

Step 3

My bedroom

4D Lesson 1

Main Language Items	Resource File	Materials Needed
Revision	17 25	word stone collection cassette/cassette player

Step 1 Word stones

a Each pupil needs their complete collection of word stones from NEW STEPPING STONES 2, as shown on page 54 of the CB.
b Divide the class into pairs. Pupils then play games with their word stones.
c Each pair chooses ten stones and places them face down. P1 turns over one stone and says the word. P2 turns over another stone and tries to make a sentence including both stones. P1 then turns over another stone and tries to make a sentence including all three stones. Repeat the procedure until all ten stones are face up.
d Pupils then store their stones for future use.

Step 2 Listen and match

a Say '**Open your Activity Book at page 70.**' Point to the phrases and pictures.
b Play the tape, one phrase at a time. Pupils listen and draw a line to match the phrase and picture.
c Play the tape again, pausing for pupils to repeat.
d Play the tape again. Pupils repeat the phrases as quickly as they can.
e Pupils practise saying the phrases as quickly as they can.
f Ask volunteers to say the phrases as fast as they can in front of the class.

Step 3 The Stepping Stones Game

a Pupils make sentences going from left to right across the stepping stones. They must begin in the first column and take one word from each column to make correct sentences.
b Work in pairs. Give the class ten minutes to make as many sentences as possible from the words on the stones.
c Check the answers with the whole class. The pair to get the most correct sentences are the winners.

tep 1

tep 3

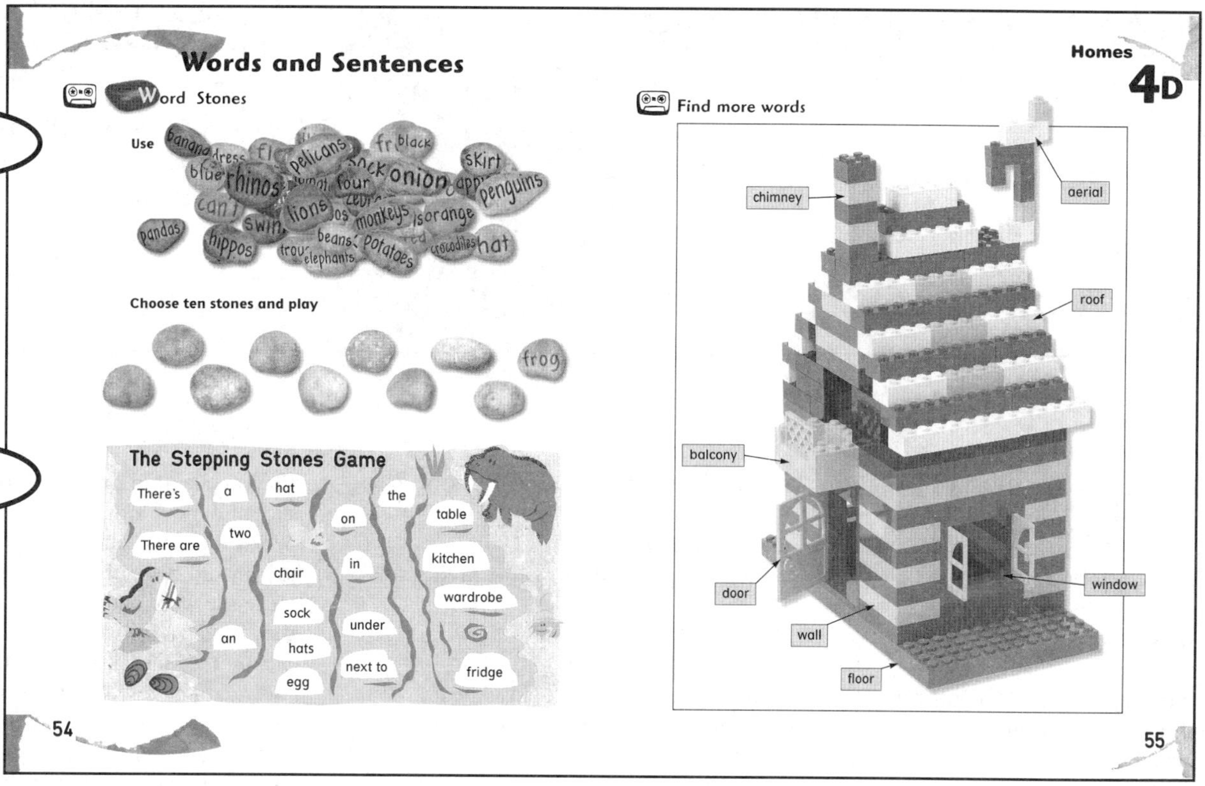
Words and Sentences

Word Stones

Use

banana dress pelicans black skirt blue rhinos sock onion four penguins lions monkeys orange pandas hippos beans potatoes crocodiles hat elephants

Choose ten stones and play

frog

The Stepping Stones Game

There's a hat the table There are two on chair in kitchen wardrobe sock under an hats next to egg fridge

54

Homes

4D

Find more words

chimney aerial roof balcony door window wall floor

55

tep 5

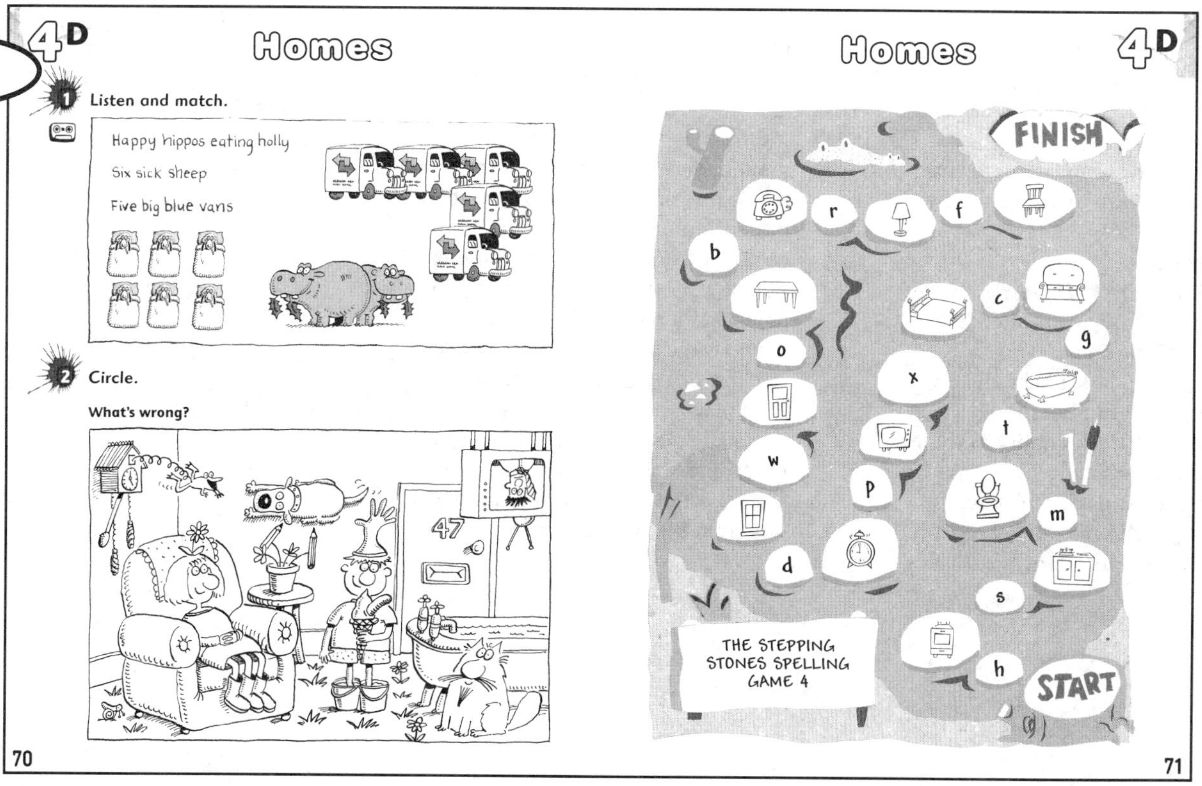
4D Homes

1 Listen and match.

Happy hippos eating holly

Six sick sheep

Five big blue vans

2 Circle.

What's wrong?

47

70

Homes 4D

FINISH

r f b c g o x t w p m d s h START

THE STEPPING STONES SPELLING GAME 4

71

4D Lesson 2

Main Language Items		Resource File	Materials Needed
Your turn/my turn What's your colour?	*Homes (Revision)*	26	Story strips 4 (see AB cut-outs section) scissors (optional) cassette/cassette player dice/counters

Step 1 Jigsaw Reading/ Listening

a Play the introductory story again. Pupils listen.

b The cut-outs 'Story strips 4' in the centre of the AB form the text to the introductory story on page 46 of the CB. Pupils should cut them out and jumble them up.

c Pupils then try to put their story strips in the correct order, without looking at their CB.

d When pupils have finished the jigsaw reading task, they should look at the pictures on page 46 of their CB to check the order.

e Finally, play the complete story again on tape to confirm the correct order.

Tapescript:

In a Dark, Dark Wood ...
In a dark, dark wood there's
A dark, dark house.
In the dark, dark house there's
A dark, dark cupboard.
In the dark, dark cupboard there's
A dark, dark shelf.
On the dark, dark shelf there's
A dark, dark box.
And in the dark, dark box there's
A ...

Step 2 Circle. What's wrong?

a Say '**Look at the picture at the bottom of page 70 in your Activity Book.**'

b Pupils circle all the mistakes they can find in the living room.

c Write the mistakes on the blackboard. Ask pupils to tell you what they have found, e.g. '**There's a frog in the clock.**' etc.

Step 3 The Stepping Stones Spelling Game 4

a Ideally this game should be played in groups. Each group needs one copy of the board game on AB page 71 and a dice. (If no dice is available, the numbers 1–6 can be written on each side of a six-sided pencil.) Each group nominates a referee. The referee's job is to check the answers and adjudicate. The rest of the group are the players. Each player needs a coloured counter (or small coloured piece of paper), a pencil and a sheet of paper.

b The object of the game is to make your way from the start to the finish.

c Players take it in turns to throw the dice and move around the board. When they land on a letter, they must say a word beginning with that letter, write the word and say each letter as they write. When they land on a picture they must say the word, write the word and say each letter as they write.

d Encourage pupils to use English as they play. They should count in English and use phrases such as '**Your/My turn**'.

e In addition, ask pupils questions about the game as your monitor their progress, e.g. '**Is it your turn?**', '**What's your colour?**'

Step 1

4 Homes
STORY
In a Dark, Dark Wood
In a dark, dark wood there's a dark, dark house.
In the dark, dark house there's a dark, dark cupboard.
In the dark, dark cupboard there's a dark, dark shelf.
On the dark, dark shelf there's a dark, dark box.
And in the dark, dark box there's a ...
46
47

Step 2

Step 3

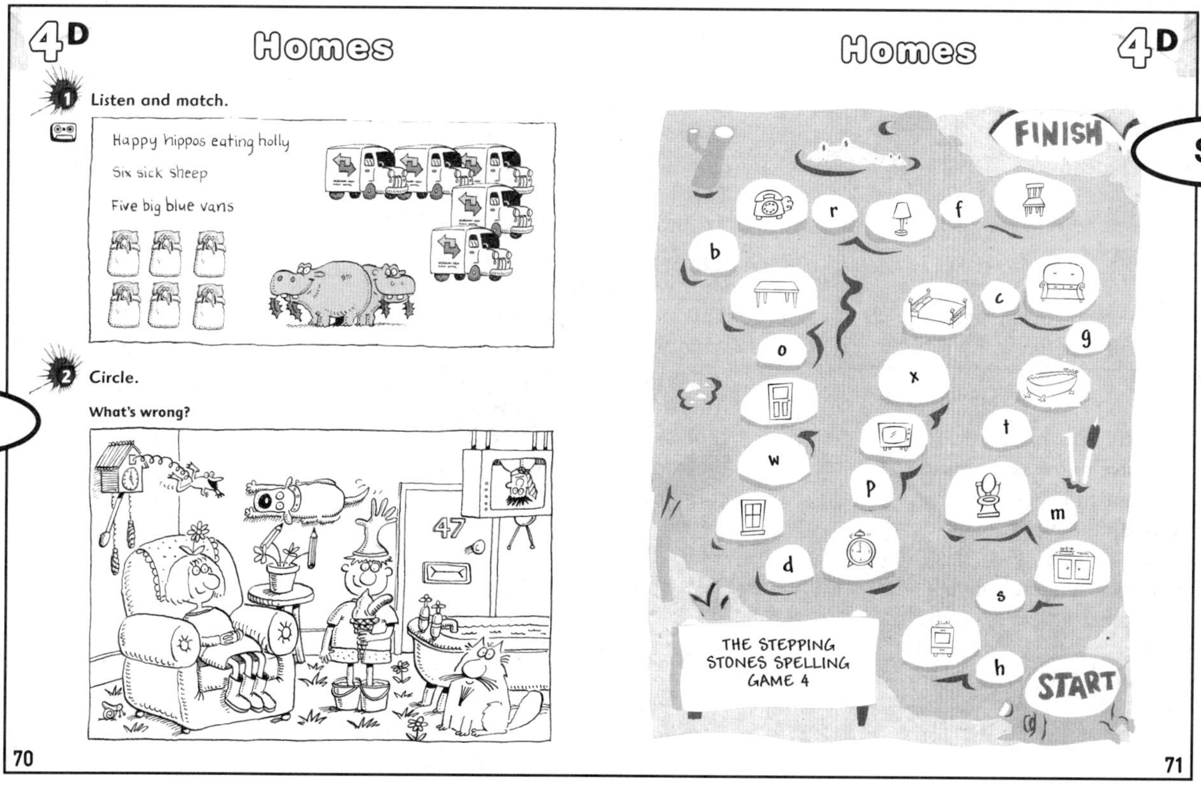

4D
Homes
1 Listen and match.
Happy hippos eating holly
Six sick sheep
Five big blue vans
2 Circle.
What's wrong?
47
70
Homes
4D
FINISH
r
f
b
c
g
o
x
t
w
p
m
d
s
h
THE STEPPING STONES SPELLING GAME 4
START
71

4D Lesson 3

Main Language Items		Resource File	Materials Needed
chimney roof aerial wall door floor	window balcony	38	cassette/cassette player

Step 1 Find more words

a Say **'Open your Coursebook at page 55 and look at the photo'**. Ask pupils in their L1 what they can see. Can they name anything in English?
b Play the tape and listen to the words while looking at the picture.
c Play the tape again. This time pupils point to the appropriate item as they hear the word.
d Play the tape again. Pupils listen and repeat the words.

Tapescript:
chimney // roof // aerial // wall // door // floor // window // balcony

Step 2 Games

a Spell the name of one of the items e.g. 'R-O-O-F'. Pupils say the word **'roof'**. Repeat with other features.
b Stand at the front, clearly visible to the class, and silently 'say' one of the items. Pupils have to guess the word using the movement of your lips as their cue and say the word aloud. Repeat with other items.
c Ask **'What's this?'** and indicate the appropriate number of letters on the blackboard, e.g. _ _ _ _ _ _ _. Pupils say the word **(chimney)**. Repeat with other items.

Step 3 Listen and draw

a Tell pupils to open their Activity Books at page 72.
b Explain that they will hear three descriptions of three different houses on the tape and they must draw the relevant house in each empty box.
c Play the tape while pupils listen.
d Play the tape again, pausing as necessary for pupils to draw the houses.

Tapescript:
1 **Draw a roof on the house. // Draw two doors // and six windows. // Draw two chimneys // and an aerial. //**
2 **This house has got one door // and three windows. // On the roof there is a chimney // and two aerials. //**
3 **This house has got four windows // and two doors. // It has got a very big roof. // And there is a window in the roof. // There is an aerial on the roof // but there isn't a chimney. //**

Step 4 Find the 12 words

a Pupils circle the words they find in the wordsquare on AB page 72 and tick them on the list.

Optional

a Pupils make a list in their exercise books of all the furniture items in their living rooms at home.
b Ask pupils **'What's in your living room? How many chairs are there in your living room? What colour's the sofa?'** etc.

Optional

a Pupils draw a plan of their living room and label all the furniture.
b Ask pupils questions, e.g. **'Where's your TV?'** etc.

Words and Sentences

Word Stones

Use

banana
dress
pelicans
black
skirt
blue
rhinos
four
onion
penguins
lions
monkeys
orange
pandas
hippos
beans
potatoes
crocodiles
hat
elephants

Choose ten stones and play

frog

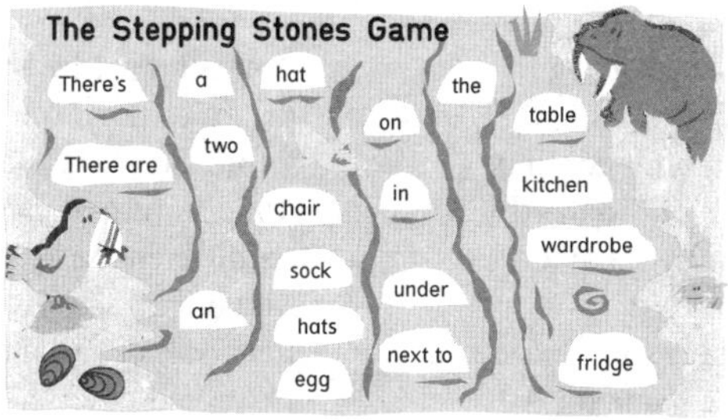
The Stepping Stones Game
There's
a
hat
the
on
table
There are
two
chair
in
kitchen
wardrobe
sock
under
an
hats
next to
fridge
egg

Find more words

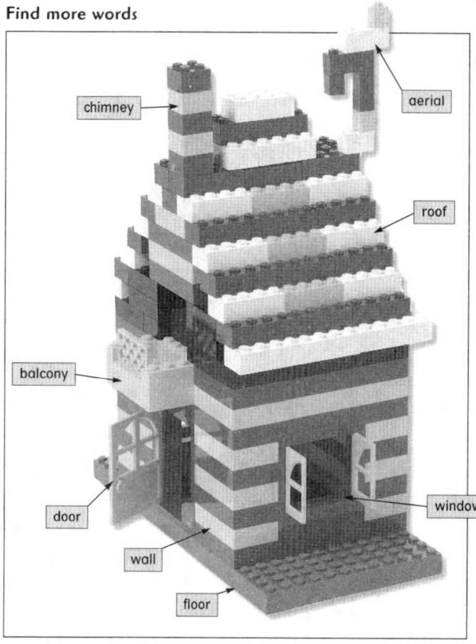
chimney
aerial
roof
balcony
window
door
wall
floor

Step 1

Step 3

3 Listen and draw.

1 2 3

Step 4

4 Find the 12 words. Look → ↓

aerial ✓
balcony
bathroom
bedroom
chimney
door
floor
kitchen
living room
roof
wall
window

l	i	v	i	n	g	r	o	o	m
i	k	i	t	d	o	b	l	a	b
w	i	n	d	o	w	e	i	e	a
a	t	c	h	o	a	b	v	r	t
l	c	i	v	r	o	o	f	i	h
l	h	k	i	n	l	f	l	a	r
b	e	a	l	t	h	r	o	l	o
w	n	b	e	d	r	o	o	m	o
c	h	i	m	n	e	y	r	o	m
y	n	b	a	l	c	o	n	y	y

1 Play the game.

You need

Throw the dice and draw.

1 Throw a 6 to start. Draw the floor and walls.

2 Throw the dice again. You need a door (⚂), four windows (4 x ⚄), a roof (⚁), a chimney (⚄) and an aerial (⚀).

4E Lesson 1 - Project

Main Language Items	Resource File	Materials Needed
Classroom furniture (Revision) door window roof chimney aerial wall		project materials dice scissors coloured paper

Step 1 Write

a Pupils make a list in their exercise books of all the furniture items in their classroom.

b Ask pupils '**What's in the classroom? How many chairs are there?**' etc.

Step 2 Draw

a Pupils draw a plan of their classroom and label all the furniture.

b Ask pupils questions, e.g. '**Where's the table?**' etc.

Step 3 Play the game

a In groups, pupils must throw the dice to draw the parts of the house. Each number on the dice represents a different part of the house (see AB page 73).

b One pupil in the group must now throw a six to start. The pupil who throws a six can draw the floor and walls.

c The game continues in each group with each pupil throwing the dice until they have drawn all the parts of the house.

Step 4 Start a project

a Tell the pupils they are going continue their work on the theme of 'homes' by creating houses of their own. Divide the class into small groups.

b CB page 56 shows an idea for a basic dice game, similar to the game on AB page 73, in which the players construct a house by throwing a dice. Pupils can make this in a two-dimensional version, shown at the bottom of the page, or in a 3-D version, which slots together as shown in the upper part of the photo.

c Help groups to organise who does what. Rather than making door and windows out of coloured paper, pupils may like to draw the door and window pieces themselves, adding doorknobs, letterboxes, window boxes, etc.

d Alternatively, a more elaborate project idea continues the idea of construction, but without the dice-throwing element. Again, the class work in small groups.

e Each group will have to think of a character in fiction and design the appropriate house for it. Their character's name must be kept secret because once the houses are ready, their classmates will have to guess who the inhabitant might be.

f The projects could involve:
• drawing fairly detailed plans of the house, including some measurements and furniture.
• making a 3-D model out of cardboard and other materials.
• explaining why the house is suitable for the character in question.

g Before they start, sit down with each group in turn and help pupils organise the different tasks and materials so that everyone is actively involved. Remind them that once they have completed the project, they will have to describe their house to the class and have their classmates try to guess who might live there. Make sure they have the necessary English vocabulary for both the materials they use and the parts of the house they construct. After they have shown their houses to the class, ask them to prepare a wall display with explanatory bubbles and a descriptive sentence or two.

h Encourage pupils to do some research on this project and to continue the work outside their English class.

Step 4

START A PROJECT

5
2
3
4
1
6
= aerial
= door
= roof
= chimney
= window
= wall

56

Homes

4E

SUPERSNAKE
Once upon a time there were three little worms.
The first little worm lived in a house made of grass.
The second little worm lived in a house made of matchsticks.
The third little worm lived in a house made of Lego bricks.
One day along came a big bad rat.
He blew down the house made of grass.
He blew down the house made of matchsticks.
And he knocked down the house made of Lego bricks.
Dinner time!
HELP!
Stop!
"Dinner time!" said the rat.
"Help!" screamed the worms.
"Stop!" shouted Supersnake.
Aagh!
Hurray!
Ha, ha!
The rat screamed. The worms cheered.
Supersnake laughed and put the rat in a house made of metal.

57

4D Homes

3 Listen and draw.

1 2 3

4 Find the 12 words. Look ↓

aerial	✓
balcony	
bathroom	
bedroom	
chimney	
door	
floor	
kitchen	
living room	
roof	
wall	
window	

l	i	v	i	n	g	r	o	o	m
i	k	i	t	d	o	b	l	a	b
w	i	n	d	o	w	e	i	e	a
a	t	c	h	o	a	b	v	r	t
l	c	i	v	r	o	o	f	i	h
l	h	k	i	n	l	f	l	a	r
b	e	a	l	t	h	r	o	l	o
w	n	b	e	d	r	o	o	m	o
c	h	i	m	n	e	y	r	o	m
y	n	b	a	l	c	o	n	y	y

72

Homes 4E

Step 3

1 Play the game.

You need

Throw the dice and draw.

1 Throw a 6 to start. Draw the floor and walls.

2 Throw the dice again. You need a door (⚀), four windows (4 x ⚄), a roof (⚂), a chimney (⚃) and an aerial (⚀).

73

4E Lesson 2 - Evaluation

Main Language Items			Resource File	Materials Needed
Prepositions	grass	screamed		
Once upon a time ...	matchsticks	shouted		test cards 4E (see photocopy master on TG p.175)
lived	lego	cheered		scissors (optional)
made of	metal	laughed		cassette/cassette player
first	blew down ...			
second	knocked down			
third				

Step 1 Listen and number

a Look at the pictures at the top of page 74 of the AB. There is a short dialogue or sentence about each of the pictures on the tape. Pupils must decide which dialogue or sentence refers to which picture and write the appropriate numbers in the boxes under the pictures.

b Number 1 is given as an example. Play each one three times.

Tapescript:

1 **Where's Sam? He's under the table.**
2 **Where's Wow? Next to the TV.**
3 **What's Wow doing? He's eating a biscuit.**
4 **There are two socks under the table.**
5 **Where's Wow? He's on the table.**
6 **Wow is between the chair and the cooker.**
7 **Where are the socks? Under the chair.**
8 **What's Wow eating? Cake.**
9 **Where's the chair? It's next to the cooker.**
10 **Where's Wow? He's under the table.**

Step 2 Write (Test)

a Working individually, pupils look at the pictures and write an appropriate sentence for each picture on a sheet of paper.

b The tests are designed to test communication as much as accuracy. Marks should be given for answers which are comprehensible and appropriate.

Step 3 Write

a Working individually, pupils read the passage, look at the picture and complete the passage with the appropriate words.

Step 4 Test yourself

a Photocopy one set of test cards 4E for each pupil (see photocopy master on TG page 175).

b Say **'Open your Activity Books at page 75 and look at the pictures.'** Hand out the test card sheets and ask pupils to cut out the cards. Alternatively give each pupil a set of cards already cut out. Pupils then fold the eight cards along the dotted line as shown in the picture.

c To do Test 1, pupils place all their cards in front of them with the pictures showing, following the visual instructions. Demonstrate.

d Pupils then read the first sentence in the left-hand list, **'The television is on the table.'** Pupils must find the card with the picture which illustrates the sentence, pick it up and read the sentence on the card. They then put a tick or cross in the box in their AB according to whether they were right or wrong. Repeat for the other cards.

e To do Test 2, pupils first cover the sentences in the left-hand list and then place all their cards in front of them again with the pictures showing, following the visual instructions. Demonstrate.

f Pupils then look at the first picture in the right-hand list. Pupils must complete the appropriate sentence in the space provided. (**'The chair is next to the fridge.'**) They then find the card with the appropriate picture, pick it up and look at the words to check. They put a tick or a cross in the box accordingly. Repeat for the other pictures. Pupils who want to test themselves further can try to write the whole sentence on a piece of paper.

g Pupils add up their scores out of eight for each test and total them. Finally, they circle the appropriate comment.

Step 5 Supersnake

a Look at the Supersnake cartoon on page 57 of the CB. Pupils listen to the dialogue, reading at the same time.

Step 1

Step 2

Step 3

Step 4

Step 5

START A PROJECT

1
2
3
4
5
6
= aerial
= door
= roof
= chimney
= window
= wall

56

Homes

4E

SUPERSNAKE
Once upon a time there were three little worms.
The first little worm lived in a house made of grass.
The second little worm lived in a house made of matchsticks.
The third little worm lived in a house made of Lego bricks.
One day along came a big bad rat.
He blew down the house made of grass.
He blew down the house made of matchsticks.
And he knocked down the house made of Lego bricks.
Dinner time!
HELP!
Stop!
"Dinner time!" said the rat.
"Help!" screamed the worms.
"Stop!" shouted Supersnake.
Aagh!
Hurray!
Ha, ha!
The rat screamed. The worms cheered.
Supersnake laughed and put the rat in a house made of metal.

57

4E

Homes

2 Listen and number the picture.

3 Write.

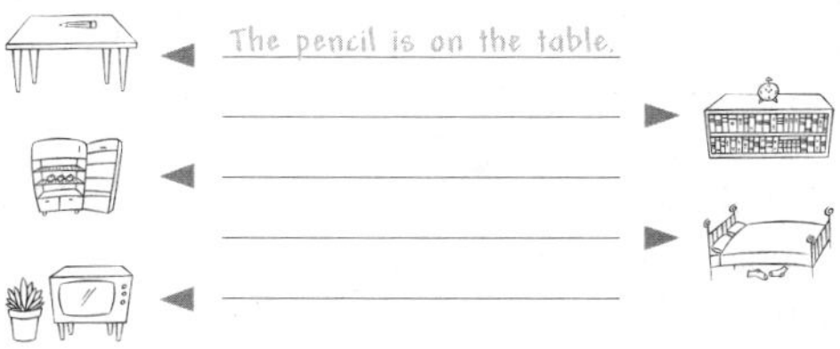

The pencil is on the table.

____

____

____

____

4 Write.

There are three chairs ______ the living room. The television is next to the ______. There's a clock ______ the television. There's a ball ______ the sofa. There's a small table ______ the sofa and a ______ on the table.

74

Homes

4E

5 Test yourself. Right (✓) or (✗)?

You need

TEST 1

- *Put the cards like this.*
- *Read these words.*
- *Find the pictures.*
- *Check. Right (✓) or wrong (✗)?*

The television is on the table.	☐
The boat is in the bath.	☐
The cat is under the bed.	☐
The sink is next to the cooker.	☐
The telephone is on the bookcase.	☐
The cupboard is between the sofa and the armchair.	☐
The chair is next to the fridge.	☐
The dress is in the wardrobe.	☐

SCORE /8

TEST 2

- *Put the cards like this.*
- *Look at these pictures.*
- *Complete the sentences.*
- *Check. Right (✓) or wrong (✗)?*

The chair is …

The dress is …

The telephone is …

The cupboard is …

The television is …

The cat is …

The sink is …

The boat is …

SCORE /8

TOTAL /16

Circle your total score

16 Excellent 15–14 Very good 13–12 Good

11–10 Quite good 9–0 Do it again!

75

Festivals – Halloween

Main Language Items			Resource File	Materials Needed
Halloween	October	brim	10	bowl/water/apples
	festival	star		materials to make witch's hat
	dress up	moon		cassette/cassette player
	witches			
	ghosts			
	party			

Step 1 Presentation

a Say **'Open your Coursebooks at page 58.'** Introduce the topic of Halloween by asking pupils in their L1 whether it is celebrated in their country. When is it? Are there any traditional activities/games played by children?

b Briefly ask some questions about the pictures at the top of the page. Use **'Who's this? Is this ...?'**

c Play the tape. Pupils listen and read at the same time.

d Then ask some questions to check comprehension, e.g.:
When is Halloween?
What do children do now?

Step 2 Play Bob Apple

a Look at the pictures and read the text on page 58 of the CB about Bob Apple. Ask pupils if they know of any similar games.

b Then play the game in the classroom. Divide the class into groups of three or four.

Step 3 Make a witch's hat

a Each pupil makes a hat following the visual instructions on page 59 of the CB.

b Pupils can decorate their hats as shown or design their own decorations.

Step 4 Start a Halloween project

Working in groups, as before, pupils can plan a Halloween party, with ghost's or witches' costumes. Alternatively, the following project on the theme of night-time may be a way to help pupils rationalise fear of the dark.

a Ask pupils to tell you in their L1 what time they go to bed at night. **'Does everyone go to bed at the same time? What about adults? Do some have to stay up and work? What kinds of jobs would they do? Do all animals sleep at night? Which ones come out and why?'**

b Divide the class into groups of three or four and explain that they are going to work together in order to describe people and animals who stay up at night. Each group will select one person and one animal, and investigate what they do during the night.

c Before they start, sit down with each group in turn and help pupils organise the different tasks and materials so that everyone is fully involved. Tell them that the project should be presented on a single piece of poster paper and include:
• a description of the night life of one worker and one animal.
• a drawing or a plan of where each one works/hunts.
• a map of the sky at night featuring some of the constellations that are visible on a clear night.

d Once they have completed their project, each group presents it to the class. The drawings are then displayed around the room. Make sure that pupils have the necessary English vocabulary and structures.

e Encourage pupils to continue their project work outside their English class; they should try to interview night workers if they know any, consult nature books and encyclopedias to uncover facts about the habits of nocturnal animals and find out something about the names and positions of the most famous constellations.

Step 1

Step 2

Step 3

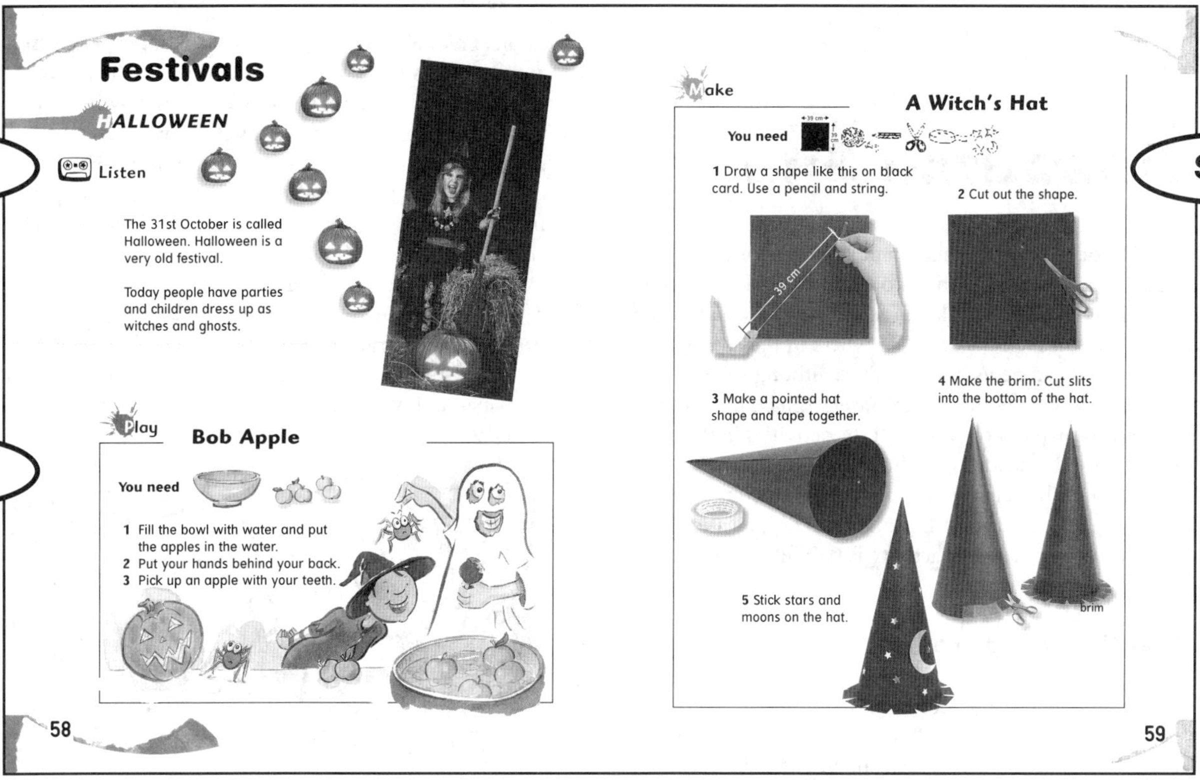

Festivals

HALLOWEEN

Listen

The 31st October is called Halloween. Halloween is a very old festival.

Today people have parties and children dress up as witches and ghosts.

Play

Bob Apple

You need

1 Fill the bowl with water and put the apples in the water.
2 Put your hands behind your back.
3 Pick up an apple with your teeth.

58

Make

A Witch's Hat

You need

1 Draw a shape like this on black card. Use a pencil and string.

2 Cut out the shape.

3 Make a pointed hat shape and tape together.

4 Make the brim. Cut slits into the bottom of the hat.

5 Stick stars and moons on the hat.

39 cm
brim

59

Resource File

The **Resource File** contains some 60 ideas for the classroom and includes ideas for Project Work and ways of handling mixed ability classes as well as many games and other activities not included elsewhere in the course. These ideas can be used at any time, although the range and variety of activities in *New Stepping Stones* makes the use of this material optional. All the activities in the **Resource File**, however, are linked to the material in the CB. Each of the activities has a number which is used for reference purposes in the Lesson Notes to indicate when a particular **Resource File** activity is helpful or suitable.

Displays and projects

The topic-based nature of *New Stepping Stones* makes it ideal for Project Work. Wall displays, classroom charts and other follow-up activities are examples of such work. Wall displays serve a number of purposes. They are attractive and create a pleasant atmosphere in the classroom. They can be used as a classroom resource to provide practice in all the language skills. They provide extra motivation when created by the pupils and especially when they are about the pupils themselves. Much of the work in *New Stepping Stones* can be expanded to relate events more closely to the pupils and their environment.

1 Personal file displays

Work created in the Personal File sections of the course makes very good displays. The work can be mounted on paper and a display made which relates to the topic itself. For example, in **Animals**, the work can be presented within a zoo with each child's work occupying a different cage. These displays can be followed up with spoken or written work which relates to the pupils themselves.

2 Block of flats

Each pupil draws a picture of a room (real or imaginary) and writes a description alongside. Display the rooms together and build a class block of flats.

3 Class collage

Pupils gradually collect pictures as the topic progresses and stick on a collage thereby building up their own reference section. These collage displays may involve vocabulary from the topic as a whole, or focus upon particular sub-categories within the topic. (In **Food**, sub-categories may include sweets, drinks, fruit and vegetables. In **Animals**, classification could be according to common characteristics.)

Displays can take the form of:

a Topic Wall Dictionary, or

b Topic Dictionary Books – tie several blank sheets of paper together, stick pictures of various objects on the paper and write the names inside. Hang these Dictionaries on the wall for class use.

Animals
Polar Bear
Giraffe
Gorilla
Dictionaries
Food
Animals

3a

A possible variation on the content of the collage displays is to use realia other than pictures cut from magazines, e.g. for **Food**, food labels and sweet wrappers, etc.

3b

Rather than simply displaying the collage pictures on sheets of paper, variety can be added by cutting the backing paper of the display into a shape which relates to the topic itself. In **Homes** this could take the form of a large furniture van:

shelves
chair
drawers
lamp
dressing table
sofa
Fred's
Furniture
Removals

4 Class surveys

The information gathered in **Surveys/Questionnaires** can be presented in wall charts, giving personal information in note form. For example, in **Food** at the start of the topic, pin a chart to the wall.

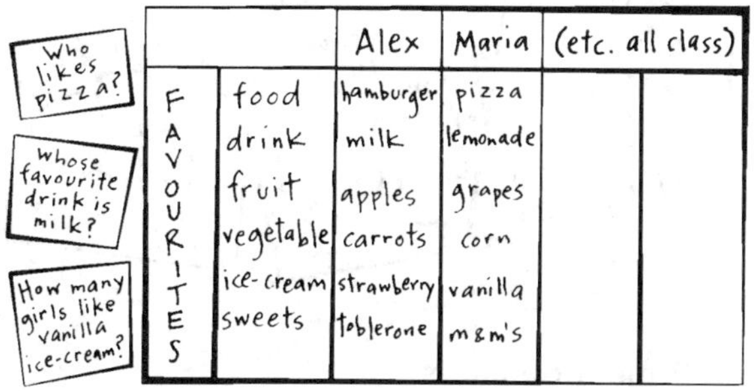

Who likes pizza?
Whose favourite drink is milk?
How many girls like vanilla ice-cream?
Alex
Maria
(etc. all class)
FAVOURITES
food
drink
fruit
vegetable
ice-cream
sweets
hamburger
milk
apples
carrots
strawberry
toblerone
pizza
lemonade
grapes
corn
vanilla
m&m's

Gradually add the information to the chart as the topic progresses. Put questions around the display to add interest and focus attention on different aspects of the topic.

Such displays can relate to any of the Topics in *New Stepping Stones*:

Animals – likes and dislikes, favourite animals.

Homes – type of home, number of rooms, total furniture in pupils' homes.

Clothes – what pupils wear, their favourite clothes, the most commonly worn items and colours, etc.

5 Food survey

Prepare a wall chart as follows:

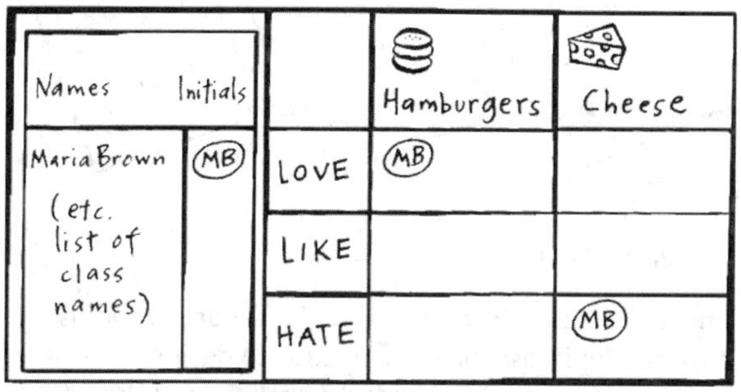

Names
Initials
Hamburgers
Cheese
Maria Brown
MB
(etc. list of class names)
LOVE
LIKE
HATE
MB
MB

Pupils go to the wall chart either individually or in small groups and record their level of preference for a particular food item by signing their initials on the chart. Questions relating to this information can then be given either on the blackboard or on workcards, e.g.:

How many children love ice-cream?
Does Anna love or hate beefburgers?
Who doesn't like cheese?

6 Meals

Each pupil needs a paper plate, or a piece of paper or card cut into the shape of a plate. Pupils draw a picture (or make a collage, if time and materials are available) of their favourite meal or the meal they hate most. These can then be displayed on the wall accompanied by a written description.

My favourite meal is spaghetti bolognese. I love spaghetti.
Maria Brown
My favourite meal is beefburger and chips.
Alex R.

7 Animals

Make a string and pin display. Pupils work in small groups. Each group needs a large picture of an animal, a large sheet of coloured paper, strips of white paper, glue, pins and string. Pupils discuss the physical appearance of their animals then make labels for each different part of the body. The picture and labels are then stuck onto the large sheet of paper. Pin this to the display board then connect the labels to the picture with the pins and string. (For weaker pupils, the labels can be prepared in advance; the activity is then a simple reading task.)

GIRAFFE
big eyes
long neck
long legs
small ears
spots on its body
long tail
by Anna, Pablo & Paul

7a

If materials are not available for the above display, then prepare large cut-outs in the shape of various animals. The characteristic of the animal is written on the part of the body being described. Supply extra vocabulary as required.

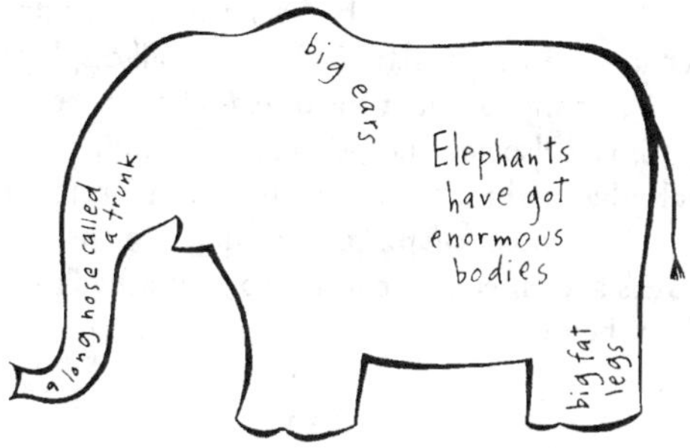

big ears
Elephants have got enormous bodies
a long nose called a trunk
big fat legs

8 Comprehension cards

All work displayed on the walls can provide the basis for a wide range of follow-up activities. One activity to practise reading and writing is to use Comprehension cards. These are worksheets made by the teacher based on the written information given within the displays, e.g. as a follow-up to **Personal File** work in **Food**.

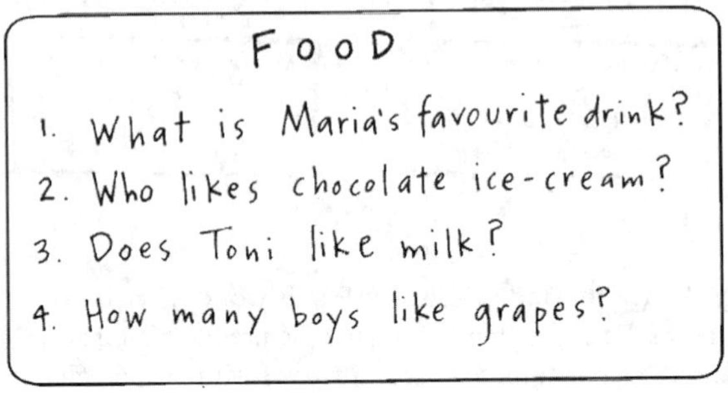
FOOD
1. What is Maria's favourite drink?
2. Who likes chocolate ice-cream?
3. Does Toni like milk?
4. How many boys like grapes?

The cards can be used for oral and/or written work, or form the basis for quizzes or even tests. They can be used for every topic and graded in degree of difficulty to suit individual needs.

ANIMALS
1. What do hippos eat?
2. Can monkeys fly?
3. Do seals eat fish?
4. Can tigers swim?
HOMES
1. Draw a table.
2. Draw a lamp on the table.
3. Draw a fridge.
4. Draw a chair next to the fridge.

The cards can be used individually or in small groups. Pupils can go to the display, read, make notes, sit down and write answers in full, then test their partner's knowledge of other class members.

9 Pupils' files

Pupils can be encouraged to keep a file of their own work, including work they do in their English lessons. This is more flexible than an exercise book, since all work done on paper can be easily stored. Work from wall displays can then be kept in the files after the displays have been taken down. This can also add another dimension to the **Personal File** activities: work from these can form part of a personal file. Pupils can practise the drawing and writing in their ABs and, after correction, display finished pieces of work in their file.

Elephants are big and grey.
Some elephants have got big ears.
Some elephants have got small ears.
African
Asian
Elephants love water.
They can swim.

10 Project booklets

Throughout the **Animals** topic (or as a round-up activity), animal profiles are gradually built up. Pupils choose one animal which they would like to study in detail and gradually build up a small reference booklet. Make the booklets by tying several sheets of paper together with string. As each aspect of animals is covered (colour, size, characteristics, food, origin, etc.) pupils add another page to their booklet. When complete, they can be displayed and used for reference and reading practice by the whole class.

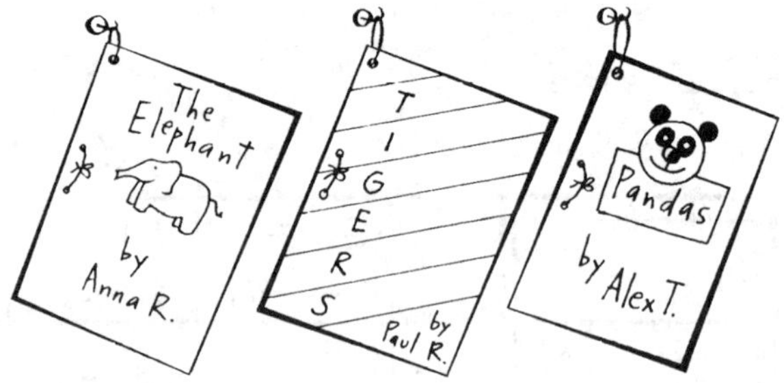
The Elephant
by Anna R.
TIGERS
by Paul R.
Pandas
by Alex T.

11 What's in the box?

The last word of the rhyme **'In a dark, dark wood'** is missing. Pupils use their imagination to decide what could be lurking in the box: **a spider! a snake! a rat!** Provide extra words as required. Pupils copy out the rhyme, completing the last line with the word of their choice and drawing the 'thing' coming out of the box. The drawings can be displayed on a shelf for added effect.

by Alex
In a dark, dark wood
there's a dark, dark house.
In the dark, dark house,
there's a dark, dark box.
And in that dark, dark
box there's a SPIDER!
by Anna
In a dark, dark wood
there's a dark, dark house.
In the dark, dark, house
there's a dark, dark box.
And in that dark, dark
box there's a GHOST!

12 Scale plans

If pupils are not already familiar with the concept, then you will need to explain scale in plans and maps.
Draw the following grid and sketch on the blackboard. Tell pupils, '**This is a bedroom**', and label the three furniture items **bed**, **wardrobe** and **table**. Then tell pupils the scale of the picture is '**One square is 100 cm**'. Write this on the board.

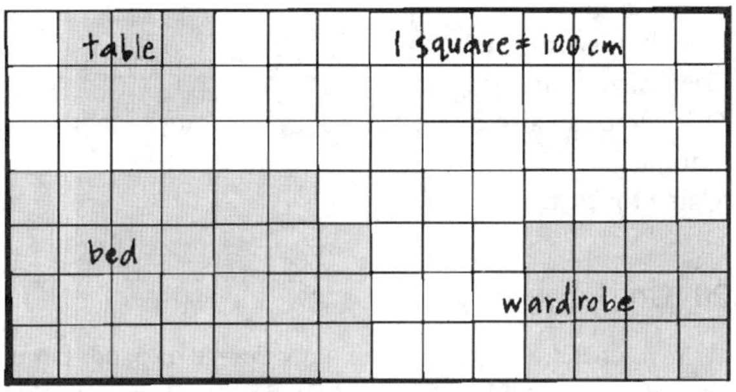
table
1 square = 100 cm
bed
wardrobe

Then ask pupils the following questions:
How long is the bed?
How wide is the bed?
How long is the table? etc.
When pupils understand the concept they can make their own scale plans. This is a cooperative activity and will generate a lot of language. The class can work together and produce a plan of the whole classroom, or pupils can work in small groups. Each group will need graph paper and measuring instruments (rulers or tape measures). String is also very useful.

12a

Pupils make a scale plan of a room in their own home. This can generate a lot of language practice in the following lesson. They can be displayed upon the wall and questions about the plans used for writing practise or in quizzes. Pupils can describe their plan to their partners who have to try and recreate the drawing exactly. If letters and numbers are added to the sides of the graph paper, then pupils can produce coloured plans using simple instructions, '**Colour D1 red**', etc.

13 Word wall

If space is available, a large scale, ongoing version of **Word steps** (see **Resource File 39**) can be created. Stick a very large sheet of paper on the wall and start a word-step. The ultimate aim is to fill the whole sheet with words. When you reach the end of the paper, turn around by adding words that end in the same letter as the previous word.

14 T-shirt display

Each pupil will need a sheet of paper cut into the shape of a T-shirt upon which they draw a design of something they can name in English, or write an English word. These can then be displayed hanging from a 'washing line'. This is good for revision of vocabulary.

Maria
Anna
Alex
Paul
Hello

15 Life-size model

You will need a large sheet of paper. One pupil lies on the paper and the teacher draws around him/her. The teacher then leads a discussion in which pupils decide what the figure in the drawing should wear, the colour of hair, etc. Decisions are noted on the blackboard. Pupils colour the drawing accordingly. Stick the completed drawing to the wall and label body parts and clothes items and give the character a name.

Games

In general, the games in this section are oral games, though some involve reading and writing.

16 I-spy

The game can be played either in pairs, groups or as a whole class activity, although initially it is only recommended as the latter. Referring either to objects in the classroom or pictures in the CB, say '**I can see something beginning with B.**' The class then try to guess the object. The pupil who guesses correctly thinks of the next object.
(Teacher-led pupil, led, whole class, teams or pairs.)

17 Battleships

Divide the class into pairs. Each pupil requires an identical grid to his or her partner. In **Food** the grid could look like this:

	fish	apple	bread
Monday		✓	✓
Tuesday	✓		
Wednesday	✓		✓
Thursday		✓	
Friday	✓		✓

There can be any number of food or drink items along the top of the grid. A total of about twenty squares is ideal. Each pupil places ten ticks at random on their grid. Pupils must not look at one another's grid. Players take it in turns to ask questions to find the location of their opponent's ticks, e.g. **'Do you eat fish on Tuesdays?'**
The first player to find all their opponent's ticks is the winner. This type of exercise can be adapted to any topic, e.g. for **Homes**:

	kitchen	living room	garden	bedroom
Mary			✓	
Tom	✓			
Ann				✓
Fred		✓		

For the above grid, use the question form, **'Is Mary in the bedroom?'**
(Pairs, game of chance.)

18 Memory chains

This game involves pupils successively adding to the length of a sentence by repeating what previous pupils have said and then adding something themselves. It is a memory game and can be used for practising a wide range of structures and vocabulary and is particularly useful for developing fluency.
P1 says a phrase, e.g. **'I like milk.'**
P2 adds to the list, **'I like chocolate and he likes milk.'**
Then P3 says, **'I like bananas, she likes chocolate and he likes milk'**, etc. If a pupil forgets the sequence or makes a mistake, the next person in line starts a new sequence.
Other possible chains include:

a P1 – **I can swim.**
P2 – **She can swim and I can jump.**
P3 – **She can swim, he can jump but I can't fly. etc.**

b P1 – **Lions eat meat.**
P2 – **Lions eat meat and hippos eat grass.**
P3 – **Lions eat meat, hippos eat grass and seals eat fish.**

18a

Weaker students may find it useful to use playing cards as prompts. (These will need to be made in advance.) Pupils take turns, turning over cards and naming the sequence. Emphasis is then taken away from remembering the sequence to simply remembering the English names for things.
(Whole class, groups, pairs.)

19 Find the link

Look at the zoo picture in the CB. Write the numbers 1–16 on individual pieces of paper and lay them face down on the table. Pupils then pick out two numbers at random and find the relevant numbered cages in the picture. The object of the game is to think of as many similarities between the animals as possible. Pupils are awarded a point for each similarity they say, e.g.:
They eat grass.
They can swim.
They have four legs.
This game can also be played using the **Games Pack (animals)**.
(Game for pairs.)

20 Colour words

Write a word (or random letters) on a piece of paper large enough to be seen by all pupils. Each letter should be written in a different colour. Think of some other words that can be made using the letters on the card. (The same letter can be used more than once.) Then give clues (either written or oral) directing pupils to make the new words, e.g.:
In this word, the first letter is blue.
The second letter is red.
The third letter is blue. etc.
What is the Word?
(Teacher-led, whole class.)

21 Verb Bingo

Elicit verbs from the pupils and write them on the blackboard. Pupils need a grid in which to write any nine verbs from the list. The teacher requires a set of call cards with each word written on. Prepare these while pupils are making their Bingo cards. To play the game, pick out a call card and mime the verb. Pupils cross out the verbs on their Bingo cards as they are mimed. The first player to eliminate all their words and shout 'Bingo!' is the winner. Pupils can then take the role of miming the bingo words.
(Teacher-led, pupil-led, whole class.)

22 Alphabet Bingo

Each pupil draws a twelve-square grid on a piece of paper and writes a letter of the alphabet in each square. The bingo caller (teacher or pupil) writes the alphabet on a piece of paper and calls out the letters in random sequence crossing them out as she does so. Pupils cross out the letters on their bingo card as they are called out. The first player to eliminate all their letters and shout 'Bingo!' is the winner. Then play the game in small groups.
(Teacher-led, pupil-led, whole class, groups.)

23 Memory sequences

Four pupils come to the front of the class. The teacher says a sequence of letters to each pupil in turn who has to repeat the exact sequence in the same order. Start with three letters and add one letter each round. If a pupil makes a mistake or can't remember the letters, he or she is out of the game. The winner is the last player remaining. Then bring four new pupils out to the front.
The game can be played competitively by dividing the class into two teams and selecting two players from each in turn and awarding points.
(Teacher-led, whole class.)

23a

Memory sequences can also be played using cardinal or ordinal numbers or any vocabulary set.

24 Spell it

This game practises the letters of the alphabet. The teacher spells out any word to the class, saying the letters in quick succession, i.e. **'D-O-G'**. The first pupil to say **'dog'** wins a point. Pupils must not write the letters down. Start off with short words and gradually increase the level of difficulty.
(Teacher-led, whole class, teams.)

25 Spelling bee

Divide the class into two teams (A and B). Team A asks one pupil in Team B: **'How do you spell apple?'** The teacher acts as referee and, if the word is spelt correctly, awards a point to Team B. If the word is spelt incorrectly, Team A wins a point. Continue the game with teams taking turns to ask the questions.
(Teacher-led, whole class, teams.)

25a

Pupils can play the above game in small groups or pairs. One pupil asks the questions and uses the word list at the back of the CB (or words elsewhere in the book) to check other pupils' answers.
(Game, groups, pairs.)

26 Busy pictures

Many of the large full- or half-page pictures in the CB can be used as the starting point for games. To practise vocabulary, pupils study the picture for one minute, close their books and see how many objects they can remember. Pupils can simply list items or add size, colour, location of objects, etc., depending on how complicated you want the task to be. Pupils can list the items orally or in writing.
(Memory game, individually, pairs, groups.)

27 Washing line

You will need two bags of clothes, each one containing similar items, and two washing lines. Divide the class into two teams. One representative from each team comes to the front. Say **'Find a white shirt.'** The first player to hang the item on the line wins a point for his team. Change players and continue.
(Teacher-led, whole class, two teams.)

28 The laundry game

This game requires an open space. Divide the class into two, three or four teams. Each team selects a 'runner'. Say **'Bring me a black shoe!'** Any pupil wearing a black shoe quickly removes it and gives it to the 'runner'. The first 'runner' to give the correct item to the teacher wins a point for their team. Repeat the instructions using other clothing items. An alternative to using pupils' clothes is to play the game with bags of clothes or even using the Game Pack pieces.
(Teacher-led, whole class, teams.)

29 Clothes race

This is a variation on **The Laundry Game**, above. Divide the class into teams. Give instructions such as **'Anyone wearing blue socks come here.'** The first player to the front wins a point for their team. Repeat the instructions using other clothing items.
(Teacher-led, whole class, teams.)

30 Body building

You will need one dice per group of four. Write the following codes on the blackboard:

1 = jumper	**1 = red**
2 = shirt	**2 = blue**
3 = skirt	**3 = pink**
4 = socks	**4 = brown**
5 = shorts	**5 = white**
6 = hat	**6 = orange**

Pupils 'win' clothes items, record what they collect, then write a description. **'I've got a red skirt ...'**, etc.
(Groups, individual writing practice.)

31 Getting dressed

This is a mime game. One pupil comes to the front of the class. The teacher whispers the name of an item of clothing to her. The pupil then has to imagine she is putting on that particular item of clothing and mime the event (fastening buttons, tying laces, etc.). The rest of the class guess the item. Can also be played in groups using the Bingo counters as word prompts for the mimes, if necessary.
(Teacher- or Pupil-led, whole class or groups.)

32 Colour memory game

Divide the class into two teams. One or more representatives from each team are blindfolded. Ask the representatives questions relating to the colour of everyone's clothes, e.g. **'What colour is X's jumper? Is X wearing a shirt? Is X's dress red or blue?'** etc. If they guess correctly then they win a point for their team. Change representatives and continue. The game is good for enhancing observation skills – pupils will rapidly look around the class trying to memorise colours but there's always the chance of a wild guess if in doubt!
(Teacher-led, teams, game of memory and chance.)

33 What were they wearing?

A game to focus attention on other people's clothes and test observation skills. Ask two pupils to leave the room for a moment; don't explain why, but make sure everyone sees them leave. Then ask **'What's Alex wearing?'**, and note the suggestions on the blackboard. Call the pupils back into the room and check the answers.
(Teacher-led, observation game.)

34

The above game can be made more challenging by limiting the number of different objects on the cards but changing the details such as the number or colour of the objects. Pupils would then have to ask more than one question, e.g. **'Have you got a door?' 'Yes.' 'What colour is it?' 'Pink.'** etc.
(NOTE This is a good way of moving students into new pairs or groups if required – when they have found their new partner they sit down together and do the next task.)
(Whole class, speaking.)

35 Battleships

Divide the class into pairs. Each pupil requires an identical grid to his partner:
e.g. for **Clothes**

	dress	trousers	socks	T-shirt	hat
Jim		✓		✓	
Tina	✓		✓		
Tom		✓		✓	✓
Jane	✓			✓	✓

There can be any number of names and clothing items on the grid. A total of about twenty squares is recommended. Each pupil places ten ticks at random on their grid. Pupils must not look at one another's grids. Players take it in turns to ask questions to find the location of their opponent's ticks, e.g.:
'Is Tom wearing a hat?' etc.
The first player to find all their opponent's ticks is the winner.

Reading and writing practice

36 Monster munch

What do monsters eat? Pupils can let their imaginations run wild in this exercise. Invent gruesome monster meals of spiders, worms, sea water, old cars … in fact, anything! Pupils draw pictures of the monster meals and write about their likes and dislikes.

37 River race

This game is to practise spelling any of the words in NEW STEPPING STONES. It is played in pairs. Each pair will need two pieces of string for the river bank and twenty small cards (stepping stones) to write on. Pupils take turns selecting a new word for their partner to write on a stepping stone. The pupil writing cannot look in their book. If the word is spelt correctly, then it is placed in the river. The first player to reach the opposite bank is the winner. Pupils must use ten cards to reach the opposite bank.

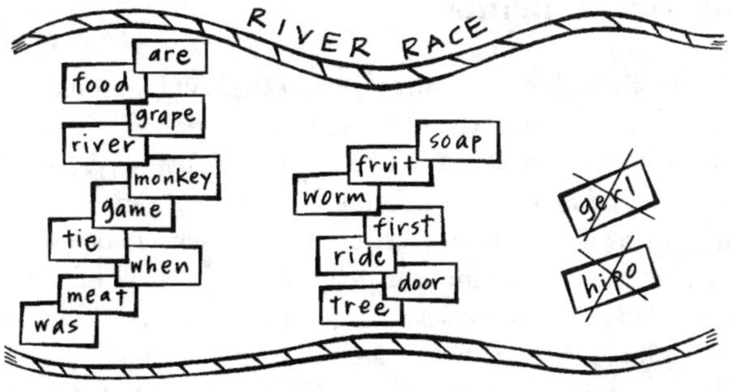
RIVER RACE
are
food
grape
river
monkey
game
tie
when
meat
was
soap
fruit
worm
first
ride
door
tree

38 Which room?

This is a simple vocabulary listing exercise. Pupils draw an outline of a house in their exercise books. List vocabulary items on the blackboard. Pupils write the furniture item in the appropriate room (there will be some overlap).

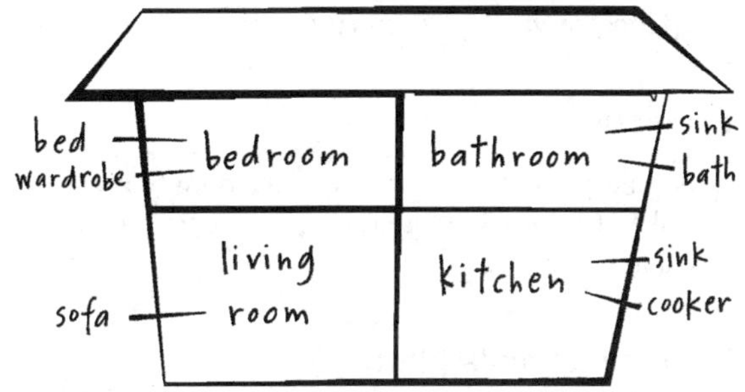
bed
wardrobe
bedroom
bathroom
sink
bath
living room
kitchen
sink
cooker
sofa

39 Word steps

This is a written version of the game **word tennis**. Divide the class into pairs or small groups. Each pupil writes a word at the top of a piece of paper then passes the paper to their partner (or the person on the left). Pupils build up word steps by adding words beginning with the last letter of the preceding word, e.g.:

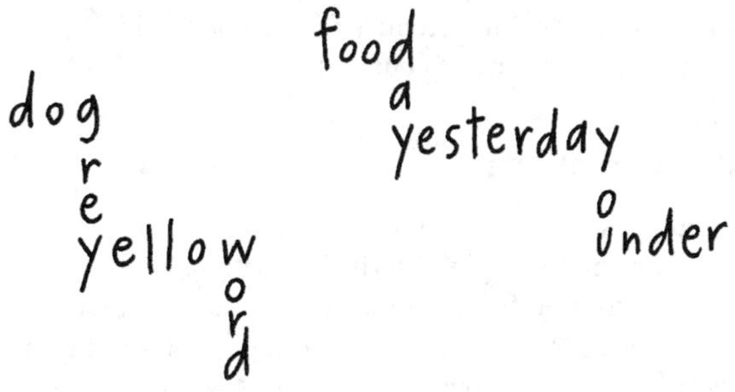
dog
yellow
word
food
yesterday
under

If it is impossible to add another word, pupils start a new set of steps.

40 Alphabetical order

This is a remedial exercise to practise alphabetising. Pupils write words on separate pieces of paper and arrange them in alphabetical order manually.

41 Number plates

For homework, instruct pupils to collect car registration numbers, making a note of the colour, size and make of the car. Ask a few questions such as:
How many did you collect?
What's the number? etc.
If car registration numbers have significance in your country (e.g. MI shows a car comes from Milan), then you can ask questions such as:
What do these letters mean?
Where does the car come from?
The main purpose of this task, is that pupils will have made their own alphabet and number dictation sequences and can dictate them to their partners.

42 Speed writing

Instruct pupils to write a set of words:
Write five words beginning with 'r'.
Write the names of four vegetables.
Write eight colours.
Write the alphabet.
Write ten things you find in a house. etc.
The first pupil to finish shouts '**Stop!**' and everyone must put their pens down while the words are checked. If correct, award a point and give the next instruction. If wrong, the race continues.

43 Crosswords

Write a word vertically on the blackboard, e.g. **ATHENS**. Pupils must quickly write one word beginning with each of the letters that make up the word, e.g.:
Animal
Tiger
Hat
Elephant
Necklace
Shell
Demonstrate the game on the blackboard. The game can then be played cooperatively in small groups, pairs or with pupils working alone.
The game can also be played competitively by stopping the activity when the first pupil finishes, checking the words and allocating points.

44 Hieroglyphics

This is a whole class activity and involves cracking a code to work out the meaning of hidden messages. The code could be as follows:

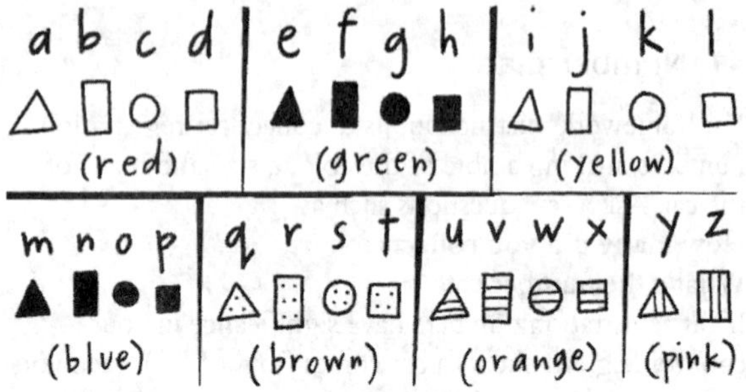
a b c d
(red)
e f g h
(green)
i j k l
(yellow)
m n o p
(blue)
q r s t
(brown)
u v w x
(orange)
y z
(pink)

Copy out each hieroglyphic with the letter it represents onto a separate piece of paper. Give each pupil one of the pieces of paper (or more than one if there are less than 26 pupils in your class). Write some coded messages on the board, i.e.:

1.
(What's your name?)

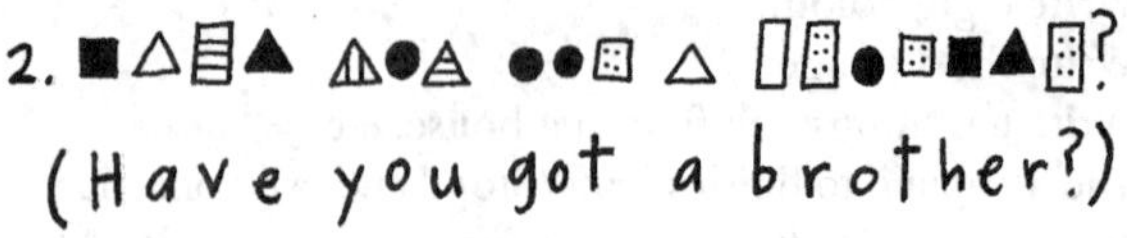
2.
(Have you got a brother?)

Pupils copy down the messages and then try to crack the code as quickly as possible by asking other class members what their symbols mean.

45 Connections

Using pictures in the CB as cue cards, pupils write a number of questions, each on separate pieces of paper and the answers on other sheets. Their partners then have to match the questions and answers.

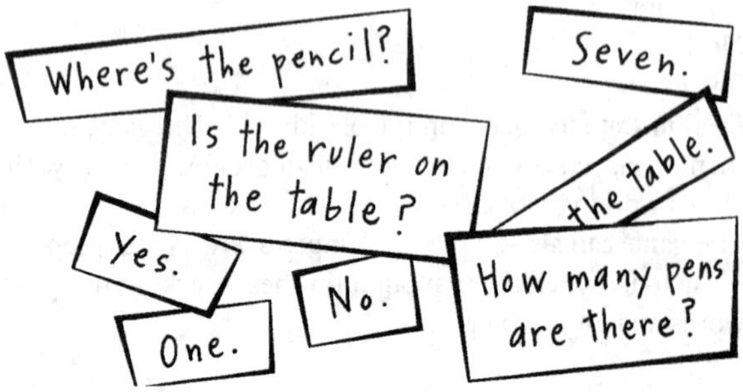
Where's the pencil?
Seven.
Is the ruler on the table?
the table.
Yes.
No.
One.
How many pens are there?

Making activities

Although **Making activities** are time-consuming, some teachers choose to expand topics into other areas of the curriculum or simply feel that there is sufficient scope to extend a particular theme further. Constructing three-dimensional displays or making things which can be used as a focus for extra language practice are two ways of doing this. Such activities are also fun. However, it is more rewarding if these activities are not simply an end in themselves but are a means to an end or part of a larger activity.
Therefore, there should be a linguistic purpose either in the task itself or as a follow-up to, or extension of, the Making activity. This can take the form of a guided reading task, prepared in advance or written on the blackboard. Alternatively, objects made by the pupils can be used in role plays or as the basis for written descriptions, surveys, questionnaires, etc.

46 Menus

Pupils make their own menu cards, including typical national and regional foods and local currency. These can be used in role plays.

47 Crazy animals photo-fit

Pupils cut out pictures of animals from magazines and then combine different parts of each picture to invent crazy animals. Encourage pupils to give their creations crazy names by putting words together, i.e. a crocodile with an elephant's trunk could become a **Crocophant** or an **Eledile** – use your imagination!

Activity Book cut-outs

This section contains activities that can be used in conjunction with the **AB cut-outs**.

48 Instructions

Use **cut-outs (Furniture) or (Clothes)**. Either make flashcards or get pupils to write instructions on paper, e.g. **'Put the sofa under the window'**, or **'Put a red jumper on the boy'**. Working in pairs or using the flashcards in a whole class activity, pupils read the instructions and put the pieces in the appropriate place on their baseboard.

49 Picture building

Use **cut-outs (Furniture)** or **(Clothes)**. Pupils work in groups of 4–6. Each pupil writes an instruction on a piece of paper, e.g. **'Put the TV by the door.'**

Each pupil places the furniture piece on their own baseboard according to the instruction. Then they pass their message to the person on their left. Read and follow the new instruction then pass the description on again. The pupils in each group will be working simultaneously on different instructions but should eventually end up with similar pictures.

50 Twenty questions

Pupils work in pairs using the furniture pieces and baseboard. P1 makes a picture. P2 asks yes/no type questions and tries to create an identical picture, e.g.:
Is there a sofa in your room?
Is the sofa by the door?
P2 may ask a maximum of twenty questions. The object is to work out their partner's picture by asking as few questions as possible. Pupils then compare their pictures. Change roles. The game can be simplified by limiting the number of pieces to be used.

51 Realia

All teachers use realia in the classroom, even if it is just picking up everyday objects and asking pupils to identify them. There are many exercises in NEW STEPPING STONES in which the use of everyday objects will add an element of realism to the language practice. The following are only suggestions and you can probably think of many more.

51a Ten Green Bottles

Line up ten plastic bottles (green ones, if possible) and 'accidentally' knock one over for each line of the song.

51b English newspapers

Many countries have a newspaper for their English speaking community, e.g. the *Athens News* in Greece. Their TV guides can prove very useful as they present authentic English within the context of the pupils' own community. (It is often highly amusing to see the foreign translation of a programme title too.)

51c Plastic animals

Small model animals can be helpful when pupils are describing physical characteristics.

52 What is it?

Use **cut-outs** animal playing cards. Pupils work in pairs. Each pair needs only one pack of cards. P1 takes a card and describes the animal:
e.g. **'It's green and it's got big teeth.'**
or **'It can swim but it can't fly.'** P2 must try to guess the animal on the card. If correct he/she wins the card.

53 Reading game

Use the animal playing cards. Pupils work in pairs with one pack of cards between each pair. Each pair will need a brief description of each playing card on a separate piece of paper. These can be prepared in advance by the teacher, or each pupil can make their own set. They will contain descriptions such as:
'It's green and it's got big teeth.'
or **'It can swim but it can't fly.'**

53a

Lay all the cards face down on the table. P1 turns over a picture and a description. If they match, P1 keeps the card and repeats the task. When she/he turns over a pair which do not match they must be laid face down and it is P2's turn.

53b

P1 takes the descriptions and P2 the pictures. P1 reads one of the descriptions and P2 must try to select the correct card. Award points.

53c

The above exercise can be done on an individual basis as a remedial reading exercise. Pupils match pictures and descriptions.

54 Search

Use the animal playing cards. Pupils work in pairs. Each pair needs only one set of cards.
Pupils spread their cards face down on the table. P1 says **'It can climb trees.'** P2 attempts to turn over a card compatible with the instruction. The object is to remember where each card is. If they turn over an appropriate card then they keep the card. P2 then gives an instruction. The winner is the pupil with the most cards.

Organising your classroom

55 Storing materials

In terms of classroom management, there are advantages in keeping each pupil's **cut-outs** and word stone collections in the classroom to avoid them being lost or forgotten.

The sheets can be cut out and stored one at a time, either the first time a particular set is used, or alternatively a lesson can be set aside early on in the course to prepare them all at once. (The Packs should be returned to pupils at the end of term.) The logistics of storing these materials will be influenced by the availability of space, class size, and the number of classes you teach. The ideas below are intended only as suggestions.

1 **If space is limited:**

a Give each pupil a large envelope. Tell them to write their name and class clearly on the envelope. Put the sheets of card inside. Collect the envelopes and store in a folder.

b When cut-outs are used for the first time, hand out the envelopes. Pupils cut out their own cards. Give each pupil an elastic band or a small envelope for storing the cards after use. (The cutting-out can, of course, be done in advance.) Always return individual envelopes to the class folder for storage.

2 **If there is more space available**, the individual packs can be stored in separate folders.

a Store the original sheets as suggested in **1a** above.

b Use a separate folder for each pack. You will need four small envelopes for each class member. Instead of returning all cut-out material to the large envelope, put it into small envelopes and store in separate folders. It is useful to colour code the folders according to the topics in the CB. Use either coloured folders or attach coloured stickers to the folder.

CLOTHES
Maria
Brown
CLOTHES
(25 pieces per pack)
BINGO COUNTERS
HOMES
ANIMALS
FOOD

Encourage pupils to take care of the materials. To avoid the problem of misplaced items, it is useful to get pupils to count the pieces before putting them away. This activity is also useful for practising counting aloud in English.

56 Bingo cards

Take a sheet of paper approximately 300 mm x 280 mm. Draw straight lines and divide the sheet into six columns of 30 mm width. Divide the rest of the sheet by drawing lines every 30 mm. Photocopy one sheet for each pupil. Cut out the cover cards relating to the particular Bingo card.

Wordlist

This wordlist contains all the words presented in *New Stepping Stones*, Level 2, and gives the pages upon which they first appear. The letters AB indicate that the words are in the Activity Book. The words in **bold type** are used actively in production and the pupils should know these words. Pupils may have an active knowledge of other words, though it is not a requirement of the course that they are able to produce them.

Photocopy master: Test cards 1F

fold

1F 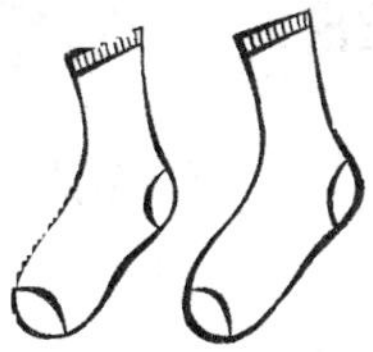	1F 	1F 	1F 
White socks.	A blue sweatshirt.	Yellow trousers.	A grey T-shirt.
1F 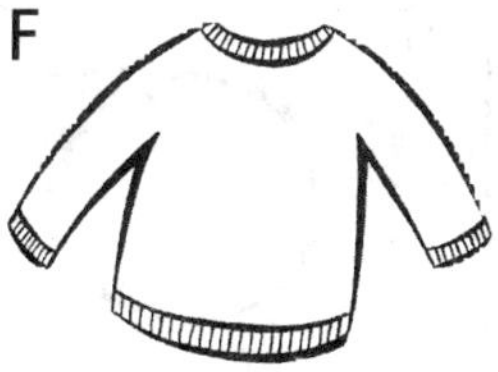	1F 	1F 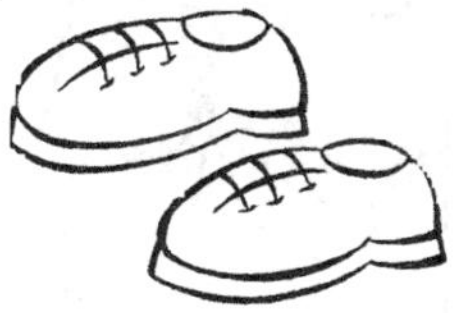	1F 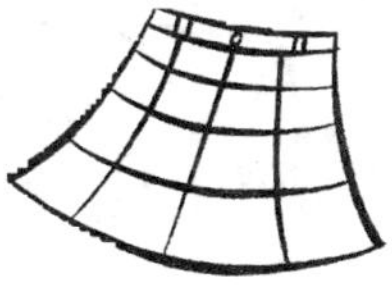
An orange jumper.	A purple dress.	Black shoes.	A pink skirt.
1F 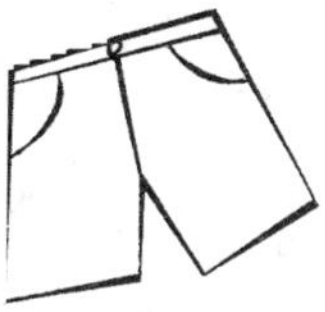	1F 		
Green shorts.	A brown shirt.		

Photocopy master: Test cards 2F

fold

2F 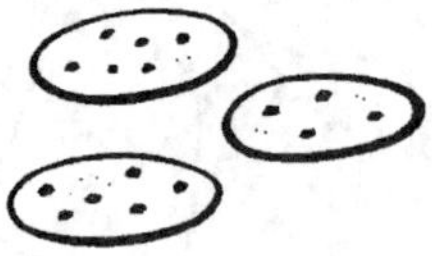	2F 	2F 	2F 
Biscuits.	Bananas.	A hamburger.	An ice-cream.
2F 	2F COLA COLA	2F 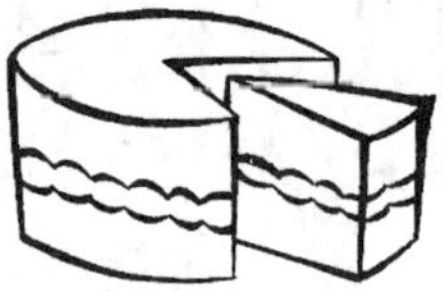	2F 
Cheese.	Cola.	A cake.	An apple.
2F 	2F 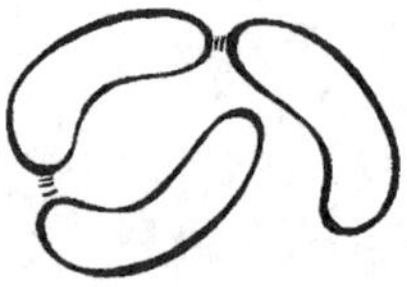		
Chocolate.	Sausages.		

Photocopy master: Test cards 3F and 4E

fold

3F 	3F 	3F 	3F 
Penguins can't fly.	Tigers eat meat.	Kangaroos can jump.	Seals eat fish.
3F 	2F 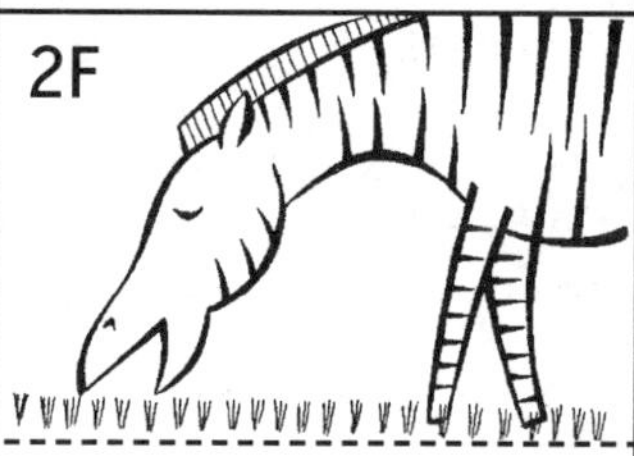	2F 	2F 
Monkeys can climb.	Zebras eat grass.	Elephants can't fly.	Giraffes eat leaves.
4E 	4E 	4E 	4E 
The television is on the table.	The boat is in the bath.	The cat is under the bed.	The sink is next to the cooker.
4E 	4E 	4E 	4E 
The telephone is on the bookcase.	The cupboard is between the sofa and the armchair.	The chair is next to the fridge.	The dress is in the wardrobe.

Addison Wesley Longman Limited,
Edinburgh Gate, Harlow,
Essex CM20 2JE, England
and Associated Companies throughout the world.

First published in this edition 1997

ISBN 0 582 31132 2

Set in 3.5mm Columbus

Printed in Spain by Graficas Estella

Cover illustration by Alan Snow

Illustrated by: Bernice Lum, *Mérel, Trevor Dunton, Julie Ashworth, David Le Jars, Lisa Williams, Chris Mould, Emma Holt, Neil Layton, Lisa Smith.*

Acknowledgements

Thanks to the following people who helped in the development of *New Stepping Stones*:

In Argentina: María Mónica Marinakis, Myriam Raquel Pardo Herrero.

In France: Christiane Fatien, Catherine Quantrell-Park, Jean-Pierre Top.

In Poland: Magdalena Dziob, Ilona Kubrakiewicz, Urszula Mizeracka.

In Spain: Ana Baranda, Mercé Barroetabeña, Maribel Cequier, Marisa Colomina Puy, Paloma Garcia Consuegra, Susana Garralda, Jordi Gonzalez, María Antonieta Millán Gómez, Immaculado Minguez, Mady Musiol, María Elena Pérez Márquez, María Angeles Ponce de León, Antonio Tejero.

In the UK: Viv Lambert, Sally McGugan.

and to those who contributed so much to the original edition:

Janet Ashworth, Sylvia Bakapoulou, Kathleen Chiacchio, Lety Dominguez, Marijke Dreyer, Peta Harloulakou, Gilbert Horobin, Mrs Ioannou, Anita Lycouri, Lucy McCullagh, John Oakley, Mr Proudfoot, Lorena Rosas, Gordon Slaven, Ray Tongue, Jo Walker.